POSTMODERNISM IN THE CINEMA

edited by
Cristina Degli-Esposti

Berghahn Books
New York • Oxford

First published in 1998 by
Berghahn Books

© 1998 Cristina Degli-Esposti

Library of Congress Cataloging-in-Publication Data
Postmodernism in the cinema / edited by Cristina Degli-Esposti.
     p.   cm.
Papers from a conference held in 1994 at Kent State University,
Kent, Ohio.
Includes bibliographical references and index.
ISBN 1-57181-105-2 (alk. paper). -- ISBN 1-57181-106-0
(alk. paper)
       1. Motion pictures--Social aspects--Congresses.
       2. postmodernism--Social aspects--Congresses.
       I. Degli-Esposti, Cristina.
PN1995.9.S6P66   1998
791.43'6113--dc21   97-46957
                                                                      CIP

British Library Cataloguing in Publication Data
A catalogue record for this book is available from
the British Library.

Printed in the United States on acid-free paper

ACKNOWLEDGEMENTS

I am sincerely grateful to Dudley Andrew, Kay Armatage, Peter Bondanella, Manuela Gieri, Marcia Landy, Dana Polan, and Maureen Turim. Serving as Advisory Board, they helped me select the papers for this collection. I feel fortunate for having had their help and support. To all of them, *grazie*.

CONTENTS

Contents

INTRODUCTION

POSTMODERNISM(S)

Cristina Degli-Esposti*

I n these introductory remarks, I will outline some of the major characteristics of postmodernism as we have come to understand it. For diversity and to reflect the range of the postmodern, I have chosen to discuss films that are not brought up in the essays of the collection, and also refer, for reasons of inventory, to the presence of a neo-baroque style in postmodern cinema.

The term "postmodernism" has fluctuating meanings. It maintains a volatile, mercurial definition that applies to our changing times. As it seeks its own definition, or definitions, it creates and then reinforces its own culture. This word has been extensively used to discuss philosophy, political thought, and the arts in general. Over the last couple of decades, an ever increasing number of books, articles, and special issues of journals have been devoted to the analysis of the concept of postmodernism. Yet many scholars still feel uneasy when encountering this term. The debate over the conception of that which may be considered postmodern and its many shapes and modes of expression is nonetheless far from being exhausted, for there are, in effect, several kinds of postmodernisms, each one pointing to different states of questioning and to diverse ways of remembering, interpreting, and representing.

The concept of postmodernity as an historical category appeared in Arnold Toynbee's 1939 edition of *A Study of History*. Articulating the idea that the modern period comes to an end after World War I in 1918, he asserts that the postmodern period begins to develop between 1918 and 1939, that is, between the end of World War I and the beginning of World War II. While others have seen the end of modernity in the seventeenth century, Umberto Eco has ironically responded in his reflections on *The*

3

Name of the Rose that if we stretch the concept we might even think that Homer's *Odyssey* is postmodern! (Eco 1985: 7-19).[1]

Federico de Onís used the word *postmodernismo* as an aesthetic category in his *Antología de la poesía española e hispanoamericana (1882-1932)* published in Madrid in 1934. The same term was used again by Dudley Fitts in his 1942 *Anthology of Contemporary Latin-American Poetry* in the context of Latin-American poetry. Leslie Fiedler and Ihab Hassan began using the term in the 1960s and questions concerning its meaning and use have not ceased since then to stir endless investigations and debates. Even critics extend the use of its controversial nature, albeit to represent the crisis of ideology and the increase of both verbal and visual codes in today's languages. When first used in a literary critical context, the term postmodernism came also to be applied to motion pictures with films such as Ridley Scott's *Blade Runner* (1981). It is only later however that the term would more frequently be used in cinematic theory.

Postmodernism still has no agreed upon genesis. If some scholars want the idea of postmodernism to appear as early as 1875 (Arnold Toynbee), others see it develop in the early 1960s (Charles Jencks). To complicate matters still further, Gillo Dorfles considers the appearance of neo-baroque forms in his 1951 reflection on architecture in *Barocco nell'architettura moderna*.[2] Postmodernism appears to be the summation of all these definitions, at times opposed in meaning but ultimately validating its own being. In 1985 Ihab Hassan noted that the term is an oxymoron. "If the term modern already illustrates the present, how can something be 'post-modern'?" (Hassan 1985: 119-132). Be that as it may, I believe our culture is indeed postmodern in this oxymoron-like manner as it transcends the notion of present. It reaches back to the past and forward to the future trying to synthesize these two "imaginary places" in narrative fashion.

Paradoxically using and exploiting the conventions of both popular and elite literature and culture, postmodern texts are generally concerned with the very act of telling/showing stories and remembering told/shown stories. Today this practice has become rather prevalent across writerly and visual constructs. It uses strategies of disruption like self-reflexivity, intertextuality, bricolage, multiplicity, and simulation through parody and pastiche. But postmodern texts, both written and visual, may also use organizational systems (as, for instance, in Italo Calvino's stories, or in Peter Greenaway's films) that develop in hypertexts that include both several levels of reality and other texts storing great quantities of information. This inclusion has reached new unprecedented levels of sophistication that point out a multiplicity of meanings. Computer graphics, the multimedial hypertextuality of the CD-ROM, computer memory, and imaging are now able to exceed human memory.

These "technological effects" distance postmodernist cinema from modernist cinema and accentuate the singularity of a new relationship between the spectator and the object of the gaze. Unlike the effects of the great stories (Lyotard 1979) of the pre-postmodern period, the very act of looking — from both sides of the screen — has become a central theme of postmodern films. There is awareness that each postmodern text/film expresses itself on several levels and that each one requires a different look, a different degree of attention, and cognitive competence from the spectator.

Memory, the archival site of the past, and intertextuality work together to reproduce a collective recollection of the past into the present. A memory game calls into question the attention/participation of the spectator. For this reason, postmodern cinema is made of and from the accumulation of information that, through memory and quotations, presents a rereading and rewriting of things so that the act of communication tends to supersede the content of the communication.

Unlike the narrator in modernist cinema, the postmodern narrator is uncertain and often looks at the audience through the camera lens. His/her knowledge of the story is ambiguous, ironic, and unpretentious and attempts to engage the spectator who is now cautious of the communicative game set up by the film. Where once, in modernism, irony was used as a distancing device, in postmodern cinema irony becomes a way of questioning truth and artificiality. Estranged by these new communicational relationships, the spectator is taken to another level of seeing. He/she is not only seeing differently, but is aware of seeing himself/herself see.

The multiple perceptions of the postmodern vary with the change of diverse interpretative systems. According to Umberto Eco's notions concerning interpretative intentions, every act of reading, and therefore of interpreting, is a rather complex transaction between the competence of the interpreter (the interpreter's world knowledge) and the kind of competence that a given text postulates. As neither holds a privileged position, these various interpretative intentions offer a multiplicity of decodifications. Yet, such freedom also leads to a practice of overinterpretation as discussed by Umberto Eco in his recent semiotics studies (Eco 1992). The loose and freewheeling nature of postmodern interpretation can, in fact, incur the danger of a random association that inevitably trespasses the limits set by the *intentio* of the author and of the text itself.

The intellectual game controlled by citational aesthetics implies various levels of spectatorial competence. As argued by Eco, each text (filmic or literary) can be enjoyed at different levels of knowledge (Eco 1985). When competence is weak, the citation may not be recognized at all; when it is strong, then the reference and intertextuality develop into a hypertext able to produce a true pleasure of recognition. One of the most distinctive characteristics of a "postmodern text" is the overt demand on the attention of the spectator whose active and indispensable participation is summoned and called upon in various levels of "interpellation."

The contamination of genres in postmodern cinema and the utilization of new media such as computer graphics and animation allow diverse fields to coexist together in hypertexts. Two directors, Peter Greenaway and Wim Wenders, who deal very closely with the concept of layering and hypertext, come to mind. Although they approach the act of film-making differently, their films carry the cross-interdisciplinary quality of current postmodern modes of representation in straight-forward hypertextual manner and are defined by their own tension to find a frame of reference. They find it across numerous citations and self-referential quotations that recall the films previously made by each director.

Since his *A TV Dante. Inferno. Cantos I-VIII* (directed with the collaboration of Tom Phillips, 1988), a postmodern adaptation of the first eight cantos of Dante's *Divine Comedy*, Peter Greenaway has been experimenting with multilayered, intertextual imaging where each frame within a frame offers both connections with and digressions from the original frame. He has explored this technique even further in *Prospero's Books* (1991) where Shakespeare's world is literally unfolded as the contents of twenty-four books come to life in front of the reader's/spectator's eyes.

Both Peter Greenaway and Wim Wenders challenge the presence of history in their films. According to Greenaway, "we probably haven't seen any cinema yet: we've seen a 100-year-long prologue" (Greenaway 1996). Convinced of the power of the word over that of the image, he has greatly experimented with the possibilities of imaging through computer graphics, believing they will balance the conflicting dyad 'word/image.' His style is importantly linked to the potentiality of computer graphics and its windows language, which will surely expand the medium of art and the way we perceive the filmic image.

In *Lisbon Story* (1995), Wim Wenders indulges in Dziga Vertov's original idea of a man with a movie camera (from the eponymous 1929 experimental film), and the film constructs its own hypertext, using both metacinematic and self-reflexive forms. The main character, Friedrich Monroe, the fictional film director of the story, is a man "in transit," obsessed with the idea of recording the purity of images. He unexpectedly shares affinities with Friedrich Munro (different spelling but same pronunciation), a film director who died at the end of Wenders's previous film *Der Stand der Dinge* (1982).

When the "Lisbon story" is about to come to an end, Wenders realizes that his director's attempts have failed. Carrying out the praxis of his obsessive idea, to the extreme of removing the eye from behind the camera, does not solve the challenge of the word/image dyad, Wenders calls into question another director who speaks his intent. It is the Portuguese maestro Manoel de Oliveira who tells us while looking in the camera that the cinema should be rediscovered through sound because sight cannot be enough. One should listen to the sounds of the world first, then remember the things of the past and show the words and sounds of life's images. However, as the maestro says, what can indisputably record things is memory, because memory is the only true thing. But memory, so he warns us, is an invention.

Intertextual and hypertextual travels and their citational aesthetics are typical features of any postmodern text. They base their very existence on repetition with a difference, on recycling the past via the rereading of every story and every meaning. But the minimalism of postmodern films diverts the attention of the spectator so that it centers on details that are often a reference to, or a quotation of something else. In so doing, those details become fragments, thereby taking on a life of their own and opening up visual digressions that manneristically point their own being to the reference of something else.[3]

A fragmented use of slow motion in films emphasizes an expanded, segmented, and reconstructed perception of real time, now given excessive, hyperbolic visibility through deconstruction. As for objects, the practice of detailing, the detailing of time in this case, attempts the impossible goal: its own iconic fragmentation. This use of the camera is often paralleled with the technique of hypertextualization, which interrupts one story line to take over another, and another, and another, and possibly goes back to the first one or alternatively any another one.

The desire to digress is what fuels the very existence of the postmodern hypertext. The attention of the spectator is focused on the digression of time, the excess of details, and fragments that become grandiose and acquire spectacular excessiveness inside the visual frame, or in the case of a written text, what I would call a "circumstantial window." The recodification of meanings through a changed perception of time diverges the attention of the spectator from the plot and from the great picture of things to center on the marvel and the stupor they can effect. They almost become more relevant than the whole to which they belong and constitute excessive, baroque, hyperbolic iconic forms of estrangement that can, in postmodern times, be referred to as "neo-baroque."[4] As baroque manners of artistic expression, they strive to reach a missing center and multiply endlessly by means of infinite replication and differentiated repetitions.

The presence of baroque orders of signification in postmodern representations can be traced in the various expressive codes of the cinema and the media that revolve around its industry: their redundancy, "baroquisms," systems of (over)interpretation, and their special subversive, disguised ways of seeing and observing through the camera lens question and displace the spectator's attention. In this kind of "carnivalized" cinema, diverse patterns of displacement and several layers of communication live together in representational forms that function as a means of interpretation or/and (over)interpretation. These fields of constitution follow the parameters of baroque aesthetics, style, and spirit. They augment the concept of postmodernism in the cinema and more specifically in films that openly deal with conceptions of history, memory, time, space, and that place modernist mechanical technology versus postmodern cybertechnology.[5]

Elements of baroque aesthetics, conceit, stupor, marvel, and metaphysical shock are all part of the game the mnemonic machinery of postmodern cinema plays with the spectator. The baroque fascination with the concept of movement, of being in transit, parallels the condition of "electronic traveling" out of time. Electronic power has broken the boundaries of the frames in and out of which the spectator can travel. In transit, he/she interacts with the content of the frame to be consumed, then moves on to another center, because movement of thought and movement in general is what makes the center of space become the element of time.

In his last film, *La voce della luna* (1990, The Voice of the Moon), Federico Fellini explores the mnemonic condition of being in transit and transitivity in the great variety of travels of the film's characters who are passing through several worlds.[6] Michel Foucault has called this variety of parallel worlds *heterotropias*. His notions of *heterotopology* and of *heterotropic* travels that can be found in a large number of recent films, shed light on the concept of space, its relationship with time, and our place in it. *Heterotropias*, the postmodern worlds that live side-by-side, represent "the space in which we live, which draws us out of ourselves, in which the erosion of our lives, our time and our history occurs, the space that claws and gnaws at us" (Foucault 1986: 23). Foucault considers museums and libraries examples of "heterotropias of indefinite accumulation of time." These centerless spaces bear a disruptive quality embedded within them for they contain innumerable parallel stories that connect to each other but also potentially diverge from one another.[7]

In this carnivalized, *heterotropian* cinema, mnemonic and inventory-like references to the past are often excessively expressed in an overblown style where displacement, fragmentation, inversion of hierarchy, and transgression live together. The awareness of such carnivalized worlds and their narratives can be seen in films such as Quentin Tarantino's *Pulp Fiction* (1994) or in Milcho Manchevski's *Before the Rain* (1994) where different narratorial worlds intersect one another. David Lynch's *Lost Highway* (1996) is another example of an *heterotropic* film in transit in which unexplained events render and disrupt narrative logic, and characters metamorphose into other people entirely, leaving unsolved the problem concerning the transferring of memory and personality.

By morphing into other entities and recreating other narratorial centers that constitute layers of *metalepses*, i.e., the worlds and their levels of reality, postmodern films become multivoiced texts ruled by shifting perspectives where puzzle-making and elaborate word/image play become the signifying space in which meanings occur. Reality seems to disperse in stories within stories within stories, and no single perspective or interpretation is necessarily the right one. Warping the viewer's expectations by moving into startling events, Lynch's film is populated by many puzzling worlds. A mystery man can both be standing in front of you, but also be at the other end of the phone line answering your questions! The film can possibly be understood in the revealing sentence uttered by the main morphing-character who hates video cameras: "I like to remember things my own way."

In the age of visual literacy — where postmodern culture seems to reproduce itself endlessly — the technologies of the real play with the concepts of time and space, and occur in fluid sets of media logic that morphe the individual into an entity that is both the self-reflexive producer and the consumer of the message. The pervasive use of the latest technology can only be contained through discursive reflection and recorded account, which function as organizing "devices." The repertoires of postmodern art forms thematize a playful eclecticism of styles and the self-conscious theorization of culture in a parodic reflexivity that in turn becomes the way — possibly the only way — to inform contemporary creativity.

The decenteredness of postmodern narratives has morphed into other forms of centrality that exist in virtue of communicative relationships. The loss of an old center becomes the gain of new centers occurring wherever a communicative exchange takes place. These sites of exchange constitute an area where an intricate network of images double and juxtapose, reflect and recall other images, while the changing of their narratives remains the powerful assertion that a center appears to be easily dispersed. The iconic knowledge that stems from the contamination of genres and metagenres, from the signs of advertising, fashion, music, television, and computers constitutes the ever changing site of the center.

In losing the center, several forms of "tourism" have manifested themselves and have proven to be substitute forms for the spectatorial recipient. In her book *Window Shopping: Cinema and the Postmodern*, Anne Friedberg argues that the different ways in which we now view the cinema provide "a paradigmatic model for postmodern subjectivity" and that "temporal *flânerie* of cinematic spectatorship has been intensified in new forms of spectatorship produced by cable television, the multiplex cinema, and the VCR" (Friedberg 1993: 125). According to Friedberg, the movement involved in watching cinema has developed into *flânerie*, a form of tourism through time. Indeed we see that postmoderism has been defined by new forms of cinematic spectation that often demand a remarketing and reselling the past. Replete with a *mise-en-abyme* of references frequently endorsed by touristic forms of parodic travesty, postmodern films recurrently offer innumerable imagings of memory often with documentaristic presence as in the case of Oliver Stone's pseudo-biographical films.

Whenever the conceptualization of time is called into question, a sense of historical perspective appears essential. Combination of past styles and future technology, seen as early as 1926 in Fritz Lang's *Metropolis*, are consolidated in George Lucas's and Steven Spielberg's *Star Wars* films and extra-terrestrial encounter films where the future is based on the categories of a medieval past. More recently cybermnemonic stories have appeared that induce transmemorial travels provided by memory-helmets which allow the placement of things in time so that they can claim a space. In revisiting the past, postmodern cinema becomes a form of memory itself with its own art of memory. "Postmodernism operates in a field of tension between tradition and innovation, conservation and renewal, mass culture and high art" (Huyssen 1993: 145).

Charles Jencks sees that the historical continuum and the present-past relationship has, in postmodern time, resulted in *anamnesis*, that is, in suggested recollections. He sees in this old rhetorical trope a goal in itself (Jencks 1987: 335-349). In fact, *anamnesis* induces dissociated and partial memories that combine into shapes and create their own storytelling. This is detectable in virtually any postmodern art form — a form that can produce its own narrative but leaves the plot up to the spectator.

These exasperated, touristic forms of memory appear in postmodern cinema in deconstructions of time and space, and present fascinating and peculiar assemblages of past styles and future cybertechnology. This style of representation, which began with George Lucas's and Steven Spielberg's films where the world of the future carries the memory of a medieval past, developed and evolved quite distinctly in the recent cybermnemonic stories of *Johnny Mnemonic* (1995), of *Virtuosity* (1995), and in the medication-induced trans-memorial travels of *Unforgettable* (1995).

The cyberpunk science fiction in these films represent forms of textuality that open a door on new cultural landscapes. Playing with the rediscovered notions of history, memory, and technology, this genre introduces techniques of communicational *trompe l'oeil* where *mise-en-abyme* representation self-consciously refers to itself. The intertextual net of references — one within the other — create a *trompe l'oeil* effect where the optical fooling of the eye as a receptive sense becomes the site of artifice. A place where the world of the real and the world of fiction merge and morphe. This happens in Kathryn Bigelow's *Strange Days* (1995) and even more obviously in Gabriele Salvatores's *Nirvana* (1997), a *noir*, Pirandellian mnemonic-techno-thriller; a unique instance in the spectrum of Italian cinema.

Nirvana takes up the tradition and themes of such films as *Blade Runner* (the *noir* detective and his raincoat array, cyber architecture, multiculturalism in the future), and *Strange Days* (the mnemonic helmet that allows the recovery of other people's memory, the end of the millennium/world condition, which had already been a communication breakthrough in Douglas Trumbull's *Brainstorm*, 1983). But *Nirvana* also retrieves, within the *noir* fatalistic cybertime of the diegesis/B-pic plotting, the Pirandellian discourse of the character-author search. A virtual character, Solo (i.e., Alone) is DOA destined. He dies every time, at the end of each game, if rules are not obeyed or modified. By virtue of a virus he becomes conscious of his identity as a character and manages to open a dialogue with his author-creator, a trench-coated detective who shares a role reminiscent of Deckard in *Blade Runner*.

As a reflection of our visual and confused society, postmodern films deliberately show their perplexed ways of telling stories through a disorienting use of editing. Fictional elements merge with the real people or facts recorded with actual footage as in Robert Zemeckis's *Forrest Gump* (1994), or earlier in Woody Allen's *Zelig* (1983). In both films, layers of representation morphe together into a self-consciously manipulated product by using alternative ways of making cinema with the combination of high-definition technology and *metaleptic*, multilayering imaging. Among the constants, layering and the use of memory are two of the most significant forms of interpretation and representation in postmodern texts.

Postmodernism appears in chameleon-like shapes as nostalgic revisitation. For instance, Fredric Jameson sees the obsessive use of the past, memories, and quotations as ways to compensate for postmodernism's lack of a history of its own. It takes history from elsewhere, from the past, from the history of others, or as Friedberg would have it, from "elsewhen" (Friedberg 1993: 177). Jameson also detects a nostalgia mode since the 1970s in revisitation films like George Lucas's *American Graffiti* (1973), Roman Polanski's *Chinatown* (1974), and Bernardo Bertolucci's *Il conformista* (1970) (Jameson 1984: 53-92). The postmodern nostalgia mode would continue in many other films of the late 1980s, for example, Giuseppe Tornatore's *Nuovo cinema paradiso* (1989).

Nonetheless, the retrieval of the past should not be seen as a negative practice altogether. In fact, historical revisitation appears indeed to be responding to the postmodern urge to find a place in history. But being so much preoccupied with being somewhere else, the postmodern often fails to focus on what is really there which is equally its strong point and its shortcoming. The postmodern view sees the metamorphoses which appear to be portrayed in the images of postmodern society. These metamorphoses are nothing else than what remains from the past and arrives to us through fiction. Linda Hutcheon has called this way of retaining the past and history "historiographical metafiction" (Hutcheon 1988: 5). These fictions are a way of reconsidering the clichés of the present like Terry Gilliam's medieval stories, or his fantastic ones like *The Adventures of Baron Munchausen* (1989), or even his intriguing travels into the future and into the past of *12 Monkeys* (1995) which includes postmodern cybertechnology filtered through a nostalgic retrieval of modernist technology.

The postmodernist obsession with memory has recently increased and has virtually unfolded in every direction. In the postmodern terrain of expressiveness and perception, electronic media send facts to memory and record via cameras and videos the cultural formations of the time. The postmodern age of replication, paradoxically, both repetitive but different, indulges in activities of replication that have turned into a real "pleasure of repetition" for which everyone can enjoy a different kind of experience where the practice of replication melts into a multiplicity of signifying worlds.

The theorization of contemporary and postmodern theory in particular has become, babushka dolls style, the storytelling of post-modernist storytelling itself. It behaves like a postmodern text in that the various layers of reality with their own narratorial component are called into question to analyze any postmodern text seen as an interpretation of series of stories, memories, and inventions.

New computer interpretative systems have opened the way for the development of the visual. Educated by the visual language of computers and by television sets that function as baby-sitters, the new generations have acquired their own systems of reading and rereading the visual language embedded within postmodern texts. We all become unconscious beneficiaries, the consumers of the products we help to create in an array of hyper-self-reflexivity.

All kinds of postmodernisms fuel the mnemonic cataloguing characteristic of our mannered minds, which continually try to organize systems of interpretation to do the impossible, i.e., to understand what really lies behind the state of things. I believe that the characteristics of the postmodern conditions will remain for a long time. Contradictory and innovative like the baroque conception of existence, postmodernism retrieves the past and shapes it into a multiple number of proleptic possibilities where the mobile, "nomadic" postmodern mind remembers and directs any thought through a never ending, multicoded legitimization of what is perceived as real.[8]

* * *

This collection by no means purports to be exhaustive on the vexed topic of postmodernism. I hope it will be seen as a contribution to forming cultural experience. The voices that speak in this anthology examine the relatedness of the many ways in which images can be postmodern and analyze distinctive aspects of contemporary cinema. They present different perspectives on what can be defined as postmodern filmic expression, and attempt overall to see beyond the most negative assumptions on postmodernism one can find in Jürgen Habermas's philosophical theories, or in Jean Baudrillard's pessimistic and paradoxical writings.

The idea of collecting these essays stems from a conference on the topic of the cinema and the postmodern I directed at Kent State University in the Fall of 1994. The essays grouped here were found, by the advisory board and myself, to be those that better investigated the particular relationship between the cinema and the category of the postmodern. Very diverse in theme and development, they consider the multiple ways in which stories are told in postmodern fashion both in motion pictures and in self-reflexive television programs like *The Simpsons*.

I have grouped them into four sections. The first section examines concepts of ideology, the mnemonic, the parodic, and the media. Cynthia Baron's analysis begins by placing Robert Altman's *The Player* (1992) in the postmodern field of representation analyzing its uses of self-reflexive techniques and the presence of a Hollywood counter-tradition detectable in the film's characters who are conceived as social types more than psychological beings. Concerned with spectatorship positioning, her study investigates the parodic aspect of the filmic techniques that bring forth the film's conflicting value system, for example, where the *noir* system of representation is set against the one used in the musical.

Marwan Kraidy's essay explores the treatment of race and gender by Hollywood's "ideological manufacturing of the Orient" in Disney's *Aladdin* (1992). The animated film presents several signs of intertextuality embedded within itself. In fact, the film offers references to the art of filmmaking at very crucial moments in a plot that revolves around the axis of race, gender and class.

Since the majority of people watch films on television, television programs have become the receptacle for the pro-filmic elements and commentaries of the big screen. The discourse of these self-reflexive television programs is the topic of David Weinstein's reading of *The Simpsons* and its representation of the hyperreal aspects of postmodern society of both the maker and the consumer of postmodern images.

Timothy Shary's piece investigates dislocation, the loss of identity and history in "young adult movies," such as *Bill and Ted's Excellent Adventure*

(1989), *Singles* (1991), *Wayne's World* (1992), *Reality Bites* (1994), in light of Fredric Jameson's theory of postmodernism. He centers his analysis on the outcome of the commodification of culture. Playing with the notion of irony, these films end up appropriating that commodity consumption that they should be critiquing.

The second section of the volume highlights essays that deal with issues of cross-cultural identity and national cinemas. Considering the changes in postmodern Japanese cinema, John Bruns's piece studies Juzo Itami's 1987 film *Tampopo*, its use and figuration of subjectivity, creative consumption, and pleasure in light of postmodern *bricolage*.

Rosanna Maule's analysis of authorship is seen through a reconceptualization of the notion of national cinemas. It maps the radical politics of European cinema, examining the concept of "interpellation" and the restored concept of *auteurism* in postmodern time. Through the examples of three films from three different European countries, Maule argues that postmodern *auteurism* can be seen as an index "to express a legitimate and necessary historical perspective," and also as a nomadic figure in light of Deleuze and Guattari's theories.

Janina Falkowska's essay focuses on "postsocialist" Polish cinema, particularly on two films that present a sort of "socialist-Hollywood thriller" and political pastiche, Konrad Szolajski's *The Pigs* (1993) and Andrzej Wajda's *The Man from* (1992). As discussed in the essay, these films are examples of the "new postmodern (un)reality in Poland" where the Western-commercial, the Eastern-idealistic, and the pastiche of political voices from the past and the present coexist.

The third section of the book centers on the notions of the past in postmodern perspective and of tourism through time. Ellen Strain's essay deals with issues of tourism, (post)history, and colonization, as well as simulated travel and tourist's gaze within the debate of postmodernism and media-travel. Her study develops in light of theoretical studies on tourism and the touristic gaze. While identifying the space of the visual position of spectators/tourists, it explores a notion of anti-tourism in the films adapted from of E.M. Forster's novels, where the political critique hinges on the claim that direct experience within tourism is unreachable.

Christine Bolus-Reichert considers the problematics of the colonial subject in contemporary French cinema as set in French West Africa, and "the recolonizing tendency of travel cinema" in *Black and White in Color* (1976), *Clean Slate* (1981), and *Chocolat* (1988). Developing postcolonial representations of the colonial period, these film render "an imaginary geography which still locates identity in the tale of travelers," where landscapes and notions of *dépaysement* are the imaginary geographies that shape the maps of travel cinema.

Barry Laga's analysis of *Barton Fink* (1991) offers an interesting reading of a film that attempts to "make sense of the past within a postmodern perspective." It centers on the postmodern strategies of paralyzed desire for closure while the film already exists, paradoxically, outside itself — as one understands from the final shot.

The final section of this volume deals with the overtness of an auteurial presence. Marshall Deutelbaum's essay investigates one of the many possible ways to convey visual autobiography in postmodern time. His reading of *Akira Kurosawa's Dreams* (1990) exposes the metacinematic and metabiographical aspects of the film especially in "The Crows," one of the film's episodes/dreams. Director Martin Scorsese plays Dutch painter Vincent van Gogh and a young would-be artist represents young Kurosawa in his desire to become a painter in a *trompe l'oeil* effect.

Philip Holden-Moses discusses possible ways of recognizing locatable events in Peter Greenaway's *Drowning by Numbers* (1988). Dealing with one of the major concerns of any postmodern art form, Greenaway's film is a perfect example of postmodern cataloguing techniques. In the film the past is reworked in postmodern fashion along the artificial and formal lines of game and role playing. These organizing devices based on defined codes of signification like that of numbers are the only sense-making references that permit an understanding of the flow of events. The essay uses its own organizing device, paralleling the film's organizational systems with an ancient icelandic numbering list.

Mary M. Wiles's postmodern analysis of Rainer Werner Fassbinder's *Querelle* (1982) sees the film as an "anti-art art film." It presents a close analysis of the film and its original source, *Querelle de Brest*, Jean Genet's 1948 novel. Considering the implications of the Genetian "theatre of the double," adaptation, and the legacy of German expressionist cinema, Wiles's essay develops a fine psychoanalytic study of Fassbinder's postmodern film and his position within the German cinema of the 1980s.

Most of the studies collected in this volume share a common concern for the crisis scenario of postmodern society. Rather than applying catastrophe theories and indulging in the apocalyptic and horrific nihilism that some theorists and critics see in postmodernism and in the age of postmodernity, these essays concentrate on the possible remedial aspects of critical analysis, and provide interesting reading strategies and different systems of interpretations that may help us in the difficult task of being postmodern.

REFERENCES

Benjamin, Walter. 1977. *The Origin of German Tragic Drama*, trans. John
 Osborne. London: LNB [original title: *Ursprung des Deutschen Trauerspiels*.
 Frankfurt a.M.: Surkamp Verlag, 1963].
Calabrese, Omar. 1992. *Neobaroque: A Sign of the Times*, trans. Charles Lambert.
 Princeton: Princeton University Press [original title: *L'età neobarocca*. Bari:
 Laterza, 1987].
Degli-Esposti, Cristina. 1994. "Voicing the Silence in Federico Fellini's *La voce
 della luna*," *Cinema Journal* 33.2 (Winter): 42-55.
——— 1996a."Federico Fellini's *Intervista* or the Neo-Baroque Creativity of the
 Analysand on Screen," *Italica* 73.2 (Summer): 157-172.
——— 1996b. "The Neo-Baroque Scopic Regime of Peter Greenaway's
 Encyclopedic Cinema," *Cinefocus* 4: 34-45.
——— 1996c. "Sally Potter's *Orlando* and the Neo-Baroque Scopic Regime,"
 Cinema Journal 36.1 (Fall): 75-93.
Deleuze, Gilles. 1993. *The Fold: Leibniz and the Baroque*, trans. Tom Conley.
 Minneapolis: University of Minnesota Press [original title: *Le pli: Leibniz et
 le baroque*. Paris: Editions de Minuit, 1988].
de Onís, Federico. 1934. *Antología de la poesía española e hispanoamericana
 (1882-1932)*. Madrid: Casa editrice Hernado.
Dorfles, Gillo. 1951. *Barocco nell'architettura moderna*. Milan: Tamburini.
——— 1984. *Architetture ambigue. Dal neobarocco al postmoderno*. Bari: Dedalo.
Eco, Umberto. 1985. "Reflections on *The Name of the Rose*." *Encounter* 64.4
 (April): 7-19.
——— 1992. *Interpretation and Overinterpretation*. Cambridge: Cambridge
 University Press.
Fitts, Dudley. 1942. *Anthology of Contemporary Latin-American Poetry*. Norfolk,
 Conn.: New Directions.
Foucault, Michel. 1986. "Of Other Spaces," *Diacritics* (Spring): 22-27.
Friedberg, Anne. 1993. *Window Shopping: Cinema and the Postmodern*. Berkeley:
 University of California Press.
Greenaway, Peter. 1996. "Peter Greenaway," in *Movie Times*, supplement of *Sight
 & Sound* (May): 15-16.
Hassan, Ihab. 1985. "The Culture of Postmodernism," *Theory, Culture & Society*
 2: 119-132.
Hutcheon, Linda. 1988. *A Poetics of Postmodernism: History, Theory, Fiction*. New
 York: Routledge.
Huyssen, Andreas. 1993. "Mapping the Postmodern," in Joseph Natoli and
 Linda Hutcheon, eds. *A Postmodern Reader*. Albany: SUNY: 105-156.
Jameson, Fredric. 1984. "Postmodernism or, the Cultural Logic of Late
 Capitalism," *New Left Review* 146 (July-August): 53-92.

Jencks, Charles. 1987. *Postmodernism*. London: Academy Editions and Rizzoli International Publications.

Lyotard, Jean-François. 1979. *La condition postmoderne*. Paris: Les Editions de Minuit.

McHale, Brian. 1987. *Postmodern Fiction*. London and New York: Routledge.

Sarduy, Severo. 1974. "El barroco y el neobarroco," in César F. Moreno, ed. *América Latina en su literatura*. Mexico City: Siglo XXI: 167-84.

Toynbee, Arnold. 1939. *A Study of History*. London: Oxford University Press.

Wollen Peter. 1993. "Baroque and Neo-Baroque in the Age of the Spectacle," *Point of Contact* 3.3 (April): 8-21.

NOTES

*   Cristina Degli-Esposti also publishes under her married name, Degli-Esposti Reinert.

1   First appeared in *Alfabeta* 49 (1983).

2   He later expanded his study in another volume, *Architetture ambigue. Dal neobarocco al postmoderno* (Bari: Dedalo, 1984).

3   For the difference between detail and fragment, see Omar Calabrese, *Neobaroque: A Sign of the Times* (Princeton: Princeton University Press, 1992). First appeared as *L'età neobarocca* (Bari: Laterza, 1987).

4   Elsewhere I have organized a filmic analysis of this kind of neo-baroque postmodernism and its observational scopic regime, its cataloguing techniques, and encyclopedic mnemonic strategies. See Cristina Degli-Esposti 1996a, 1996b, and 1996c.

5   Other scholarly contributions to the re-evaluation of baroque aesthetics include Omar Calabrese 1987, 1992; Peter Wollen 1993; Walter Benjamin 1977 [original title: *Ursprung des Deutschen Trauerspiels* (Frankfurt a.M.: Surkamp Verlag, 1963)]; Severo Sarduy's "El barroco y el neobarroco"; Deleuze's 1993 [original title: *Le pli: Leibniz et le baroque* (Paris: Editions de Minuit, 1988)].

6   I have discussed this issue at length in my article. See Degli-Esposti 1994.

7   Michel Foucault discusses at length the concept of *heterotropia* in: "Of Other Spaces," *Diacritics* (Spring 1986): 22-27. Also see Brian McHale in *Postmodern Fiction* (London and New York: Routledge, 1987).

8   I am borrowing the concept of "nomadology" from Deleuze and Guattari.

Part I

The Ideological, the Mnemonic, the Parodic, and the Media

The Player (*Columbia Tristar, 1993*) *Robert Altman*
Movie studio executive Griffin Mill (Tim Robbins) receives anonymous death threats from a
rejected screenwriter. Still courtesy of Jerry Ohlinger's Movie Materials.

CHAPTER 1

THE PLAYER'S PARODY
OF HOLLYWOOD
A Different Kind of Suture
Cynthia Baron

The alienation effect "has nothing whatever to do with ordinary stylization, on the contrary, the achievement of an A-effect absolutely depends on lightness and naturalness of performance."

Bertolt Brecht, *Brecht on Theatre*

In spite of all they reveal, poststructural analyses of *suture* consider spectator positioning in relation to only two types of film practice: classical-realist texts that lead audiences to identify with fictional characters, gendered subject positions, and dominant ideological perspectives; or modernist texts that disrupt conventional modes of narration and identification to foreground their production of meaning, and thereby estrange or alienate spectators from the text. The poststructural paradigm might seem useful for analyzing not only classical-realist and modernist texts, but postmodern modes of spectator positioning as well. Yet its (high) modernist vantage point makes it ill-suited for analyses of text/spectator relations in cases of postmodern cinema that require us to consider different types of suture, for example, instances in which spectators are alienated from the diegesis but not the text. With its emphasis on text-as-process, a film such as *The Player* requires us to reconsider existing conceptions of suture, for it generates a type of postmodern pleasure that does not arise from identification with characters, the camera, or a reality present elsewhere, but instead occurs in the course of making one's way through continually shifting levels of fiction.

As originally formulated by Jacques-Alain Miller, suture names the process whereby a thinking and speaking "subject is 'stitched' into the chain of discourse" (Stam et al. 1992: 169). Miller proposed that while philosophers from Descartes to Husserl have argued for the validity of the cogito (the principle that awareness of one's own thoughts is evidence of one's existence), subjectivity is in fact produced by the miscognition that one has a "real" and "unique" identity. Miller, echoing the views of Sartre and Lacan, argued that subjectivity exists only in so far as it represents a logical position that is not identical to the content of thought or discourse. Neither the content of thought, nor the awareness of thought, a thinking and speaking subject is, according to Miller, necessarily divided, alienated, and defined by lack or negation. A unified subject, an effect rather than a cause, is produced by repressing the "real" terms of its existence.

Seeing connections between the process of subject formation described by Miller, and the way shot/reverse shot editing patterns in Classical Hollywood Cinema mask the artifice of cinematic "reality," and position spectators to assume the literal (and therefore often figurative) point of view of fictional characters, Jean-Pierre Oudart, and later Daniel Dayan used Miller's notion of suture to characterize relationships between spectators and the classical-realist texts central to Hollywood cinema of the studio era. The equation between cinematic suture and point of view editing proved to be overly schematic, for as John Frow notes, "it collapses a general conception of enunciative relations into the single figure of the absent one" (1986: 241). Yet the work of Oudart and Dayan led scholars to consider the notion of suture more broadly, as the range of procedures by which classical-realist films establish a "position for the viewing subject which necessitates not only its loss of being, but the repudiation of alternative discourses" (Silverman 1983: 205-206). Amplifying the implications of the earliest formulations of suture in classical-realist texts, Laura Mulvey, Jacqueline Rose, Claire Johnston, and others demonstrated that "the classic film text distinguishes sharply between the male and the female subjects, and that it does so on the basis of vision" (Silverman 1983: 222). Modifying the original formulations of suture in slightly different ways, Nick Browne, Stephen Heath, and others explained that classical-realist narration "transforms cinematic space into dramatic place, thereby providing the viewer not just with a vantage point but a subject position" (Silverman 1983: 214). Moving the discussion beyond questions of suture in classical-realist texts, Heath argued that suture can be understood as any text's "play for a subject" (1978: 64). His position is that any text can be considered as discourse that is incomplete and necessarily directed to a subject at every moment. Framed this way, suture describes a text's "play of incompleteness-completion" (Heath 1978: 63). My analyses of suture in one form of postmodern cinema takes Heath's position as its starting point.[1]

Given that discussions of suture in Classical Hollywood Cinema have come to examine not only shot/reverse shot editing patterns, but camera movement, framing, sound/image relations, and more, analysis of suture in a postmodern text would also seem to benefit from study of undertheorized elements, for example, the role that character, casting, and performance play in text/spectator relations. Moreover, because we can "read against the grain" of classical-realist texts, and because "modernist" devices such as self-reflexivity, narrative intransitivity, aperture, and multiple diegesis do not necessarily establish emotional and ideological distance, it is possible to see that formal strategies in any text need to be examined in relation to issues surrounding reception. The fact that audiences bring with them different reading or interpretive habits requires us to ask, what are the various relationships between a specific text and the field of presuppositions that shape reading practices? Differences between the production and reception of classical-realist texts, modernist texts, and postmodern texts demand that we consider the existence of perhaps very different horizons of expectation, and they invite us to ask, for example, how might we best describe relationships between spectator positioning, Hollywood films produced in the postmodern era, and the conventions that now shape contemporary mass audience expectations?

The Player (Robert Altman, 1992) is a film which allows us to consider aspects of the relationship between audiences and postmodern texts that have been overlooked. Its parodic project "fails" to achieve conventional suture because (1) the film's conception of character is at odds with classical-realist conventions of psychological realism, (2) its manipulation of star images often runs counter to expectations created by the industry's use of the star system, and (3) the pastiche of performance styles and levels of performance creates an emotional distance from the characters in the fiction, and opens a space for reflection on the values that have shaped Hollywood films. Yet the film does not conform to patterns established by modernist "counter-cinema."

Prevailing views of suture in classical-realist texts have led film scholars to discuss identification largely in terms of editing patterns and subject positions, and have contributed to making the concept of character the most undertheorized category in (film and literary) narrative theory. Yet as the work of Jonathan Arac, John Frow, Murray Smith, and Bert States suggests, character is in fact a central figure to contend with in any analysis of suture. It is an especially pertinent issue in *The Player* because the film's conception of character is a source of alienation. In contrast to the Hollywood tradition, characters in the Altman film are not psychological essences. Instead, they are social types, shaped and delineated by their environment and historical circumstance.

Viewed as an "organized apparatus of identification" (Frow 1986: 249), the star system provides other material pertinent to my discussion of suture in *The Player*. Here, too, the film represents a departure from the classical-realist model, for its use of star images often has an alienating effect. Rather than marshaling star images to enrich fictional characters, *The Player's* stars often draw attention *away from* the narrative.

The film's collision of performance styles and levels of performance (actors playing characters, actors using their star images to play characters, and actors playing themselves in cameos) also plays a part in its parodic "play for a subject." The (slight) disjunction between the tightly-wound performances of actors playing fictional characters, and the off-hand casualness of actors playing themselves in cameos disrupts conventional modes of identification. In addition, the (slightly) different ontological status of the fictional characters bound to the diegesis, and the cameo actors defined by their trans-textual star images further disrupts conventional modes of identification and has an alienating effect.

To say that these strategies create distance is not to suggest that the film generates modernist estrangement or unpleasure. *The Player* can be read as a film that seems to use strategies central to Classical Hollywood Cinema, but in fact shifts audience involvement to a different register, to the relationship between itself and its spectators. The strategies that draw attention to the film's various ways of making a "play for a subject," and the effect created by its shifting the basis of audience involvement, echo both the methods and effect of what is known as epic theatre, the theatrical form first developed by Bertold Brecht and Erwin Piscator in Germany in the 1920s.

Modernist applications of Brecht's theories of drama, most notably by Godard, make it difficult to see connections between Brechtian theatre and a film such as *The Player*. Yet it is important to understand that for Brecht, the alienation effect is *not* inextricably connected to formal devices that make a text "difficult" or "unpleasurable." Articulating strategies for an approach to drama that creates emotional detachment from characters in order to generate an intellectual awareness of social realities, Brecht argued that alienation from conventional emotional engagement "absolutely depends on lightness and naturalness of performance" (1964: 95). For epic theatre of the 1920s, the goal was not to create or recreate a sense of existential alienation. As conceived by Brecht and Piscator, for epic productions that seek to reform rather than reinscribe cultural norms, the alienation effect, achieved by a variety of means, is not an end in itself, but instead is "principally designed to historicize the incidents portrayed" (Brecht 1964: 96).

A film like *The Player* makes it possible to understand the central features of epic theatre in ways that were not made apparent by modernist projects. The film does, for example, depend on a narrative structure that is marked by interruption, digression, and the "jutxaposition of self-contained units" (Stam et al. 1992: 199). Making a stronger point as an argument about representation in commercial cinema than as a representation of "real" people found in a reality present elsewhere, the film presents us with characters that are nothing more than "epiphenomenon of social process" (Stam et al. 1992: 198). Emphasizing rather than masking social contradiction, the film is structured in terms of what Brecht called "the radical separation of elements" where each scene is "radically separated from its 'neighboring' scenes," and each "track" exists "in tension with other tracks" (Stam et al. 1992: 199). The film's thoroughgoing use of realistic detail does represent a break with the alienating strategies of modernist cinema, but it does not place the film at odds with the premises of epic theatre. As Stam, Burgoyne, and Flitterman-Lewis point out, Brecht's "critique of realism centered on the ossified conventions of the nineteenth-century novel and naturalist theater, but not on the goal of truthful representation" (Stam et al. 1992: 202).

The Player does make a "play for a subject," but it does not depend on suture in the conventional sense. Rather than generating identification with characters or subject/object positions, the film engages spectators by presenting them with continually shifting levels of fiction. Its excessive intertextuality, more intriguing than the narrative itself, becomes a game that rewards insider knowledge and multiple viewing. The film's encyclopedic presentation mobilizes conflicting perspectives and allusions, with the result that spectators are positioned, addressed, inscribed as unifying/unified subjects of reading.[2]

Positioning *The Player* in the Postmodern Field

Maurice Yacowar points out that earlier Altman films from *M.A.S.H.* (1970) to *Quintet* (1979) represent contrasting positions on the shared metaphor of play (see 1980). *The Player* extends that investigation by playing with the notion of play on a number of levels. First, the film is about gamblers who cannot resist making a play, about the players who make the deals that make Hollywood run. Second, the film is about playing with Hollywood conventions, in particular those surrounding the actors, the stars, the players who make Hollywood films come alive. The film can be seen as a spoof of the star system, and at the same time, an homage to the work of performers. Third, the reverberations of play extend to the audience as well, for the film can be read as positioning spectators as players, or in Viola Spolin's words, as "fellow players, and the last spoke in the wheel which can then begin to roll"(1983: 13).[3]

The Player is quite different from the sort of postmodern cinema discussed by Fredrick Jameson and others which evokes "not an actual past, but rather the kinds of narrative experience — the adventure story, the science-fiction movie — that seem to typify the experience of the 1950s" (Connor 1989: 177). Unlike the "retro" films that are charged with a nostalgic desire for a reality "present elsewhere" (Derrida 1978: 211), *The Player* can be read as a fiction that presents us with *traces* of other fictions. Rather than establishing its presence through repetition or re-presentation, Altman's post-Absurd comedy is an expression of a postmodern "aesthetics of absence" (Sayre 1983: 174).[4] The film can be read as embracing its fictional, contingent status. Rather than lament the loss of the "real," the film seems to take as a given its status as a text, that is it, to use Derrida's terms, nothing more (or less) than a "network of textual referrals to *other* texts, a textual transformation in which each allegedly 'simple term' is marked by the trace of another term" (1972: 33).

In addition, unlike some postmodern texts, *The Player* is not simply stylized or self-reflexive. It is parodic, for it begins with the Hollywood tradition, and creates a distance between itself and its model in its *unfaithful* imitation. Distance between *The Player* and its models seems to be endemic to the film. For example, it "fails" to be a faithful adaptation of Michael Tolkin's novel, *The Player*. Tolkin's novel is a bitter critique of Hollywood, while Altman's film is shot through with a lighthearted sense of humor. Tolkin's novel ends with the mysterious "postcard writer" quitting the business (as *Sunset Boulevard*'s Joe Gillis would have done, had he not been shot by Norma Desmond), but the film, in Altman's words, is "structured like a snail" (Altman 1993) that turns into itself and becomes itself. In the concluding scene, studio executive Griffin Mill (Tim Robbins) hears a pitch for a film that is the film we have just seen. In contrast to the linear narrative of the novel, the film forfeits closure in the conventional sense. Instead, this final move deconstructs the film's diegetic world and playfully calls attention to its "failure" to represent anything but itself.

The film is also quite different from self-reflexive films about filmmaking or the creative process that seem to suggest modernist negotiations with the postmodern era. For example, while Altman's film raises the problem of subjectivity by positioning spectators as the source of the text's unity, *The Player* is not (as Cristina Degli-Esposti writes of Fellini's *La voce della luna*) "a study of the Subject at the mirror" for whom "remembering is living" (1994: 43, 50). Instead, Altman's film is a Hollywood film about Hollywood, its conventions, its business, its mythological status as home to crass entertainment, and finally perhaps its more prosaic role as a site for creative interaction. *The Player* can be best understood in relation to a collection of films that Charles Affron refers to as "showbiz films" (1982: 132–157).

Showbiz films are always about "making it in the business." Films like *What Price Hollywood?* (1932), *All About Eve* (1950), and the three versions of *A Star is Born* (1937, 1954, 1976) use characters' generational differences to naturalize the culture's ambivalent perspectives on ambition. In the two Hollywood stories, the old star is the one destroyed by fame; in the Broadway story, young Eve represents the evils of ambition. Most showbiz films are more univocal in their commentaries on "the business" and the drive to "make it." Some of the best known showbiz films, *Sunset Boulevard* (1950), *Day of the Locust* (1975), *Barton Fink* (1991), present a markedly dystopic view of Hollywood. Others take precisely the opposite perspective and recount Broadway or Hollywood success stories in films like *Footlight Parade* (1933), *Singin' in the Rain* (1952), and *Hollywood Shuffle* (1987).

Like the often noir-inflected studies of fame and dark ambition, Altman's work presents us with a normal world that is in danger of being

27

overturned by a parallel, shadow world of guilt, perversion, and lack of control. But unlike "retro" neo-noir films such as *Body Heat* (1981) and *House of Games* (1987), *The Player's* plot twists do not lead the "hero," Griffin Mill, to some dismal ending.[5] Instead, like the success stories of Hollywood's backstage musicals, *The Player* is largely about the complications of putting on the show, and the circuitous path that finally unites "the perfect couple." Still, while Altman's film is like many backstage musicals in providing plausible narrative reasons for the films-within-the-film (the studio executives are continually screening rushes and preview prints), *The Player* exploits and heightens its theatricality by calling attention to its own techniques: as, for example, when the dialogue that opens the film tells us about cinema's famous tracking shots while we watch *The Player's* byzantine opening shot.

The Player does not privilege any of its antecedents or allusions. By drawing on the dystopic vision imparted by the studies of ambition and the utopian world suggested by showbiz films' success stories, *The Player* complicates its text/spectator relations. The film is and is not a critique of ambition. It seems to pay homage to the noir tradition at the same time that it pokes fun at values embedded in the noir genre (the sense of doom, the power of fate, the idea of a diseased world that must be cured). Similarly, the film can be read as an ambivalent critique of its own star-studded spectacle and joining of "the perfect couple." It seems to be an homage to Hollywood's stars and the tradition of excess at the same time that it maintains a parodic distance from the values associated with a genre like the musical (in particular, the self-serving, blissful confidence that success is predestined, and the idea that anything can be accomplished through an act of will and a good performance).

The Player's conflicting value systems (noir versus musical) create the possibility for a different kind of suture. First, they are part of the text's parodic project that establishes a distance between the film and its models. Second, the conflict between the two "languages," the two perspectives of the showbiz films (or the two genre systems) establishes a distance between spectators and the film's diegesis, for in the process of putting into play Hollywood's dark studies of ambition *and* its stories of glib success, the film's narrative comes to have a reduced importance. As Mikhail Bakhtin points out, in texts that develop parodic stylization, "the plot itself is subordinated to the task of coordinating and exposing languages to each other" (1981: 365). Third, because the film is irreducible to either of its discursive poles, *The Player's* point of view remains continually *in play*. While stylization (double-voiced but faithful to its models) in itself simply generates another minor enigma, *The Player's* parodic stylization contributes to destabilized spectator positioning, and as a consequence disrupts conventional modes of identification.

The film's "lack" of conventional suture is not best understood as an effect of modernist self-reflexive strategies disrupting an illusion of reality. In *The Player*, self-reflexive elements do create momentary ironic distance. For example, the narrative timing of shots that feature the poster for the film, *Highly Dangerous*, in Griffin's office insures that the title of the 1950 film will function as sly commentary. Similarly, framing that eventually reveals that the initial full-frame images of certain scenes are actually from films being screened by the executives (in the first instance, from the *Lonely Room*, in the second from *Habeus Corpus*) disrupts conventional suture by calling attention to the film's own status as a film being screened. Yet given the horizon of expectations in the postmodern era, it seems that strategies such as these are easily recouped, that they readily become just another enigma, another detour in a spectator's encounter with the text's hermeneutic code.

Modernist and postmodernist texts have struggled, it seems, with precisely this problem of negotiating a spectatorship that is continually adapting to changes in representation. One solution has been to combine modernist distancing effects with excessive violence, as in *Blue Velvet* (1986). Altman's film takes a rather different track. *The Player's* self-reflexivity complicates spectator positioning, but it is not joined to other elements that create (modernist) unpleasure. Instead, the self-reflexivity is so excessive that it simply shifts attention to the surface of the text. The film unmasks its process of production, from originating pitch to preview-audience approved ending. And when Griffin explains to June (Greta Scacchi) that a Hollywood script must have "suspense, laughter, violence, hope, heart, nudity, sex, happy endings," the "elements" that the film borrows from the Hollywood tradition are laid bare. In *The Player*, the fact that self-reflexivity easily becomes an enigma is *not* a problem to be overcome. Instead, it is something to (literally) build on — such that the sheer weight or volume of self-reflexivity tips the balance of attention from the diegesis to the film's discursive practices.

In contrast to some postmodern cinema, *The Player* is parodic because it presents us with a critical distance between itself and the tradition of Classical Hollywood Cinema. Rather than being faithful to its models, or simply looking at its status as a text, the film first looks (critically) at earlier Hollywood films and the classical-realist tradition. Moreover, the film is excessive in presenting us with the distance between itself and its models. *The Player* is built out of explicit and implicit allusions to other films, including pointed references to films like *Sunset Boulevard* (1950) and Godard's *Le Mepris* (1963) that are about the film business.[6] Echoing its excessive self-reflexivity, *The Player's* parodic allusions are so numerous that they compete with the story for attention, destabilizing and denaturalizing the central narrative.

Yet the film makes a play for the subject, and spectators are sutured into the text. Spectators are drawn in, however, not by identifying with characters or the camera, but instead by becoming engaged in the disruptive process of the narration itself. The film's endless allusions alienate spectators from the film's diegesis, but not from the film which presents itself as a game. *The Player's* game-like strategies seem to model a certain (postmodern) ideological position, one which recognizes, on the one hand, that game-playing can be deadly, and on the other, that play can be life-sustaining — especially in a post-Absurd world.

An Alternative and Alienating Conception of Character

Classical Hollywood Cinema has depended on conventions of psychological realism where characters' experiences reveal their unique personalities. Settings often simply exist as backdrops for action, and at most, serve to reflect characters' inner lives and states of being. *The Player* "fails" to imitate this strategy. Instead, the film's conception of character depends on an essential unity of character and setting. Here situation takes the place of psychology; type replaces the individual.

Marsha Kinder describes Classical Hollywood Cinema's tradition of representing characters as unique individuals caught in moments of dramatic crisis as an "intoxication with the singular" (1990: 4). *The Player* suggests a break with that tradition, for rather than masking the formulaic typicality of its narrative and characters, from the beginning of the film, it calls attention to its typicality. The opening tracking shot that is accompanied by discussions between Walter Stuckel (Fred Ward), Jimmy Chase (Paul Hewitt), and Buck Henry on tracking shots in other films is not simply a self-reflexive move; it also points to the typical dimensions of *The Player*. The typicality of the film's narrative situations is underscored in the scene where Walter, Griffin, and defense attorney, Gar Gerard (Kevin Scannell) leave the Pasadena Police Station after the witness identifies Detective DeLongpre rather than Griffin Mill as the man she saw the night of Kahane's murder. Walter reminds the others that the situation is just like a movie, *Witness for the Prosecution* (1957). Hardly unique, the scenario simply replays the story of unreliable witnesses and characters who get away with murder.

The film points out that it is not just the scenario that is typical. The characters are typical as well. *The Player* humorously but explicitly tells us that its studio executives are not individuals, but rather character types. In the scene in which Griffin's breakfast meeting with studio head, Joel Levitson (Brion Jones), follows on the heels of Levitson's meeting with Griffin's rival, Larry Levy (Peter Gallagher), Larry and then Griffin stop to say hello to Burt Reynolds and Charles Champlin. After Griffin has moved on, Reynolds calls Griffin an asshole under his breath, to which Champlin replies, "one of a breed." Reynolds responds, "not one of a breed; there's a whole breed of them; they're breeding them actually." Later, when Griffin is at the hotel to meet the writer who has been sending him threatening postcards, Griffin happens to meet Malcolm McDowell. McDowell makes a point of stopping Griffin to tell him that the next time Griffin wants to bad mouth him, he should have the courage to say it to his face. McDowell adds, "you guys are all the same."

The writers in the film are also presented as types. In the opening sequence, we are introduced to writers well positioned enough to obtain a meeting with an executive like Griffin. The stories they pitch are presented as patchworks pieces of familiar films. One project is entitled *The Graduate Part II*, another is a cross between *Pretty Woman* (1990) and *The Gods Must be Crazy* (1980). The writers' pitch style is also laughably consistent. They are all fast talkers, excessively agreeable, and invariably eager to demonstrate their insider connections. At David Kahane's funeral, we meet the other kind of writer. The eulogy, given by a struggling writer who, like Kahane, is unshaven and wears loose-fitting proletarian clothes of muted colors, mounts a diatribe against the "shit-bag producers" who fail to appreciate the talent of those whose screenplays are about "reality."

Throughout the film, even the stars become types. *The Player* consistently refuses to tap into their unique star images, and instead presents famous actors and actresses as "generic" stars. At the gala affair organized by Griffin, we watch the now conventional footage of stars going from curbside to auditorium entrance while we listen to the hackneyed theme from "Entertainment Tonight" and Lisa Gibbon's comically conventional commentary: "It's a who's who of stars; no id's necessary; they're all household names."

The film's conception of character which deviates from the norms of classical-realism has precedents in both American and international cinema. Eric von Stroheim's use of environment to define character was fundamentally at odds with Classical Hollywood Cinema, and there is a connection between his concern with character-as-social-type and character in Altman's film.[7] The conception of character in Altman's film also follows the model established by the Neorealist conception which emerged in direct opposition to Classical Hollywood Cinema's psychological realism. As André Bazin points out, Neorealism and its use of character typage "stands in opposition to the traditional dramatic systems and also to the various other known kinds of realism in literature and film" (1971: 97). While the conceptual distance between a film like Stroheim's *Greed* (1924) and *The Player* seems quite possible to bridge, the disparity between Neorealism's investigation of social conditions in postwar Italy, and *The Player*'s look at the opulent world of Hollywood, obscures the connection between their approach to character. Yet in the same way that the Neorealists "replaced psychological inquiry with depictions of external struggle with the social environment" (Kolker 1983: 272), Altman's film presents us with types who are nothing but their role in the Hollywood game. The integral relationship between character and setting in *The Player* is illustrated in a simple but telling moment: at a lunch meeting early in the film, Griffin suggests that the people at the table talk about something besides business; an uncomfortable silence follows, then laughter — there is nothing else for them to discuss.

To argue that the characters in *The Player* are presented as types rather than unique individuals does not mean that the film completely denies emotional access to the characters (it seems quite likely, for instance, that spectators "feel for" Bonnie when she is dumped by Griffin and fired by Larry), nor that it breaks entirely with Hollywood's commerce with scopophilia and narcissism. Laura Mulvey's analysis of identification along gender-specific subject positions accurately describes text/spectator relations in the scene where Griffin talks to Kahane's girlfriend, June, on the phone while standing outside on the dark street, watching her move about in the brightly lit house.[8] The fact that the film's characters are types does, however, mean that the integral relationship between characters and environment is indicative of a conception of character which breaks with conventions codified by Classical Hollywood Cinema. That departure is significant. Brecht calls attention to the role that environment plays in different kinds of theatre. He sees two types: (classical) theatre "where the environment is remarkably unimportant, treated simply as a pretext" (1964: 97), and theatre that calls attention to the social-political structures of the environment.

Unlike the classical-realist tradition, and like Stroheim's films and the cycle of Neorealist films, characters in *The Player* emerge from a concrete, historical situation. In contrast to the formulaic types Hollywood has borrowed from stage melodrama and the nineteenth-century novel, characters in *The Player* are not psychological essences symbolizing a range of conventional, transcendent, ahistorical moral categories. Instead, characters in the Altman film are social types defined by a specific environment. The fact that Hollywood has a mythical status should not foreclose the possibility of our considering that *The Player* presents us with characters who are social types — whose conflicts call attention to the *causes* rather than the expression of Hollywood spectacle.

In the scene where Griffin talks with writer David Kahane (Vincent D'Onofono) at the Rialto Theatre after the screening of *The Bicycle Thief* (1948), Griffin tells Kahane that his studio should consider doing a remake of DeSica's film. Kahane scoffs that the studio would require that the film have a happy ending. Given that characters in *The Player* are defined by their environment, it seems to me that Altman's film is, in some sense, a remake of the Neorealist film — with a "happy ending" that telegraphs its conventionality as clearly as any Douglas Sirk melodrama.[9] Like a Stroheim or Neorealist film, *The Player* seems to rechannel conventional avenues of emotional access. Rather than generating identification with characters, the social types in Altman's film focus our attention on the shaping forces of the social environment.

The characters not only "fail" to function as suturing agents because they are presented as types rather than unique individuals. The emotional distance created by the film's social-type characters is underscored by the distancing strategies of the film's manipulation of star discourse and performance. Characters in the Altman film can be seen, finally, as epiphenomenal, as pretexts "holding together dispersed moments of plot" (Frow 1986: 237).[10] The net effect, I believe, is what Brecht would call alienation.

Parodic Play with Star Discourse and Performance

The Player's use of players, in character roles and cameo parts, mirrors the strategies that produce the film's postmodern suture; for even though the actors cannot break the fourth wall by addressing the audience directly, or by coming down off the stage, *The Player* seems to approximate these theatrical devices by toying with star discourse. Hollywood films have often used star images in ironic ways, and they have depended on the intertextual associations of star images to individualize formulaic conceptions of character. In an essay on Jimmy Stewart, Marlon Brando, Gary Cooper, and others, Maurice Yacowar analyzes the star system's "fertility of cross-reference" (1979: 46). In a piece on Altman's films, Yacowar points out that the director's manipulation of star images reveals a "personal vocabulary of stars," as well as an ironic use of "the public language of familiar stars" (1980: 18).

In *The Player*, star images do serve to enrich fictional characters. For example, Whoopi Goldberg's star image individualizes the character of Detective Avery, and makes it seem "natural" that Detective Avery leads the anarchy at the Pasadena Police Station in the infamous tampon scene that ends with Griffin demanding to see his lawyer while the cops enjoy a good laugh. Star images also provide "narratives" for some of the cameo performances. For example, Cher is "cast" as the celebrity who comes to the elegant black-and-white attire dinner banquet in a flame red gown. But the film also does something quite different from its play with specific star images: it generates a parody of star images and the star system itself.

In the Altman film, cameos function in markedly unconventional ways. First, there is the central irony that stars have been cast in bit parts and as "background." Second, there are sixty-five people, almost all stars, listed in the credits as playing themselves. This virtual avalanche of stars shifts the focus of attention to *star discourse itself*. The overwhelming number of stars defuses the erotic charge normally built into star performances, and the "cavalcade of stars" underscores, rather than naturalizes, the inherent tension between star images that transcend specific texts, and fictional characters in classical-realist films.

The film's denaturalization of star discourse does not, however, entail an attack on star performances, for *The Player* seems to reject the standard view that Hollywood actors are "bad" actors just playing themselves. Instead, the film demonstrates the profound difference between in-character star performances, and instances, such as in *The Player*, where stars are in fact just playing themselves. For example, the film makes it possible to see that Jack Lemmon as the alcoholic in *Days of Wine and Roses* (1962) or the bewildered father in *Missing* (1982) is different from Jack Lemmon playing the piano in the background at the party given by Dick Mellen (Sydney Pollock).

The wealth of cameo performances does provide verisimilitude and a sense of authenticity for the film's story of Hollywood development deals.

But the stars playing background roles in an ensemble piece counters (industry-generated) assumptions about stars' egos, and their utter dependence on "personality" and "natural talent." What is interesting is the view of collaborative players that emerges from the stars' bit part performances. The image of stars working together as an ensemble presents us with a counter-weight, an alternative, a Derridean supplement to exposés about Hollywood stars, *and* to the film's own narrative which emphasizes the machinations of relentlessly competitive Hollywood corporate players.

The stars in the background insure that there will be (at least) two opposing images of Hollywood in play throughout the film. On the one hand, the film's diegetic world presents us with an image of Hollywood that is defined by the power plays of executives who refuse to be members of a team. On the other hand, the film's performative register presents us with an image of Hollywood where stars work together to create the background fabric. The net effect of the cameos is that spectators are positioned, but in relation to a point of view that is dialogic rather than fixed.

The Player's parodic use of star discourse counters the conventions that have come to define classical Hollywood cinema. The "cavalcade of stars" draws attention *away from* the narrative by inviting spectators to engage in a game of "name that star." At the party at Dick Mellen's, the dialogue identifies people like Harry Belafonte and Rod Steiger. But it casually "fails" to pick out people like Steve Allen and Jayne Meadows for us. At the glitzy banquet, the dialogue and voice over identify people like Cher and Teri Garr, but we are teasingly left on our own to name people like Sally Kellerman and Karen Black.

The endless cameos also disrupt classical-realist suture by helping to denaturalize the performances of the actors playing characters in the film. They create a Brechtian distance between the lead actors and their characters because the excessive number of cameos calls attention to actors as actors. They become an excessive presence that intermittently ruptures the seamless performances given by actors playing specific parts. Rather than there being a primary connection between actor and character, in *The Player* there comes to be a more primary connection between all the actors in the film. The connection between the actors playing on different registers disrupts classical-realist conventions that mask the performative work of actors.

The distance between actor and character is reinforced by hyperbolic elements of scenes' *mise-en-scene* that underscore significance to the point of parody. In the scene at the kariaoke bar where Griffin has a drink with David Kahane, the sentimental lyrics of the song mimic and mock Griffin's effort to placate Kahane. As Griffin apologizes for not getting back to Kahane, saying that he would like to start over again in their working relationship, the karaoke screen in the background prints out the words, "let's begin again." In the scene where Griffin's co-worker and erstwhile girlfriend, Bonnie Sharow (Cynthia Stevenson), confronts him about taking "June what's her name" to the gala affair hosted by Griffin's studio, Griffin's rattlesnake tie and the poster for Fritz Lang's thriller *M* (1931) seen in close-up at the end of the scene telegraph the meaning of the exchange so emphatically that the costuming and decor become ironic elements creating emotional distance rather than involvement in the conflict between Griffin and Bonnie. Rather than letting us decide that Griffin is a thoughtless guy, his clothes tells us he is a (rattle)snake, and the poster's tag line tells us he's just committed "the worst crime of all."

In this scene and elsewhere, Tim Robbins and Cynthia Stevenson give "realistic" performances, performances normally found with other textual strategies designed to engage the spectators' emotional involvement. But in *The Player*, because the "realistic" performances are juxtaposed with strategies like the hyperbolic *mise-en-scene* and the endless cameos, suture in the conventional sense is forfeited and replaced with conflicting representational modes that seem to generate an awareness of players *performing* parts. If there is suture, it is a different kind of suture.

The "realistic" performances of the actors playing characters are also brought into relief by being made to seem sometimes rigid, sometimes overwrought in contrast to the relaxed performances of the stars in cameo parts. The stars' bit part performances have an improvisational feel and are marked by signs of "naturalness." The feeling of natural spontaneity is enhanced by Altman's signature approach to dialogue and sound mixing. The overlapping lines and conversations in the background connote a sense of spontaneity or "live" performance, and require active participation on the part of the audience. Spectators must select what to pay attention to; they are engaged but in a way that is quite distinct from classical-realist suture, because attention is drawn away from the central narrative.

The Player's improvisational performances also play a role in disrupting conventional suture by providing ironic distance and commentary on its noir-inflected story about Hollywood ambition, for the stars' ensemble performances are completely at odds with the film's narrative portraying the intense competition in backstage Hollywood.[11] That the improvisational "feel" of the cameo performances works against the central story of controlled, obsessive ambition, and as a consequence has an actual *meaning producing function*; it echoes strategies employed in earlier Altman films. Virginia Wright Wexman has observed that in other Altman films, improvisational performances have led to the kind of textual indeterminacy that seems central to *The Player*'s break with Hollywood conventions. She points out that in the earlier Altman films, it is the form rather than the content of improvised performances that creates meaning (see 1980). Here in *The Player*, as perhaps elsewhere in Altman's work, we are given a demonstration of Brecht's point that the alienation effect "absolutely depends on lightness and naturalness of performance" (1964: 95).

Resistance in an Aesthetics of Absence

The Player presents us with a barrage of "messages": conflicting allusions, self-reflexive moves, hyperbolic use of casting and *mise-en-scene*. These discursive strategies are mirrored by the outpouring of communication in the diegetic world. Griffin's world is awash with messages: phone calls in his office, in his car; the angry writer reaches him by phone, postcard, faxes to his office and his car. In spite of (or perhaps because of) all these "messages," Griffin kills the wrong writer but "gets the girl." If a parallel is to be drawn, the film seems to be underscoring the problem of interpretation, at best a "game" where re-presentation is neither possible nor perhaps prudent.[12]

The integral role that spectators play in *The Player*'s "game" of interpretation comes to the foreground in the second of two carphone pitch sequences, for the scene can be read almost as a moment of direct address, where the film lays bare its incompleteness, and the spectator's role as the unified/unifying subject of reading. The first call is initiated by Griffin who plans to dupe Larry Levy into taking on a project that will bomb at the box office; the second, from Larry to Griffin, leads to the close of the film. In this second scene, the writer pitching the script is "the king of suspense himself," the postcard writer who had been harassing Griffin earlier in the film. The writer explains that his script is about a "shit-bag producer" who murders a writer he thinks is harassing him; the producer finds out he has murdered the wrong writer, so has trouble with blackmail and the police, but gets away with it and marries the writer's girlfriend. Griffin wants to know if the writer can guarantee the ending. The writer tells Griffin he can, *if* the price is right. Griffin makes the bargain, then turns the threat into a validation of his success — he even likes the script's title, *The Player*. The call and the deal concluded, Griffin steps out of his Rolls Royce into the arms of his beautiful, very pregnant wife, June. The music swells as the couple embrace, framed by an American flag and the blooming roses of their estates' sumptuous garden.

The scene can be read as a happy ending that valorizes spectacle, power, and the American flag. But we can, I believe, note signs of resistance. Given that it follows the scene where executives screen the new happy ending to *Habeus Corpus* demanded by the Canoga Park preview audience, it is difficult *not* to notice the Sirkian hollowness of *The Player*'s happy ending. Moreover, one of the most telling elements is the musical phrase that plays over the couple's embrace. It is from Roman Polanski's *Rosemary's Baby* (1968), and so identifies Griffin as the "actor" who sells out to the coven of devil worshipers to further his career. A reading that sees signs of resistance takes into account differences between what Thomas Elsaesser calls the upper register of the story and the lower register of montage, music, and structural parallels. The film ostensibly gives audiences their cherished happy ending, but by loading the lower register with signs pointing in the opposite direction, it criticizes "the streak of incurably naive moral and emotional idealism in the American psyche" (Elsaesser 1972:12).

A certain reading of the ending can also locate signs of resistance because the film's participation in the postmodern "aesthetics of absence" marks a complete departure from the suturing strategies of Classical Hollywood Cinema. While a classical-realist narrative presents itself as a transcription of a reality present elsewhere, *The Player* announces that, as a film on the screen, it is not even the representation of a screenplay, a fiction. In other words, the film completely rejects the notion of re-presentation, and so differs even from narratives with trick endings that finally present themselves as the hallucination of a character in the film. Instead, *The Player* destroys is own presence by suggesting that the film on the screen is a film that is yet to be produced — *by the spectator*. The film presents itself as incomplete, and unmasks the play it has been making for the spectator/subject.

It may be that here, and elsewhere, *The Player* offers "a cultural critique so subtle and endlessly skeptical ... it finally does little else than deconstruct itself" (Sarvan 1991: 53).[13] It is true that the film risks complicity with the conventions it subjects to critique, yet I believe that the effect is, finally, to bring them out for examination. Perhaps we should ask, what is it that we expect of a text? What would constitute resistance in the postmodern era? A rather different project than that found in Godard's *Weekend* (1967), *The Player* does not mount an open attack on late-capitalism. But it does represent a film marked by oppositional practices, for *The Player* breaks with classical-realist conventions and places text/spectator relations center stage.[14]

I think it *is* a mistake to equate a film's use of retro-classical or modernist formal strategies with resistance. Given postmodern audiences' horizon of expectations, can we determine whether a film's use of classical-realist conventions is read as inscribed or as inscribed-but-put-under-erasure? What is the effect of a text's stylization and self-reflexivity? If a film is parodic, is the critique directed toward traditions, texts, or the ideological inscription carried by the models? I think it is problematic to look for a full-blown attack on aesthetic or cultural traditions in an era that has rejected the notion of master narratives.[15] It is probably useful to recall that the attacks mounted on existing systems in the modernist era were inextricably bound to their latent utopian visions.

There is, however, yet another misstep, and that is to reject the possibility of resistance in postmodern cinema, to overlook resistance when it in fact exists. Throughout the film, *The Player's* parodic stylization and excessive self-reflexivity confound our efforts to see the film as representing some quotidian or fictional reality. Its conception of character as social type, its parody of the star system, and the shifting levels of performance that arise from its combination of star-cameos and actors-in-character work against our habit of seeing Hollywood film performances either as extensions of stars' personalities, or representations of characters who inhabit real or imaginary worlds. *The Player* uses standard Hollywood elements, "suspense, laughter, violence, hope, heart, nudity, sex, happy endings," but deploys them in ways that problematize spectator positioning, for these elements become, finally, *traces* of a classical suturing system that is set at a parodic distance. In place of classical suture, a film like *The Player* offers a different kind of suture. It engages audiences in *theatrical games* that turn viewers' attention to text/spectator relationships. The film seems to offer a look at the Absurd fictional status of text *and* spectator, and in the "lightness and naturalness" of its cameo performances, a model for responding to that glimpse.

REFERENCES

Affron, Charles. 1982. *Cinema and Sentiment*. Chicago: University of Chicago Press.

Altman, Robert. 1993. "One on One." Interview. Produced by Denise Farley and New Line Home Video.

Arac, Jonathan. 1988. "Hamlet, Little Dorritt, and the History of Character." *South Atlantic Quarterly* 87, no. 2: 311-328.

Bakhtin, Mikhail. 1981. *The Dialogic Imagination*. Austin: University of Texas Press.

Bazin, Andre. 1971. "The Evolution of the Language of Cinema." In *What is Cinema Vol I*. Berkeley: University of California Press.

———— 1971. "In Defense of Rossellini." In *What is Cinema Vol. II*. Berkeley: University of California Press.

Brecht, Bertold. 1964. *Brecht on Theatre*. New York: Hill and Wang.

Connor, Steven. 1989. *Postmodernist Culture*. Cambridge: Blackwell Press.

Dayan, Daniel. 1974. "The Tutor-Code of Classical Cinema." *Film Quarterly* 28, no. 1 (fall).

Degli-Esposti, Cristina. 1994. "Voicing the Silence in Federico's Fellini's *La voce della luna*." *Cinema Journal* 33, no. 2 (winter).

Derrida, Jacques. 1972. *Positions*. Chicago: University of Chicago Press.

———— 1978. "Freud and the Scene of Writing." In *Writing and Difference*. Chicago: University of Chicago Press.

Elsaesser, Thomas. 1972. "Tales of Sound and Fury." *Monogram* 4: 2-15.

Frow, John. 1986. "Spectacle Binding: On Character." *Poetics Today* 7, no. 2: 227-250.

Heath, Stephen. 1978. "Notes on Suture." *Screen* 18, no. 4 (winter 1977-78).

Kinder, Marsha. 1990. "The Subversive Potential of the Pseudo-Iterative." *Film Quarterly* 43, no. 2 (winter 1989-90).

Kolker, Robert. 1983. *The Altering Eye*. New York: Oxford University Press.

Miller, Jacques-Alain. 1978. "Suture: Elements of the Logic of the Signifier." *Screen* 18, no. 4 (winter 1977-78): 24-34.

Mulvey, Laura. 1975. "Visual Pleasure and Narrative Cinema." *Screen* 16, no. 3.

Oudart, Jean-Louis. 1978. "Suture and Cinema." *Screen* 18, no. 4 (winter 1977-78): 35-47.

Polan, Dana. 1978. "Brecht and the Politics of Self-Reflexive Cinema." *Jump Cut* 17: 29-32.

Ray, Robert. 1985. *A Certain Tendency of the Hollywood Cinema, 1930-1980*. New Jersey: Princeton University Press.

Sarvan, David. 1991. "Revolution ... History ... Theater: The Politics of the Wooster Group's Second Trilogy." In *The Performance of Power*. Iowa City: University of Iowa Press.

Sayre, Henry. 1983. "The Object of Performance: Aesthetics in the ." *Georgia Review* 37, no. 1.

Silverman, Kaja. 1983. *The Subject of Semiotics*. New York: Oxford University Press.

Smith, Murray. 1994. "Altered States: Character and Emotional Response in the Cinema." *Cinema Journal* 33, no. 4: 34-56.

Spolin, Viola. 1983. *Improvisation for the Theater.* Illinois: Northwestern University Press.

Stam, Robert, Robert Burgoyne, and Sandy Flitterman-Lewis. 1992. *New Vocabularies in Film Semiotics.* New York: Routledge.

States, Bert. 1992. *Hamlet and the Conception of Character.* Baltimore: Johns Hopkins University Press.

Wexman, Virginia Wright. 1980. "The Rhetoric of Cinematic Improvisation." *Cinema Journal* 20, no. 1 (fall): 29-41.

Wyatt, Justin. 1994. *High Concept: Movies and Marketing in Hollywood.* Austin: University of Texas Press.

Yacowar, Maurice. 1979. "An Aesthetic Defense of the Star System in Films." *Quarterly Review of Film Studies* 4, no. 1 (winter): 39-52.

——— 1980. "Actors as Conventions in the Films of Robert Altman." *Cinema Journal* 20, no. 1 (fall): 14-28.

Notes

1. The term "suture" moved into Anglo-American film theory with the publication of Daniel Dayan's "The Tutor-Code of Classical Cinema," published in *Film Quarterly* (1974), the translations of Jacques-Alain Miller's "Suture: Elements of the Logic of the Signifier," and Jean-Pierre Oudart's "Suture and Cinema" in *Screen* (1978). Certain analyses of suture have not only considered suture in classical-realist texts, but also the way that the dynamics of suture persist in the face of modernist strategies. In "Brecht and the Politics of Self-Reflexive Cinema," Dana Polan demonstrates that self-reflexivity can become part of what Roland Barthes calls the enigmatic or hermeneutic code, functioning simply as a delay, a detour, or introduction of a minor enigma that does not create emotional distance or ideological awareness (see Polan 1978). That the kind of suture found in classical-realist texts is not disrupted by modernist formal strategies is also indicated by the fact that they are part of commercial television. Summarizing Peter Wollen's views on counter cinema, Stam, Burgoyne, and Flitterman-Lewis list the central "modernist" strategies as narrative intransitivity, estrangement, foregrounding, multiple diegesis, aperture, unpleasure, and reality (see Stam et al. 1992: 198).

2. See Frow 1986. Frow makes the same point I am in arguing that linguistic discontinuity "constitutes the condition of inscription of the reader as the *unified* subject of reading" (237).

3. Viola Spolin developed a system of improvisation that began from premises fundamentally distinct from those of Konstantin Stanislavsky's "System" and Lee Strasberg's "Method." Spolin's approach to performance was popularized by groups such as Second City. *The Player's* improvisational strategies might be compared to the work of directors like Spolin and Joseph Chaikin, whose improvisational theatre advocated a continual circuit of interchange in place of the re-presentation of a text.

4. Analyses of postmodern performance by Henry Sayre and Steven Connor suggest starting points for an integration of film theory, and the significant body of work on postmodern theatre and performance.

5. The character's first name, Griffin, conjures up the image of a griffin, an emblematic, fantastic, polymorphous figure. The last name, Mill, suggests a connection between the character in Altman's film and Hollywood mogul Cecil B. DeMille. Putting the two names or terms together allows us to consider power brokers in Hollywood through and in terms of connotations surrounding the figure of the griffin.

6. *The Player* draws these films into its orbit in the scene where the executives screen the rushes from *The Lonely Room*, the film-within-the-film with Lily Tomlin and Scott Glenn.

7. For discussion of character in von Stroheim's films, see Andre Bazin, "The Evolution of the Language of Cinema," *What is Cinema Vol 1.*, p. 27; and Robert Kolker, *The Altering Eye*, p. 38.

8. The normative gender positions are perhaps complicated further on when June, taking photographs of Griffin, become the one who looks. Yet Altman's film is quite different from a work such as Nicolas Roeg's *Track 29*, which not only engages in a postmodern investigation of representation, but also a feminist critique of phallocentric theory. For a discussion of the film, see Cynthia Baron, "Nicolas Roeg's *Track 29*: Acting Out a Critique of Theory in a Postmodern Melodrama," *Spectator* 14, no. 1 (fall 1993).

9. *The Player's* happy ending is perhaps even more problematic than those found in Sirk's films. The happy endings in the Sirk melodramas carry the absurd but socially sanctioned message that victims of social circumstance can lead lives that end happily ever after. By comparison, the happy ending in Altman's film carries the message that cads like Griffin and the postcard writer not only can but should "get away with murder."

10. Discussing character in the eighteenth-century novel, John Frow explains that characters hold together "dispersed moments of plot, anecdote, and digressive reflection" (237). Like Frow's work, Elizabeth MacArthur's analysis of eighteenth-century epistolary novels in *Extravagant Fictions: Closure and Dynamics in the Epistolary Form* (1990) provides counter examples to dominant paradigms in narrative theory, and as a consequence suggests ways to conceptualize narrative in the postmodern era.

11. The situations Viola Spolin describes as antithetical to improvisation suggest a diagnosis of the problem that plagues *The Player's* studio executives. Spolin explains that "a highly competitive atmosphere creates artificial tensions, and when competition replaces participation, compulsive action is the result" (1983: 10).

12. The film seems to make the Lacanian point that misreadings produce meaning. Departing perhaps from a Lacanian perspective, the film seems to suggest that misreadings produce both conventional stories, as well as useful material for reflection.

13. *The Player's* shifting levels of fiction, and its continual interplay between text and intertext can be compared to work by the Wooster Group whose productions often intercut seemingly unrelated fragments of texts to provide new contexts for material and exemplify what Steven Conner calls "theatrical deconstruction" (1989: 145).

14. The process of spectator positioning in *The Player* is, I think, fundamentally distinct from that of high concept films like *Flashdance* (1984) or *American Gigolo* (1980) which, as Justin Wyatt explains, generate identification with characters who offer entry into an exciting lifestyle, and throughout their narratives tell audiences that "style" is a way of life, a utopian way of life. The high concept films reactivate strategies found in

classical-realist films which suture spectators into identifying with fictional characters, gendered spectator positions, and the ideological perspectives of consumer culture.

15. Robert Ray makes a similar point in his discussion on American cinema. Ray argues that for film practice to effectively counter the conservative tendencies of Hollywood cinema, American films cannot follow the model suggested by "the Godardian/Straubian film of unmitigated dislocation, disruption, and estrangement," but instead should "make use of American culture's Imaginary" and draw on Hollywood's thematic and formal paradigms precisely for the purpose of criticizing them (1985: 362, 363).

Aladdin *(Walt Disney, 1992) Animation*
Wish-giving genie (voice of Robin Williams) will turn street-smart Aladdin into a prince.
Still courtesy of Jerry Ohlinger's Movie Materials.

CHAPTER 2

INTERTEXTUAL MANEUVERS AROUND THE SUBALTERN

Aladdin as a Postmodern Text

Marwan M. Kraidy

"When politics is cloaked in the image of innocence, there is more at stake than simple deception. There is the issue of cultural power and how it influences public understandings of the past, national identity, coherence, and popular memory as a site of injustice, criticism, and renewal" (Giroux 1993: 84). This statement by Henry Giroux postulates popular culture as a hybridized arena where cultural strategies of representation, negotiation, and resistance have been fiercely fought. Moving to a specific example, Giroux proceeded: "Under the rubric of fun, entertainment and escape, massive public spheres are being produced, which appear too "innocent" to be worthy of political analyses. Such is the case of the Disney Company." Disney has indeed attained a legendary status in world popular culture and has become an enduring icon in the global cultural pantheon. Disney's *Aladdin* (1993) displays an aura of playfulness and innocence positing a utopian age of purity. Beneath this harmless surface, however, a myriad of semiotic constellations engage a plethora of signs in a powerful field of signification where constructions of race, class, and gender are imbricated in monolithic formulae and reductive conventions converging in the power dyad of a glamorized Self and a postulated Other.

The racist, capitalist, and patriarchal subtexts intertwine and interconnect through semiotic configurations which subvert signs and symbols into a postmodern carnival of intertextuality and illusion. These webs of semiosis are engaged in a process of intervalidation and reciprocal naturalization, thus perpetuating prevailing ideological dichotomies.

In this paper I expose and scrutinize *Aladdin's* three subtextual constructions of race, gender, and class. This is followed by a deconstruction of the webs of signification operating to validate these three subtexts and the unravelling of the ideological underpinnings concealed within the film's textual structure.

Race

Hollywood's ideological manufacturing of the Orient is one of the most enduring sites of Otherness in American popular culture. A plethora of cartoons, starting amidst the colonial era, constructed the Orient in all "its barbarities, its eccentricities, its unruliness" (Said 1979: 290): *Aladdin and His Wonderful Lamp* (1934), *Sinbad the Sailor* (1935), *Ali Baba* (1936), *Popeye the Sailor Meets Sinbad the Sailor* (1936), *Sahara Hare* [a Bugs Bunny piece] (1955), and Woody Woodpecker in *A Lad in Bagdad* (1962) (Smoodin 1993: 23).

The latest to date, Disney's *Aladdin* (note that the series started with an Aladdin) is no exception to the rule. The narrative unfolds in Agrabah, a stereotypical Arabland. Phonetically, the word Agrabah is rugged and heavy, "barbaric." Etymologically, the root "Agra" denotes an agricultural/agrarian society with a connotation of "underdevelopment." The movie opens with a song, "Arabian Nights," howled by a storyteller riding a camel with a disproportionate bump, which goes like this:

> *Oh, I come from a land,*
> *From a faraway place,*
> *Where the caravan camels roam,*
> *Where they cut off your ears,*
> *If they don't like your face,*
> *It's barbaric, but hey it's home.*

This "barbaric" land is deployed in all its unruly exoticism. It is inhabited mainly by wicked greedy thieves, shyly salacious harem girls, and acrimonious unscrupulous merchants. The Souk is a place of complete chaos, where vendors display everything from pearls to fruits and vegetables. Colorful laundry hangs on ropes criss-crossing vertically and horizontally above narrow and tortuous alleys. Jars of all shapes, sizes and colors fill the corners, and chaotic herds of sheep block the narrow streets. Other exotic spectacles include fire-spitting, sword swallowing, and tanned and skinny fakeers lying on their nail-spiked planks. Plunging camera-tilt shots display the place as low and debased, but alive and bustling. Vendors have huge bulbous or sharply hooked noses, sinister looks and retarded accents.

Said (1979) identified these features, including the ugly mustachioed chins and idiotic faces, as obvious reminders that for years in Western popular culture, Semites were considered the cause of all troubles. Be it a gasoline shortage, a stock exchange crash, or even natural disasters, the Semite played the role of the ideal scapegoat, the wicked anti-hero.

The guards chase Aladdin in large groups, similar to an animalistic herd. They appear to be oversexed, degenerate, and abusive. The vendors have idiotic accents, ugly beards, and a pervert gleam in their eyes implying that they would sell their mothers for a fistful of silver coins. When Jasmin takes an apple for the noble cause of feeding a starving child, the vendor immediately brandishes a sword, belting: "Do you know what is the penalty for stealing?" He was about to cut Jasmin's fist, in a gross misrepresentation of Islamic laws.

The Arab-American Anti-Discrimination Committee (ADC) strongly reacted to the movie, reading it as a blatant example of "unconscious racism" (Shaheen 1993) against Arabs. Closer scrutiny reveals that *Aladdin's* subtext is not restricted to Arabs, but extends to other traditionally stereotyped minorities and subcultures, ultimately encompassing all that is not male, Western, White, "civilized," and "developed."

In his writings on Mandelshtam, Taranovsky postulated the concept of a literary subtext (*podtekst* in Russian) as any latent meaning that can be recovered behind the surface meaning of an utterance (Tammi 1991: 316). Subtextuality assumes that any subtext relies on an *already existing* utterance which has been reconstructed (Sil'man, in Tammi, emphasis mine). Thus *Aladdin* reconstructs pre-existing prejudices and stereotypes. Radio host Casey Casem (*LA Times*, November 14 1993, cited in *Cahiers du Cinéma: Aladdin*) wrote hypothetical lyrics inspired from "Arabian Nights," as they might apply to other ethnic groups. According to him, his aim was to show that there was no more truth to the lyrics he created than to the opening song of the movie. He began with "anti-Native-American lyrics":

> *Oh, I come from the wide-open,*
> *Spaces out West,*
> *Where the Indian ponies roam;*
> *Where they scalp you dead,*
> *If they don't like your head,*
> *Its barbaric, but hey, it's home.*

He then proceeded with "anti-Latino lyrics":

> *Oh, I come from a land,*
> *Where they sleep in the sun,*
> *And the gangs of bandidos roam;*
> *where they hang you in jail,*
> *If you don't pay the bail,*
> *It's barbaric, but hey, it's home.*

And finally concluded with "anti-Jewish lyrics":

> *Oh, I come from a land*
> *Where religion is law,*
> *And the prophets and rabbis roam;*
> *Where they stone you to death*
> *If you question the faith,*
> *It's barbaric, but hey, it's home.*

Again, Casem's aim was to show that there was no more truth to the above lyrics than to those of "Arabian Nights." His rhetorical maneuvers help illustrate the all-encompassing reach of *Aladdin's* racist subtext, revealed by a series of more or less subtle codes in the movie. Thus, many vendors have a distinctly exaggerated Indian (and not Arabic) accent. A series of stereotypes of Black Americans (treated later in the paper) shows up at the end of the movie: when the genie becomes Jaffar's slave and obeying thus the orders of evil, the genie's color swiftly switches from blue to black, and his face espouses African traits. Along those same lines, neither clothing nor architecture are distinctly Arab or Islamic. They are rather a mixture of Persian, Islamic, and Indian features and include other random elements. The feathers and the diamonds on some turbans evoke India's maharadjas; other turbans definitely represent Sikh sartorial customs. The towers of the Sultan's place are a mixture of Persian, Islamic, and Indian architectural styles. These hybrid elements lead a French critic to refer to Agrabah as a Persian city (*Cahiers du Cinéma* 1994). Other codes, such as the stereotypical animals with stereotypical names (Rajah the Indian tiger and Abu the Arab monkey), the exotic parrots, and the extravagant water fountains, all contribute to the painting of the colonial landscape of exotica.

Class

A second subtext of *Aladdin's* narrative is a movement of "upward social mobility," as developmentalists would label it — to the Whole New World. Richardson (1994) demonstrated that *Aladdin's* storyline is interweaved with the American power mythos through which the shabby "street rat" turns out to be the "diamond in the rough." This reincarnation of the myth of the American dream stages Aladdin's efforts in his rags to riches journey.

Early in the movie, Aladdin has a confrontation with one of Jasmin's pretenders. After a verbal clash, Aladdin ends up in a muddy pit as the prince exclaims: "You're a street rat, you'll always be a street rat, you'll die as a street rat, and only your fleas will mourn you." Aladdin's humiliation is depicted with an extreme low angle shot, making Aladdin look minuscule and wretched as he thinks to himself: "I'm not worthless." Back to his humble abode, Aladdin thinks: "There's so much more to me." His only companion is his pet monkey Abu, to whom he speaks: "One day Abu, we're gonna be rich, live in a palace, and never have any problem at all." This point of attack marks the beginning of Aladdin's struggle to prove to himself and to others that he is not worthless. His only weapons of ascension are his shrewdness and his acute sense of self-reliance.

Aladdin is street-smart. He saves Jasmin from having her wrist cut by telling the merchant that she is mentally deranged. Aladdin and Abu are always seen executing sophisticated plots to steal food. When escaping the guards, a group of women, who obviously know Aladdin rather intimately as shown by their large smiles and shivering eyebrows, help him hide from the guards. Aladdin even manages to trick the genie of the lamp into getting him and Abu out of the cave without exhausting one of the three wishes he is entitled to as the master of the genie. Aladdin's chef-d'oeuvre remains nonetheless his trapping the evil Jaffar in an oil lamp. When Jaffar, having stolen the lamp and enslaved the genie, proclaims himself as the most powerful sorcerer in the universe, Aladdin reminds him that the genie, who gave Jaffar his power, remains more powerful than him. Jaffar's ego leads him into ordering the genie to grant him his third wish, making him the most powerful genie of all. As a genie can never come without a lamp, Jaffar the genie becomes a prisoner of his lamp and thrown faraway in the desert. Aladdin's ascension to a better world is also depicted visually, where Aladdin is increasingly seen climbing ladders and stairs.

Early in the narrative, Jasmin becomes the ultimate dream to Aladdin, the sine qua non condition for him to step into the Whole New World. She becomes the materialization of his wildest fantasies. At the same time, Aladdin turns out to be Jasmin's savior, her only way out of the kingdom's rigid traditions and Jaffar's evil plotting. Jasmin's confinement is shown in an early scene where she opens the window, causing doves to fly toward the sun, while she raises her hand, reaching out for freedom. When she talks to Aladdin for the first time, they discover that they both have the feeling of "being just trapped." However, they will eventually be free and happy, since they are both handsome and speak "correct English," i.e., without an accent, or more precisely with an urban middle-class American accent. Besides, Aladdin and the genie are the mind-body dyad, representing Science and Technology, which in modernist terms constitute a guaranteed entry to the Whole New World of material prosperity and conceptual supremacy.

Gender

Disney's *Aladdin* posits a seemingly "progressive" narratively constructed femininity compatible with political correctness. Princess Jasmin's character embodies the politically correct discourse of feminine emancipation and incorporates gender equality signifiers which are projected at the movie's textual surface. These codes seemingly signal new semiotic and narrative strategies posited against previous Disney animation movies such as *Snow White* and *Cinderella*, where female protagonists were blatantly passive, victimized, and dependent.

The narrative strategies and semiotic codes by which Jasmin's gendered character is constructed within the symbolic order of patriarchal ideology are unraveled here. *Aladdin's* pseudo feminist subtext, deconstructed, will demonstrate that the narrational shift posited in the film is not embedded in an ideological "awakening," but rather is a redeployment of the conventional codes of signification into new semiotic configurations.

I will begin by focusing on Jasmin's narrative agency, on the surface strong and independent but in fact submissive and dependent. I will then proceed with the examination of other textual elements that operate as intertexts naturalizing the patriarchal subtext. Finally, *Aladdin* will be treated as a *hysterical text*, defined by Modleski (1991), as a text so heavily repressive of its sexual impulses that these sexual undertones emerge in textual elements such as dialogue and mise-en-scène.

Jasmin is depicted as a beautiful and rich princess, a lonely shining beauty. Nonetheless, she is repeatedly portrayed as a strong woman: when the guards catch Aladdin, executing Jaffar's orders, Jasmin takes off the veil on her face and orders the guards, "by order of the Princess," to let Aladdin go. Later on, after Aladdin's metamorphosis into Prince Ali Ababwah, Jasmin jumps in the room where the sultan (her father), Jaffar, and Prince Ali/Aladdin are discussing her marriage, and shouts: "How dare you, all of you?...I am not a prize to be won!" Later on, she derides and disparages Prince Ali/Aladdin and compares him to her numerous stupid and arrogant pretenders. Finally, Jasmin bodily participates in the final battle against Jaffar, showing "manly" fighting skills. The film's "strong woman" discourse is also enacted when Jaffar, who regularly calls Jasmin "pussy cat" addresses her: "You're speechless, I see. Fine quality in a wife!" Jaffar's utterance of sexist comments will be espoused with resistance since Jaffar's character is constructed and postulated as evil.

Under this pseudo feminist politically correct text lies a highly patriarchal subtext. When Jasmin orders the guards to release Aladdin, it is only in the name of her father's status that she does so. The preeminence of the father in the movie barely hides the absence of the mother. Jasmin does not have a mother in the movie. Rumors circulating at the moment of *Aladdin's* release assert that the original script had a mother character which was later eliminated, with no apparent justification. Dorfman and Mattelart (1971), studying early Disney comics, have pointed out that the mother is not merely missing in the comics; rather, she simply does not exist as a concept.

Dorfman and Mattelart carried out a psychoanalytical explanation of the absence of the mother in Disney cartoons. Investigating Walt Disney's personal life, they discovered that he hated and resented his parents and was extremely reluctant to mention his childhood. Consequently, the child in Disney texts operates as a mask of adult anxieties. The sultan is a naive, jolly, and hypopituitary old man whose rotundity suggests harmlessness. He is repeatedly seen playing with construction games and trains. He is cute, circular, and infantile. The existence of the father and the absence of the mother anchor *Aladdin's* patriarchal subtext, thus ensconced in a "myth of patrilineal filiation without the mother," a "male parthogenesis" (Forgacs 1992: 373). The movie's protagonist and antagonist are males, as are their pets.

Exceptions include the veiled women who help hide Aladdin, unsuccessfully, in the market and the salacious and oversexed black woman who tries to take Aladdin from the guards. The veiled women in the market give Aladdin their best smiles and their sexiest looks, while the big black women who grabs him, uttering salacious words from her ridiculously large mouth constitutes a re-enactment of two of the oldest and most persistent stereotypes of African-American women: the large nanny with the raucous voice, and the fat, oversexed, man-devouring female. Another exception is Rajah, the massive Bengali tiger. Rajah is constructed as a female character: his overwhelming tenderness, uncompromising faithfulness, and his protective behavior toward Jasmin posit Rajah as a loving and protective mother/confident. Rajah is however the only non-speaking animal character in the movie, embodying Jaffar's words that "speechlessness is a fine quality in a woman." These narrative trajectories, dialogue bits and character constructions are part of a web of signification that latently constructs Jasmin as "a price to be won." The ostentatory feminist subtext projected at the textual surface functions as a mask of the hidden patriarchal subtextual meaning.

Aladdin's patriarchal text is also highly repressive of any sexual tones, accomplished with narrative twists and diversions, best illustrated in the scenes in which Aladdin and Jasmin are about to kiss, a kiss that is always interrupted by an abrupt upheaval. The first kiss is about to occur in Aladdin's humble nest, when the palace guards suddenly interrupt them, invading the place with revolving swords and warlike screams. The second kiss is interrupted by the arrival of the Sultan in Jasmin's quarters, after Jasmin and Aladdin have just returned from a flight on the magic carpet. Seeing them together, the sultan explodes with joy, after having repeatedly expressed his anguish about the fact that Jasmin was not getting married, as he wants to make sure that "[She is] taken care of" and "provided for."

The film's repressiveness of sexual impulses can be said to mark a re-enactment of the "hysterical text." Modleski, borrowing the concept from Nowell-Smith, forwards the "hysterical text" as a text so highly repressive of its sexual content that the sexual tone will inevitably manifest itself in the narrative, the dialogue or the mise-en-scène (Modleski 1991: 137). The patriarchal preeminence and the emergence of the sexual content are embodied in the final song, when flying on the magic carpet, Aladdin sings:

I can show you the world…
I can open your eyes,
Take you, wonder after wonder,
Over, sideways and under…
Don't you dare close your eyes…

The song puts Aladdin in a dominant position: he is the leader, the commander who "show[s]" Jasmin the world. He is also the knowledgeable educator who "open[s]" her eyes. He is also the sexual stallion who "take[s]" her to "wonder after wonder," and with every wonder takes on a new position. He thus takes her "over," then "sideways," and finally "under," leading her to "undescribable feelings." This strong sexual connotation leads to Aladdin ordering Jasmin to keep her eyes open: this will allow (or force) her to see the Whole New World, and also admire and appreciate Aladdin's prowess.

Aladdin is an exemplar of a politically correct text with an apparently progressive and emancipatory direction, whereas in fact, the seemingly progressive textual surface operates as a mask for latent reactionary meanings. The misogynist ideological reach is even more pervasive because it is coated with the sugarlike texture of societal progress and gender equality. Thus *Aladdin's* ostentatory pseudo feminist discourse, apparently reflecting an "ideological awakening," or a "gender difference awareness," is in fact a reactionary text whose patriarchal subtext is built by novel and more subtle semiotic configurations.

Intertexts

In *Revolution in Poetic Language* (1984), Kristeva coined the term *intertextualité*, i.e., intertextuality, as her translation of Bakhtin's dialogism (1981), defined as "the necessary relation of any utterance to other utterances" (Stam et al.1992: 203) and traced to the Socratic dialogues, which staged two competing dialogues. By utterance, Bakhtin (1981) referred to any "complex of signs," be it a film, a song, a picture, or a poem. The concept of dialogism postulates that any text constitutes an intersection of textual surfaces. These textual surfaces are usually anonymous, conscious or unconscious citations and inversions, imbricated in a multitude of texts. Thus, potential intertextual connections involve all possible communicative processes within a culture, which work on a more or less latent process of never-ending dissemination of signifiers. Thus, every text is a "palimpsest" of traces

(Genette 1982), where other texts are constructed, decoded, and recoded. In other words, intertextuality can be defined as the reader's perception of the relations between a text and all the other texts that have preceded or will follow it (Rifaterre, in Stam et al. 1992).

In his study of Native-American myths, Lévi-Strauss (1969) demonstrated the conceptual necessity of intertextuality by showing that no particular myth could be comprehended unless it is connected to intricate webs of other myths, symbols, and cultural codes and practices. Eco (1979) refers to the diverse factors that orient and allow interpretation as "intertextual frames." The merit of intertextuality is that it relates the singular text to other frames of representation, floating and discursive, rather than restricting the text to a physical and amorphous context. Intertextual maneuvers operate latently to make *Aladdin's* three subtexts appear real and natural: 1) the deployment of an unruly and dangerous world of the Other, 2) the myth of the American dream and 3) the patriarchal discourse. These turn the film into a carnival of intertextuality where magic, consumer culture, Hollywood motion pictures, and other U.S. electoral campaigns and American foreign policy, disseminate a quasi-infinity of signifiers.

Children adore magic. The same goes for some adults, but magic will always bear a connotation of childhood. Disney animation movies characterize themselves as "movies for children." Genette (1982) refers to a text's willingness to define itself as belonging to a certain genre as architextuality. This generic designation orients and induces a preferred reading of the text. *Aladdin* begins with a gesticulating story-teller narrating his story about a "dark man, in a dark light, with a dark purpose." The narrative builds up an atmosphere of magic and esoterism. Then, the story-teller claps his hands and sparkles of gleaming and shimmering powder fly from the top of his fingers. This, with the sound of a minor chord played as an arpeggio on a harpsichord, is a conventional code for magic, easily identifiable by children. Other magical codes include the genie's impersonations of music-hall musicians, and the ultimate magic formula "Abracadabra," relentlessly repeated in the genie's songs. The genie's performance is also accompanied by ringing bells and smoky clouds. Other codes include the massive recipe book that permits the genie to turn Aladdin into a prince. Jaffar's wooden cobra is also an evil version of the magical stick which turns Rajah the tiger into a pitiful puppet and imprisons Jasmin with a sand-clock. Finally, fireworks, used regularly by animators, suggest the enchantment of magic.

Other consumer icons float on *Aladdin's* textual surface. The Tupperware in the story-teller's hands, the boxing ring, the game-shows and musicals contribute to the intertextual wealth of the film. The hard angles and steep flight of Aladdin and Abu riding the magic carpet in the cave are intertexts to video-games (such as Sega and Nintendo). The Harlem Globe-Trotters are also alluded to with the apples hidden in Aladdin's hair, and the Caesar's salad is offered by the genie while green imperial laurels spring on his head. The machine on which Iago sweats to activate his master's crystal ball strangely resembles advertisements for Nordic Track and the like. Other codes include Chinese dragons, the genie's olympic dive and Aladdin's leitmotiv: "You can call me Al." The genie also becomes a red-haired Italian sailor uttering passionate thoughts in a languorous French: "Ami, c'est l'Amour." Finally, the genie's wake up call to Aladdin, "wake up and smell the humus," is a sarcastic allusion to the fashionable "multicultural" or "ethnic" food which has flooded American mass culture.

Aladdin also bears an intertextual network connecting with Hollywood and the star system, labeled by some as "celebrity intertextuality." The Aladdin and genie characters refer to two of Hollywood's biggest current stars: Aladdin facial traits are modeled after Tom Cruise, who posed for Disney artists, and the voice behind the exuberant genie is Robin Williams. The genie's facial traits also evoke Keating's leprechaun eyes in *Dead Poets Society* and the cuddly and dedicated nanny/daddy in *Mrs. Doubtfire*. The overall ambiance, especially in scenes occurring in caves and deserts, connects with the Indiana Jones series and its hidden traps, labyrinths and mazes, while Jaffar's stick and the parrot on his shoulder allude to *Treasure Island's* wicked captain. The scene where Aladdin and Abu, although hungry, give the bread they have to a poor woman and her child evokes the famous scene in Charlie Chaplin's *The Circus*, and the jagged wheel that snatches Iago's feathers is a residual reminder of *Modern Times*.

Aladdin also connects with contemporary Hollywood productions. Jaffar and the *Three Musketeers'* Richelieu wear the same black and purple gown, have the same twisted goatee, the same precious and pretentious language, and the same gross voice articulation. Bram Stoker's *Dracula* also wears a similar gown, and the movie cites *Arabian Nights* as a performative stage for luxury, perversion, and depravation. Besides, when Jaffar takes power, he moves his castle to the top of a steep hill, just like Dracula. This could also be read as a reference to *Count Duckula*, the cartoon version of the vampire tale, very popular with children. Finally, hands severed from their arms juggle and dance around the genie, in a reference to the mysterious and hilarious hand from *The Addams Family Values.*

Signs of "intratextuality" connect in *Aladdin*, through which the movie refers to itself as a cinematic production. In the exposition scene, the story-teller asks the audience to come closer to him. As his face grows bigger on the screen, something hits his nose, the camera lens, and he rubs his hurt nose and angrily says : "Too close! That's too close." When the genie is discussing the potential for him to be set free by Aladdin and does not get the desired answer, he grabs a script (conventional Hollywood technical format) and tells Aladdin "Your line is..." Finally, with the final scene in which Jaffar turns into a huge and frightening snake, cheerleaders are intercut to remind the audience, most specially children, that they are just watching a movie. Autocitations are also used, referring to Disney's previous animation movies. One of the genie's impersonations is *Pinocchio*, an early Disney animation. *Cinderella* is obviously evoked when the genie turns Aladdin into a prince and Abu into a "deluxe-elephant-sedan." The genie also cites Sheherazade and Ali Baba, other features from the *Arabian Nights*, *Aladdin's* key inspiration.

Finally, a last series of intertexts connects with American politics, especially the 1992 presidential campaign and the (second) Gulf War. In Aladdin's first encounter with Jasmin, when they are both driven to the brink by the guards, Aladdin takes a step forward, turns to Jasmin, and asks her: "Do you trust me?" As Jasmin mutters an inaudible "yes," Aladdin screams: "Then jump!" before dragging her down with him. The same "Do you trust me?/yes" reoccurs later. This question sounds very much like the question that both Bush and Clinton were eager to see answered by "yes!" in their 1992 electioneering. Besides, the genie's impersonations are a series of promises he make to Aladdin, with his main statement: "just make your wish, and anything you desire shall be yours." This sounds like the key electoral claim: "elect me, and everything will be better." The allusions to the Gulf War are enacted in the last part of the movie with the genie, enslaved by Jaffar, telling Aladdin not to rely on him anymore since he was under the orders of "Zeeno Psychopath." Then Jaffar starts singing, mocking Aladdin who had become powerless when "his assets [were] frozen" just like Saddam's bank accounts in Switzerland. Even if the allusion is not directed at the Gulf War in particular, the spectator is familiar with the portrait of the "Third World Dictator," subdued by the West's "peacemaking" efforts. This is an example of an intertextuality that does not require a specific familiarity with the singular texts involved, but is a reading which occurs between texts.

As to Jaffar's song, "Read my lips/and come to grips/with reality!" it constitutes a direct allusion to Bush's famous failed campaign promise, one of the most cited, ridiculed, and exploited electoral formulae in American culture.

In Conclusion

Other intertexts contribute to make *Aladdin's* subtexts appear real and natural: sales figures, videotapes and soundtracks, reviews and critiques, the airing of "The Making of *Aladdin*" on television, Aladdin video games and Aladdin "meal deals for kids" at McDonalds, Aladdin on cereal boxes and the Emmy Award for Best Song for "A Whole New World." And to top it all, a follow-up video, "The Return of Jaffar."

Although the movie claims and displays an ostentatory political correctness, I have argued that it functions as an apparatus perpetuating prejudices and inequalities along the axes of race, gender and class. In fact, *Aladdin* is perfectly compatible with other ideology-laden Disney animations and cartoons.

The deconstruction of *Aladdin's* three subtexts of race, class, and gender exposes the film's racism, capitalistic ideology, and sexism. Still, *Aladdin's* subtextual substance can be better understood from a postcolonial perspective, since all three subtexts operate along a Self/Other dichotomy shrouded with distant, intriguing, and dangerous exotica. Whereas *Aladdin's* subtextual streams invite a postcolonial reading, the excessive semiotic activity at the film's textual surface make it also a postmodern text. The argument that late capitalist societies work on perpetuating self-preserving stereotypes in the realms of race, class, and gender has itself become a stereotype. These power inequalities can still deploy a "semiotics of excess" where intertexts are encoded, decoded and recoded, naturalizing totalizing systems of signifiers.

Collins (1994) describes that "Bombardment of Signs" as a key symptom of postmodernism and underscores its latent political thrust. As Collins puts it, the "postmodern condition" is marked by an ever increasing surplus of texts, all of which demand our attention in varying levels of intensity. The resulting array of competing signs shapes the very process of signification, a context in which messages must constantly be defined over and against rival forms of expression as different types of texts frame our allegedly common reality according to significantly different ideological agendas… (331).

Aladdin is a postmodern text because of the semiosis of excess flooding the textual surface of the movie with chaotic streams of intertextual references, harnessing signs from a variety of popular culture domains such as Hollywood's film industry, American (U.S.) political life, the music industry, and more mundane consumer items. These intertexts become signifiers floating and wandering, free from any bond to their signifieds. This carnival of signification is a site, in Jameson's words, marking "the effacement…, of some key boundaries or separations (1983: 112).

The tension between *Aladdin's* subtextual politics and its textual aesthetics underscores an uneasy cohabitation between postcolonialism and postmodernism (During 1993). The plethora of signs and symbols deployed in *Aladdin* to depict Agrabah dilutes the possibility of spatial and temporal identity for the city, reducing it to a subaltern entity with no clear identity. This reflects the postmodern tendency to "more or less intentionally wipe out the possibility of post-colonial identity" (During, 1993: 449). As a postmodern text with a colonial subtext, *Aladdin* embodies the semiotic practices by which the subaltern is dehumanized, dehistoricized, and denied agency. In other words, it is a predictable output of a system which perpetuates itself through its representational apparati in terms of the alienation, marginalization, and silencing of the Other.

REFERENCES

"Aladdin." *The ADC Times* 14, no. 4 (1993):8.

"Aladdin." *Cahiers du Cinéma* 475 (1994):64.

Bakhtin, Mikhail. 1981. *The Dialogical Imagination*. Translated by Michael Holquist, edited by Michale Holquist and Caryl Emerson. Austin: University of Texas Press.

Collins, Jim. 1994. "Television and Postmodernism." In *Channels of Discourse, reassembled: Television and Contemporary Criticism,* 2nd edition, edited by Robert Allen. Chapel Hill: University of North Carolina Press.

Dorfman, Ariel and Armand Mattelart. 1971. *How to Read Donald Duck: Imperialist Ideology in the Disney Comic.* New-York: International General.

During, Simon. 1993. "Postmodernism or Postcolonialism Today." In *Postmodernism: A Reader.* Edited by Thomas Docherty. New York: Columbia University Press.

Eco, Umberto. 1979. *The Role of the Reader: Explorations in the Semiotics of Texts.* Bloomington: University of Indiana Press.

Fiske, John. 1987. *Television Culture*. London and New-York: Routledge.

Forgacs, D. 1992. "Disney Animation and the Business of Childhood." *Screen* 33, no. 4: 361-379.

Genette, Jean. 1982. *Palimpsestes: La Littérature au Second Degré*. Paris: Seuil.

Giroux, Henry. 1993. "Beyond The Politics of Innocence: Memory and Pedagogy in the 'Wonderful World of Disney'." *Socialist Review* 2: 79-107.

Harlow, Barbara. 1992. "Travel Documents: Redelegating Representation. A Review of Timothy Mitchell, *Colonizing Egypt* and Ella Shohat, *Israeli Cinema*." *Social Text* 27, 72-87.

Jameson, Fredric. 1983. "Postmodernism and Consumer Society." In *The Anti-Aesthetic*, edited by Hal Foster. Port Townsend, WA: Bay Press.

Kristeva, Julia. 1984. *Revolution in Poetic Language*. New-York: Columbia University Press.

Lévi-Strauss, Claude. 1969. *The Raw and the Cooked*. New York: Harper and Row.

Modleski, Tania. 1991. *Feminism without Women: Culture and Criticism in a Postfeminist Age*. London and New York: Routledge.

Ohmer, Susan. 1993. "That Rags to Riches Stuff: Disney's Cinderella and the Cultural Space of Animation." *Film History* 5: 231-249.

Richardson, S.A. 1994. "A Whole New World: Walt Disney's Aladdin and the Resurgence of the American Power Myth," Eighteenth Annual Conference on Literature and Film, Tallahasse, Florida.

Said, Edward. 1979. *Orientalism*. New York: Vintage Books.

Shaheen, Jack. 1993. "Aladdin: Animated Racism." *Cinéaste* 20, no. 11, 49.

Smoodin, Eric. 1993. *Animating Culture: Hollywood Cartoons from the Sound Era*. New Brunswick, NJ: Rutgers University Press.

Stam, Robert, Roger Burgoyne, and Sandy Flitterman-Lewis. 1992. *New Vocabularies in Film Semiotics: Structuralism, Post-Structuralism and Beyond*. London and New York: Routledge.

Tammi, P. 1991. "Text, Subtext, Intertext: On Applying Taranovsky's Analytic Method (with examples from Finnish poetry)." *Semiotica* 87, no. 3/4, 315-347.

The Simpsons (20th Century Fox) Animation
Homer (dad), Marge (mom), Bart (the boy), Lisa (the girl), and Maggie (the baby). Still courtesy
of Jerry Ohlinger's Movie Materials.

CHAPTER 3

OF MICE AND BART:
The Simpsons and the Postmodern
David Weinstein

Consider the following series of television images: A man who answers to the name "Pee-Wee" talks like a little kid and wears a loud leisure suit with an even louder bow tie. He presides over a "playhouse" populated by campy characters and animated objects. CLICK. David Addison and Maddy Hayes sing an old Motown duet because, they tell us, the writers for their detective series, *Moonlighting*, do not know how to end the week's episode. CLICK. Max Headroom, a computer-generated talking television head, helps his alter ego, Carter Edison, expose video crimes in a future dominated by television. CLICK. Two animated teenagers, Beavis and Butt-head, watch an Anthrax music video. Beavis turns to Butt-head, "That was cool." Butt-head agrees. CLICK. Jerry and his sidekick George try to convince NBC executives to begin producing a series that looks suspiciously like the Seinfeld program that we are watching. CLICK. A young animated boy, Bart Simpson, stages an all-star television special — with performers including Johnny Carson, Bette Midler and the Red Hot Chili Peppers — to save his favorite television show, *Krusty the Clown*, from being canceled due to low ratings.

What do these scenes have in common? They are all from the wave of self-reflexive television programs which, since the mid-1980s, have offered viewers new ways of watching and understanding television. *The Simpsons*, which has aired in prime-time on the Fox network since

January 1990, has been among the most consistently creative and intelligent of the many postmodern television programs.[1] The animated series, on which I focus my analysis for the remainder of this essay, illustrates the way video producers have recently attempted to articulate television's position in a postmodern, image-inundated culture.

The Simpsons is on the sort of postmodern mission, defined by Linda Hutcheon, to "de-naturalize some of the dominant features of our way of life; to point out that those entities that we unthinkingly experience as natural. . . are in fact 'cultural'; made by us, not given to us" (1989: 2). Like many postmodern texts, *The Simpsons* begins this "de-naturalization" by articulating, through its mise-en-scene, dialogue, animation style, and narrative structure, the technical processes and generic rules through which television shows are constructed. *The Simpsons* further shows the way television positions viewers as consumers of both television shows and commercial products, addressing broader questions regarding the relationship between popular media, consumerism, and identity.

In examining representation and calling attention to culturally constructed categories, *The Simpsons* recognizes that it is complicit with discourses of power, domination, and representation. The postmodern "cannot escape implication in that which it nevertheless wants to analyze and maybe even undermine. The ambiguities of this position are translated into both the content and the form of postmodern art" (Hutcheon 1989: 4). Indeed, the program's self-reflexive opening sequence announces that *The Simpsons* is a commercial television product: the five family members are rushing home to watch the show on television. "There are dizzying dolly shots and tracking shots that mock the limitations of real life cameras and actions and make these seem visually, and informationally, impoverished by comparison" (Herron 1993: 19). Immediately following this opening, an upbeat voice-over informs viewers of the episode's chief sponsor, making an explicit connection between the show and the commercials that follow. Episodes also frequently refer to the animation and character merchandising processes. For example, the criticism of Disney as the creator of fantasy worlds meant primarily to sell products is equally applicable to *The Simpsons*. In short, the show "exploits its 'insider' position in order to begin a subversion from within, to talk to consumers in a capitalist society in a way which gets us where we live, so to speak" (Hutcheon 1989: 114).[2]

Not only does *The Simpsons* dismantle and examine realistic television form and content, but it also probes the effects of television on viewers' psychic realities: their thoughts, fantasies, dreams, desires. In the 1950s,

Marxist philosophers and cultural critics first addressed the problem of the power of the new mass medium. Frankfurt School critics decried the way television created an homogenized, mass audience with a "false consciousness" (Adorno 1957; Marcuse 1964). Adorno, for example, writes about the hidden meanings of mass culture, which "handle the audience" by influencing the unconscious mind (1957: 479-80). In the last twenty-five years, thinkers from a wide range of disciplines (philosophy, American studies, communications, cultural studies, psychology, anthropology, literature) have extended and focused the Frankfurt School questions by theorizing the way specific types of television images affect the individual viewer's perceptions of reality. J.G. Ballard asks, for example: "What actually happens on the level of our unconscious minds when, within minutes on the same television screen, a prime minister is assassinated, an actress makes love, an injured child is carried from a car crash?" (1990: 89). These recent works also tend to look more specifically at agency than did the Frankfurt School studies, probing who is creating and who is consuming these powerful images.

To answer Ballard's question, we must realize that, like the Simpson family, we have internalized values and modes of perception from the surrounding pop culture spectacle (movies, television, magazines, computer networks, and roadside billboards). It is no coincidence that television, the most powerful purveyor of images, became especially self-critical during the presidency of Ronald Reagan, who frequently confused the world depicted in his films with real events from beyond the screen (Rogin 1987: 7). Ironically, Reagan's attempted assassin, John Hinckley, also conflated movies and reality. He had a fantasy relationship with movie actress Jodie Foster, carrying pictures of her in his wallet and writing love letters to her. In his final letter, Hinckley "made it clear that his attempt to 'get Reagan' was designed to impress Foster" (Caughey 1984: 5). Such fantasy relationships with media figures, far from being abnormal, are "characteristic of contemporary American society" (Caughey 1984: 7). For many of us, these imaginary relationships with media figures may have prosocial effects: they lift us out of bad moods, give us advice on how to live, and help us develop traditional American values (Caughey 1984: 7, 66-7). *The Simpsons* recognizes the importance of imaginary social worlds formed through television and questions the values which these fantasies support and promote.

I will closely analyze a *Simpsons* episode that characteristically explores the technical apparatuses of television representation, the line between fantasy and reality, and the various manifestations of a consumer culture in which thought and experience are commodified.³ In this episode, the family's trip to Duff Gardens, an amusement park operated by Springfield's Duff Beer Company, is postponed when Marge's great Aunt Gladys dies. Marge, Homer, and the kids attend the funeral along with Marge's sisters, Patty and Selma. Through a videotaped will, Gladys implores the single women not to die childless, as she did. Selma takes the message seriously, scouring Springfield for a suitable father. When Homer contracts food poisoning after eating a spoiled sandwich, Selma temporarily tests motherhood by taking Bart and Lisa to Duff Gardens.

The program opens by moving from an apparently real event to a television commercial. It first appears that Daredevil Lance Murdock's jump over sixteen burning school buses, and crash into a wall, is one of the show's incidents, but a friendly voice-over signals that it is only a commercial: "Hey, Lance Murdock, you just jumped over sixteen burning school buses. What are you going to do now?" Lance, body and face contorted, answers that he is going to Duff Gardens. Murdock, who as part of his profession must regularly endure and even enjoy pain, is an apt spokesman for the fun center, which has a Whiplash roller coaster and an anguishing spinning wheel, the Washing Machine.

This Duff Gardens spot parodies the popular Disney commercials in which athletes cap victorious performances by going to Disney World. More broadly, it mocks the countless advertisements in which an upbeat announcer tells the hard-working figure that he, and by extension the audience who identifies with the character, deserves a break. In the world of *The Simpsons*, Duff Gardens does not appear especially relaxing or fun. Lance's grimace and the anxiety on people's faces as they spin around the Washing Machine suggest that the theme park does not even offer visitors masochistic pleasure: they are not enjoying the pain. The sequence criticizes the way advertisements distort the essential nature of the products that they sell. In the Duff commercial, soothing, positive narration, celebrity endorsements, and fast editing of exciting scenes make the dangerous theme park into a site for adventure. A more honest pitch, "go to Duff Gardens and hurt yourself," probably would not appeal to many viewers. Furthermore, such a campaign would probably provoke moral and legal authorities — religious groups, public interest activists and police — to close Duff Gardens.

The next shot, a quick cutaway to Homer, Bart, and Lisa Simpson watching television with big smiles on their faces, assures us that the previous sequence was, indeed, not part of the "real" action. The commercial then returns, now framed by the Simpson family's television, further removing us from the "reality" of the program by this reminder that the advertisement, like an actual *Simpsons* episode, is a construction.

The spot shows us "the happiest fish in the world," in the fabulous Duff Beeraquarium [sic], a beer-mug shaped tank. The commercial implies that being dropped in a vat of beer is heavenly, but the fish do not look happy. Tourists surround the giant mug, watching the pitiful, drunken movements of the fish, who swim crookedly and keep crashing into the tank's glass walls. One has a sick, greenish tint and belches mournfully. Thus the commercial parodies the fantasy of happy drinkers everywhere, a dip in a pool full of beer, and uses the voice-over to conceal the miserable realities of drinking too much. These bloated creatures are drinking themselves to death, and the happy visitors, like viewers at home conditioned by years of media representations glorifying beer, do not recognize what they are plainly seeing.

The Simpsons excitedly plan to visit Duff Gardens, but Gladys's funeral prevents them from going. On the way to the burial home, Marge reminisces about her great aunt, only to find that film representations have supplanted her "real" memories. The character flashes back to her childhood with two other young girls, holding hands in a lake, as soft music plays. In the next shot, the grown-up Marge looks worried, "Oh, wait a minute. That was *Prince of Tides*." A similar confusion of movie fantasy and psychic reality occurs later in the show. After he and Marge watch a porn movie, *The Erotic Adventures of Hercules*, Homer dresses in a toga and attempts to carry Marge away. Marge plays her role by seductively resisting at first. "I can't. The beans will burn," she says with a smile. Homer replies, "Homercles [sic] cares not for beans." He then picks up his willing wife and heads towards the bedroom.

These fantasies show the way memory and even sexual desire are sparked by movies. They do not advance the show's narrative, which at the time of Marge's reverie finds the characters approaching the funeral home. They arrive to confront the commodified rituals surrounding Gladys's death. The minister gives a generic speech in which he refers to Gladys as a "he." Marge's sister Patty admonishes the speaker, "That eulogy better not show up on the bill." When Patty mentions that "Gladys wasn't a rich woman" during her own talk, the mourners clear out, leaving the Simpson family.

The person who apparently stands to gain the most from Aunt Gladys's death is her stereotypically smarmy lawyer and executor, Lionel Hutz. He attempts to alter Gladys's video will by dubbing his voice over the dead woman's. When Marge objects, he sheepishly explains with a smile, "You'd be surprised how often that works." Indeed, the lawyer's trick is part of the show's broader criticism of video technology, and the people who profit from it. While this ploy may have failed, as the lawyer proudly tells the bereaved family, he earns his fee simply for pressing the play button on a VCR.

The will shows how technology alters barriers between life and death. Through videotape, Gladys uncannily returns to life after her funeral to dispense advice and the remainder of her worldly possessions. However, the program shows that, rather than giving Gladys a ghostly, supernatural authority over mortals, the video trivializes and undercuts her attempt at sincerity and meaningful communication. Thus, when Gladys starts to read a "serious" poem, Robert Frost's "The Road Not Taken," Homer fast forwards to the part of the video in which the dead woman divides her possessions and dispenses parting nuggets of wisdom. The family members want to see what they are receiving from their dead aunt, but they are also more comfortable watching this portion of the video because its mixture of gift giving and pithy advice is familiar to such avid television watchers. Gladys's accumulation of potato chips that look like famous people, including her prized Jay Leno chip, is the type of idiosyncratic collection, revolving around acquisition and consumption, encouraged by television advertisements, local news broadcasts, news magazines, infomercials, shopping networks, and talk shows. Indeed, with the right agent, Gladys might have even landed herself and her chips a spot on Leno's *Tonight Show*.

The only part of Gladys's will that makes an impression on anyone, however, is the old woman's cliched admonition to her single nieces, "Don't die lonely like me. Raise a family." The dead woman's advice grabs Selma. She wants to have a baby, but first must find a father. Love is commodified through her attempts to buy it. First, she tries the Low Expectations Dating Service. In Selma's amateurish video, shown through a camcorder viewfinder, she advertises herself as a "free lunch." For her big finish, she eats a cigarette, ties it up in her mouth, and then opens her mouth to reveal the still-lit cigarette. The stunt would not be out of place on *America's Funniest Home Videos*. However, Selma's act is screened before a tough potential suitor, Groundskeeper Willie, who hurls the video away in disgust. Selma next attempts to buy love from Princess Opal, a woman who peddles a number of essential products to this postmodern world: potions, hexes, and fax machines. After she mistakenly drinks truth serum, Opal admits that her products are useless. Like most consumer goods in *The Simpsons* world, these potions cannot fulfill their promises to satisfy characters' emotional desires. Finally, following an unsuccessful date, Selma tries the Springfield Sperm Bank. The company's newsletter, "Frozen Pops," offers product from top media figures: a basketball star, a Nobel Prize winner, even a Sweathog from *Welcome Back Kotter*. However, Selma and her sisters are wary of ordering anything through a catalogue. This sequence parodies a culture in which everything has a price: technology has made it such that choosing a father is no different from choosing an ice cream pop. But while it mocks the sale of love, it repeats and reifies the dominant media stereotype that women in their thirties who want children have few, if any, viable options.

The episode solves the problem of Selma's maternal desire when she takes Bart and Lisa to Duff Gardens, an experience which teaches her that she does not want kids. During the Duff Gardens visit, the episode makes its strongest attack on consumer culture, which creates psychic needs that can only be satisfied through the consumption of goods and products. The Disney enterprise (feature films, cartoons, merchandise, amusement parks) is, in many ways, "emblematic of capitalism itself" (Willis 1993a: 2). The Disney World theme park, in particular, is the symbol of a larger cultural commodification of play: "the wholesale use of architecture and decor as a means for promoting consumption — in an environment where there is probably more surveillance per square inch (both technological and human) than in any of today's underfunded prisons" (Willis 1993b: 121). The animated characters add to the artificial magic of Disney World by literally coming to life and playing with kids. These "products (of adult imagination) live to sell, to be consumed, to multiply" (Willis 1993b: 125). Furthermore, Disney parks create a utopian past, eliminating negative, unwanted elements of the history that they reconstruct. "The Disney people don't consider this retrospective tidying up an abuse of the past; they freely admit its falsification, pointing out that it is, after all, just entertainment" (Wallace 1985: 36). However, this "entertainment" frequently glorifies business, technology, and capitalism. The EPCOT Center, for example, exists so that a number of huge corporations may sell their optimistic solutions to current social and environmental problems (Wallace 45-49). In short, Disney World represents a magical climate of total control and safety in the service of capital. "To get your money's worth, you have to do everything and do it in the prescribed manner. Free play is gratuitous and therefore a waste of the family's leisure time expenditure" (Willis 1993b: 126).

The television program dissects Disney and Disney World on two levels: it articulates the way in which this artificial environment works and introduces chaotic actions which disrupt the theme park's order. In the real Disney World, "there is no possibility of an awful thrill, like being stuck at the top of a ferris wheel" (Willis 1993b: 124). At Duff Gardens, however, Bart and Lisa enjoy breaking the rules, even though their transgressions sometimes put them in physical danger.

The second Duff Gardens advertisement, making Bart, Lisa, and Homer further anticipate their visit, parodies the Disney security deployed to create good, clean, family fun. "Come to Duff Gardens," the friendly announcer hails viewers, "where roving gangs are not a big problem any more." During this voice-over, a friendly policeman waves mechanically at the camera, grin frozen on his face, while three handcuffed youths glumly stare into space. The announcer then invites us to experience the clean-shaven sounds of the group Hooray for Everything. The act parodies Up With People, a popular singing group that performs at Disney World, holiday parades, and the half-time festivities of bowl games. In the advertisement, the group — three boys (one Asian, one black, one white) and two women (one Asian, one white) — performs on a stage shaped as a giant beer mug. *The Simpsons* thus calls attention to the way that beer companies associate youth, health, positive feeling, and beer consumption. The advertisement also parodies the way such pop groups both call attention to and erase racial, gender, and ethnic differences in the service of unity behind products. These singers appear to be different, but Duff brings them together.

The group's version of Lou Reed's "Take a Walk on the Wild Side" is purged of sinful and offensive meanings. In the original, Reed's laconic, gritty, rasp articulates a catalogue of urban transgressions, many of them sensual and sexual: prostitution, blow jobs, transvestism, drug use. In the chorus, "the colored girls" — a phrase as flagrantly racist in 1972, when the song was released, as it is today — watch the action around them with a detached resignation, matching Reed's laconic, wordless chorus: "Do da do do do." Hooray for Everything converts the original's musical narrative to a celebration of unity. The colored girls in Reed's song become "all the races," as the upbeat, updated chorus. Everybody is safe, happy and united at Duff Gardens.

As Lisa and Bart approach the actual Duff Gardens with their aunt, the show questions the nature and reality of Duff's vision of unity. The first evidence of the theme park is the Duff Beeramid, Duff's equivalent to Cinderella's Castle. After seeing the aluminum pyramid glorified on television, Bart finally gets to see the original. "There it is," he says with happiness and awe. Rather than basking in the structure's aura, as Bart does, Lisa earnestly recites facts from the guidebook, "Twenty-two immigrant laborers died in its [the Beeramid's] construction." As she says this, the camera cuts to a guidebook photo of tourists gathered around a small graveyard in front of the structure. Selma's nasty and shocking answer to Lisa: "Big deal. They were only immigrants." The reply exposes the tacit cultural assumption that immigrants and working people must sometimes suffer and even die for the good of the country. It is only by not thinking about these casualties — ignoring and/or subconsciously minimizing the conditions of production, and the exploitation inherent in most products — that people can enjoy any goods, services, or tourist attractions.

Bart and Lisa then tour the Beer Hall of Presidents, an example of theme park history in the service of corporations.[4] A robotic Abe Lincoln, also a feature at Disney's Hall of Presidents, turns the Emancipation Proclamation into an assertion of the freedom to drink Duff. "Four score and seven years ago," begins the Lincoln figure somberly, "we took a blend of the finest hops and barley to brew a refreshing, full-bodied lager." He then switches to a rap as a drum machine kicks in, "I'm rapping A.B. and I'm here to say, 'If you want a great beer Duff's the only way.'" He concludes his spiel by smashing a beer can into the side of his head. The sequence ends with Bart once again exposing the park's dark side by pulling down George Washington's pants. The father of our country's robotic father's eyes flash red, as he turns to Bart with a sinister expression.

In the Hall of Presidents, as elsewhere in Duff Gardens, the kids and Selma are bored unless they make their own fun and break the rules. This need to violate the park's laws is most apparent in the "Little Land of Duff," a parody of Disney's "It's a Small World." The tourists sail on a small boat through the world. Figures in "native" costumes serenade them, "Duff Beer for Me. Duff Beer for You. I'll Have a Duff. You'll Have One Too." On a dare from Bart, Lisa breaks the monotony by drinking the black, bubbly liquid on which the boat is sailing. Lisa hallucinates. An electric guitar gives a bluesy edge to the Duff song; brightly colored spots appear; Aunt Gladys becomes a lizard; Lisa shrieks at the figures around her, "They're all around me. No way out." Although Lisa's experiences are not marked as an acid trip, her perceptions are informed by the typical pop culture representations of the LSD experience, in which hallucinating characters enjoy psychedelic music, bright colors, and new ways of seeing themselves and the world around them. Our understanding of the incident, which again is not labelled as an LSD trip, is similarly dependent on pop culture. As the scene progresses, her experience becomes even more mass mediated: she interrupts the patriotic parade with the 1960s cliche, "I can see the music," as she waves her hands and traces designs in the air, like a Deadhead. The scene winds down when the Duff police return to their security station with Lisa, who proclaims regally that she is the "Lizard Queen," an echo of Jim Morrison's nickname, the Lizard King. Throughout the sequence, all of the other people are notably static as they wait in line and watch the parade.[5]

In taking control of the situation by drinking the liquid, Lisa breaks the park's rules and refashions this tightly regimented leisure space into a place of excitement and unpredictability, even though she does not know what will happen after imbibing the strange substance. Furthermore, hallucinating visitors are less likely to follow the park's carefully constructed order: like Lisa, for example, they might run into the middle of a parade. At the very least, they might not consume the park's messages about Duff's place in history and the world.

While Homer is not central to this episode's plot, as the Simpson who watches the most television, he is the one whose psychic life is most centered on consumption. Indeed, the morning that his family is scheduled to visit Duff Gardens, Homer is unable to attend because he is ill from eating a giant hoagie. As he is sickly lying in bed, an apparent flashback illustrates the way Homer stages a fantasy centering on his desire to consume the phallus-shaped sandwich. The sequence starts, amidst dreamy xylophone music, at the company picnic. Homer smiles fondly at the giant leftover and pats it fondly, "I'll give it a good home." Next, he is sitting on the couch, as the sub protrudes from between his legs. Marge asks with annoyance if he is still eating that sandwich and warns him that it is going bad. However, Homer won't give it up, "Only two more feet and I can put it in the 'fridge," he insists. When his wife later finds the now-shriveled sandwich behind the radiator, she once again tells Homer to get rid of it. Homer refuses. Finally, the couple is in bed together. Homer turns to Marge, "I'd like to be alone with my sandwich." Marge answers angrily, as the sandwich completes its displacement of her, "Are you going to eat it?" Homer does not hesitate, "Yes."

The next shot returns us to the bedroom the morning of the Duff Gardens trip, yet there is no transition to mark the end of the "fantasy," and the return to the show's realistic narrative. The scene ends with a sick Homer angrily removing the deformed sandwich from the garbage can. "This is all your fault." Suddenly his tone and facial features soften. "Oh, how could I stay mad at you?" he asks, as he moves the hoagie tenderly to his cheek. Marge angrily slaps her rancid rival away from Homer, ending the sequence. However, the three "real" food commercials which immediately follow ironically add to the scene's impact by showing how food satisfies emotional, if not sexual, needs. In the first two advertisements, Corn Chex Cereal and Sucrets cough drops allow fathers to please their young daughters. In the third, McDonald's brings office unity, as workers engage in friendly banter over who will pay for their delicious and inexpensive lunch.

The Simpsons thus attacks capitalist culture in general, and television in particular. The show's narratives celebrate the way individuals and corporations in positions of power — ranging from Homer to Mr. Burns, the owner of Springfield's nuclear power plant, to Duff Beer — can never entirely control their environments. Indeed, instruments and technologies that enable the exercise of power (money, video, nuclear energy) are rendered useless in the face of human unpredictability. Furthermore, a host of formal devices — non-linear narrative, verbal and visual puns, non-sequiturs, parody, animation, montage — suggest that not only television, but life itself, may endlessly be remade.

REFERENCES

Adorno, T. W. 1957. "Television and the Patterns of Mass Culture." *Mass Culture*, edited by Bernard Rosenberg and David Manning White. New York: The Free Press.

Ballard, J. G. 1990. *The Atrocity Exhibition*. San Francisco: Re/Search Publications.

Caughey, John. 1984. *Imaginary Social Worlds*. Lincoln, NE: University of Nebraska Press.

Herron, Jerry. 1993. "Homer Simpson's Eyes and the Culture of Late Capitalism." *Representations* 43: 1-25.

Hutcheon, Linda. 1989. *The Politics of Postmodernism*. New York: Routledge.

Marcuse, Herbert. 1964. *One-Dimensional Man*. Boston: Beacon Press.

McNeil, Alex. 1991. *Total Television: A Comprehensive Guide to Programming from 1948 to the Present*. 3rd ed. New York: Penguin Books.

Parisi, Peter. 1993. "'Black Bart' Simpson: Appropriation and Revitalization in Commodity Culture." *Journal of Popular Culture* 27, no. 1: 125-42.

Rogin, Michael Paul. 1987. *Ronald Reagan, the Movie*. Berkeley: University of California Press.

Wallace, Mike. 1985. "Mickey Mouse History: Portraying the Past at Disney World." *Radical History Review* 32: 33-58.

Willis, Susan. 1993a. "Critical Vantage Points." *South Atlantic Quarterly* 92, no. 1: 1-6.

———— 1993b. "Disney World: Public Use/Private State." *South Atlantic Quarterly* 92, no. 1: 119-38.

NOTES

1. The Simpson family first appeared in short, animated segments of Fox's *The Tracy Ullman Show* (1987-1990). The pilot for the *Simpsons* series aired as a holiday special on 23 December 1989. See McNeil (1991: 689-90; 785-6).

2. Hutcheon makes this point about postmodern film, but it is equally applicable to *The Simpsons*.

3. The episode under discussion here is "Selma's Choice", episode 9F11 from the show's fourth season, first aired on 21 January 1993.

4. Many corporations, such as John Hancock Insurance, use historical figures as part of their identities. Others structure advertising campaigns around respected people and events from the past.

5. Of course, due to the show's animation style, backgrounds are frequently static, but in this scene, as Lisa skips in front of people, their lack of animation is especially apparent.

CHAPTER 4

REIFICATION AND LOSS IN POSTMODERN PUBERTY:

The Cultural Logic of Fredric Jameson and American Youth Movies

Timothy Shary

In 1984 Fredric Jameson published his seminal essay "Postmodernism, or the Cultural Logic of Late Capitalism" in the *New Left Review*, thereby formally entering the debate on this contemporary cultural description. With the subsequent publication of a book with the same title, as well as two books on cinema and many articles on postmodernism in theory and in practice, Jameson became one of the most visible and vocal critics of the postmodern manifestations of economics, history, and sociology. While most of the films he formally discussed were diverse but specific examples of 1970s and 1980s international cinema (e.g., *Perfumed Nightmare, Diva, The Shining*), Jameson's commentaries on reification in mass culture and the loss of identity and history offer an opportunity to apply his influential critiques to more recent cinematic trends.

Movies about teenagers and young adults have clearly followed trends over many generations, portraying varying degrees of lost innocence, depicting the dangers of delinquency, and sometimes celebrating the sweetness of care-free youth. Current Hollywood youth movies — a term

I use since the studios (and most critics) seem to consider the "young" audience as everyone under thirty — are not altogether different from those of the past in terms of their themes, but their visual and narrative styles, and attitudes, reveal a distinct postmodernist operation at work. While this condition applies to virtually all of Hollywood's young adult movies at least from *Fast Times at Ridgemont High* (1982) to the present, for the purposes of this essay I will focus on two different pairs of films that rely on particular generic traditions, the buddy comedy as portrayed in *Bill and Ted's Excellent Adventure* (1989) and *Wayne's World* (1992), and the ensemble romance as represented by *Singles* (1991) and *Reality Bites* (1994). In their pursuits of fun, love, and to a certain extent, knowledge, the young characters in these films navigate familiar cultural terrain: they still have to go to school or get jobs, their boyfriends and girlfriends fulfill both dreams and nightmares, and in the end, they just want to be accepted for who they are and on their own terms. However, my argument will show that these picaresque journeys are particularly rife with postmodern realizations and references, making Jameson's observations all the more relevant to this specific contemporary genre.[1]

Below I offer an account of Jameson's work on postmodernism to provide a necessary foundation upon which an examination of the postmodern youth film may be built. While Jameson is by no means the only (or even most important) critic of postmodernism, many of his arguments are especially germane to the phenomena of Hollywood's recent practices. My discussion of the films herein is meant to demonstrate the relationship between certain theories of the postmodern and their ongoing activation within a particular cultural practice, which in this case is the cinematic representation of contemporary American youth.

Fredric Jameson

Jameson's early works in the 1970s were characterized by passionate textual exegeses and theoretical arguments in which he developed and defended a Marxist hermeneutics, so that when he began to take on postmodernism in the mid-1980s, his attack on the postmodern manipulations of economy, art, and history was of no great surprise. Jameson first grappled with what he envisioned as the current cultural morass of de-centering and detached postmodern conditions in "Pleasure: A Political Issue," published in an anthology on pleasure a year before his *New Left Review* article. Here Jameson is all but ready to lay out his critique of postmodernism, although he is loyal to the subject at hand: "...it becomes clear that the question of the originality of our own situation — consumer capitalism, postindustrial society, or better still, what Ernest Mandel calls 'late capitalism' — will have to be reckoned into any discussion of the relationship between pleasure and politics" (1983a: 2).

Jameson was quick to adopt Mandel's phrase into his own vernacular on the issue, and in his 1984 article, "The Politics of Theory: Ideological Positions in the Postmodernism Debate," Jameson attempts at once to objectively discuss the debate while defending his position. "The problem of postmodernism," he begins, "— how its fundamental characteristics are to be described, whether it even exists in the first place, whether the very *concept* is of any use, or is, on the contrary, a mystification — this problem is at one and the same time an aesthetic and a political one" (1984a: 53). And while he rather clearly covers the artifacts (visual arts, films, literature) and theorists of postmodernity (providing an explanatory chart which divides such "pro-post-modernists" as Lyotard from "anti-postmodernists" such as Habermas), he also makes his suspicions clear, albeit in cavalier and sarcastic fashion, saying that perhaps postmodernism "is not so new a story after all: one remembers, indeed, Freud's delight at discovering an obscure tribal culture, which alone among the multitudinous traditions of dream analysis on the earth had managed to hit on the notion that all dreams had hidden sexual meanings — except for sexual dreams, which meant something else!" (1984a: 65)

While Jameson had not thoroughly detailed his ideas about architecture in his *New Left Review* essay, an article he published the next year, "Architecture and the Critique of Ideology," further established how the aesthetic of postmodernism he was now addressing was really a matter of space and form, and he would return to this issue in cinema as well. As Martin Donougho has said, "...the postmodernist crisis is primarily *spatial*. There is no longer any *here* here: and that goes for the life-world of a now 'decentered' subject just as much as for the styles of contemporary art" (1985: 186). Thus, if we "subjects" of postmodernism are engulfed in such a physiological dilemma as that posed by the systemic "ideologies" of the buildings in which we live and work, then we are in quite a paradoxical debacle: we submit to our environments rather than creating them, while we seemingly have more control over how they look and function. This is all part of the facade (pun intended) of postmodernism vis-à-vis architecture, and it is even more applicable to our economic conditions.

"To put it most dramatically," Jameson says, using the architecture of Manfredo Tafuri as an example, "if the outer limit of the individual building is the material city itself, with its opacity, complexity, and resistance, then the outer limit of some expanded conception of the architectural vocation as including urbanism and city planning is the economic itself, or capitalism in the most overt and naked expression of its implacable power" (1985: 67). Jameson's full conception of postmodernism emerged from his examination of architecture, and it brings us to the heart of Jameson's ultimately economic polemic about postmodernism.

As much as Jameson is occupied by the aesthetics of postmodernism, his central concern is the deceptive fragmentation of subjects and the disruptive severing of cultural production from personal reception that has taken place under capitalism. This has caused an identity crisis that leads to the reification of subjectivity: our very existence has become composed of products, and they seem to have no origins. And this reality exists because of our current global economy, which cannot be ignored regardless of how one views postmodernism. Jameson says, "...every position on postmodernism in culture — whether apologia or stigmatization — is also at one and the same time, and *necessarily*, an implicitly or explicitly political stance on the nature of multinational capitalism today" (1991: 2). Jameson's zeal for what is obviously an otherwise Marxist position on the scope of postmodernism is not shared by all, despite his claim to the contrary. Antony Easthope (1990: 61) takes issue with Jameson's overarching economic assessment:

> If, however, [cultural] analysis proceeds on another basis altogether, one that accords a specific effectivity to each mode and recognizes the social formation as a decentered structure in which each social and discursive practice acts within its own time, then such overall assessments [as Jameson's] become much harder to make. Architecture, film (whether Godard or Hollywood), literature — and within literature, poetry — must be considered in terms of that particularity.

But Jameson *is* a Marxist, and so perhaps such criticisms are merely a matter of misplaced prejudice. If so, there nonetheless remains a particular obstacle inherent in his call for the recognition and reformation of capitalist economies: Jameson offers no *modus operandi,* or even hope, for that recognition or reform. As John McGowan (1991: 157) has said:

> ...we find [Jameson's] theory of postmodernism depriving him of any politically active subject. Neither the working-class nor any other agent steps

forward as harbinger of a future beyond late capitalism or as the group that can lead us from necessity to the realm of freedom.

Another realm of Jameson's critique of postmodernism is not so problematic, although it may be harder to understand; this is the "loss" of history. As if the rather chaotic fragmentation of subjectivity through capitalism was not enough of a threat to cultural and individual identity, Jameson sees a movement away from historical periodizing which would have us believe that virtually everything happens without effect, that we live in a time detached from time, or more specifically, "a perpetual present" (1983b: 125). Donougho (1988: 187) describes this as "the vanishing of existential or historicist pathos and its replacement time by new intensities, free-floating and random, based on the new electronic media." Jameson has described this as the process by which "cultural production has been driven back inside the mind, within the monadic subject: it can no longer look directly out of its eyes at the real world for the referent but must, as in Plato's cave, trace its mental images of the world on its confining walls" (1983b: 118).

The walls of Plato's cave, as Jameson would have it, were replaced by screens earlier this century, first in the cinema, and then with television and video. The bombardment of the present which we face in our current media erases our concepts of past and future, and as soon as a product becomes "old" or "out of fashion" it is suddenly rendered "new" again while remaining "old" at the same time. This is what Jameson refers to as "nostalgia for the present," which is particularly evident in contemporary films. The postmodern aesthetic posits this process as an effective cycle in the evolution of "art," whereby we are constantly evaluating, consuming, and recycling products (although the evaluation step is virtually eliminated), absent from an historical perspective. Jameson sees this as beginning in the 1950s, and notes that "it is by leaving out, by ignoring, by passing over in silence and with the repugnance one may feel for the dreary stereotypes of television series, that high art palpably issues its judgments" (1991: 280). However, even these judgments seem to have become worthless in the face of constant commodity production and consumption.

Jameson says that "the only adequate way out of this vicious circle, besides praxis itself, is a historical and dialectical view which seeks to grasp the present as History" (1984a: 65). If we cannot actually depart from or destroy our postmodern condition, we can at least change our view in order to work against its continuing cycle. To this end Jameson has proposed his disputed theory of "cognitive mapping," which connects with the psychological aspect of postmodernism that he analyzes. His dilemma remains textual, that is, he sees a way "out" of postmodernism through the very texts which are a part of it. McGowan explains that Jameson's "refusal to allow history to be completely swallowed into textuality has given him an epistemological grounding for his theorizing a Marxist hermeneutic, but his concession that we always approach history through texts has left him without a model of nontextual action" (1984a: 152). Yet I would challenge McGowan on this point, for it seems that if there *is* a means to "saving" history and our cultural identities, it is through nontextual models of psychology, which Jameson does propose.

Simply put, postmodernism has so diffused our senses of space and time that we need "maps" to find out where and when we are. Jameson cites such sites of dislocation as MTV, the Bonaventure Hotel in Los Angeles (which for him typifies postmodern architecture), the proliferation of "news and information" channels, and of course, multinational capitalism itself. Cognitive mapping is the theoretical, aesthetic, and political means of reorienting our perspective to grasp the origins of artifacts and the ramifications of acts. In "Postmodernism, or The Cultural Logic of Late Capitalism," Jameson suggests it thus: "Disalienation in the traditional city, then, involves the practical reconquest of a sense of place, and the construction or reconstruction of an articulated ensemble which can be retained in memory and which the individual subject can map and remap along the moments of mobile, alternative trajectories" (1984b: 89). Jameson is not calling for a revolt so much as for a retreat: he says that it is vitally important for us to recognize our postmodern roles (as he himself has done reluctantly), if we are to "achieve a breakthrough to some as yet unimaginable new mode of representing [the world space of multinational capital], in which we may again begin to grasp our positioning as individual and collective subjects and regain a capacity to act and struggle which is at present neutralized by our spatial as well as our social confusion" (1984b: 92). Indeed, if there is to be *any* political form of postmodernism, Jameson concludes, it "will have as its vocation the invention and projection of a global cognitive mapping, on a social as well as a spatial scale" (1984b: 92). This will not come easily, if it comes at all, although Jameson's firm belief in a Marxist methodology remains clear. As John O'Neill (1990: 295) has said, Jameson argues that such postmodern dangers as "the death of the subject, the end of humankind, the migration of reason into madness, the collapse of social and historical narratives into schizophrenic case histories, are acceptable *only* if we work for a renewal of Marxist history and hermeneutics."

Even with his beloved Marxist dialectic, Jameson remains rather cynical, realizing that his idea of cognitive mapping may itself be already outdated and reconsumed within the postmodern: the "maps" which he proposes must have some representational existence, but the very nature of representation has been ruptured. "The question is not so much as to whether representation is noxious," Jameson said in 1982, "but rather as to whether and under what conditions it is *possible* at all" (Green 1982: 90). By 1991 he had conceded that "'cognitive mapping' was in reality nothing but a code word for 'class consciousness' — only it proposed the need for class consciousness of a new and hitherto undreamed of kind, while it also inflected the account in the direction of that new spatiality implicit in the postmodern" (1991: 418). Yet Jameson retains a strained hope that the dialogue on postmodernism will continue in the face of its paradoxes and paralyses. He concludes his book on postmodernism thus:

> The rhetorical strategy of the preceding pages has involved an experiment, namely, the attempt to see whether by systematizing something that is resolutely unsystematic, and historicizing something that is resolutely ahistorical, one couldn't outflank it and force a historical way at least of thinking about that. 'We have to name the system': this high point of the sixties finds an unexpected revival in the postmodernism debate. (418)

How appropriately postmodern for Jameson to find the debate on postmodernism revived with ideological concerns of the 1960s. Perhaps we have arrived at the historical era from which there is no escape, and for which there will be no accounting whenever it is over. To be perfectly postmodern, we find ourselves in a *Twilight Zone* of history, on a *Dog Day Afternoon* in politics, and dealing with a perfidiously *Untitled* aesthetics.

By the early 1990s, cinema had become a meta- and/or megadiscipline for Jameson's aesthetic, historical, and theoretical considerations of culture. He notes that "film itself has never been more alive than it is globally, where in the new world system a host of local voices have found the most sophisticated technical expression" (1990: 6). Film, and now video, have become problematic media messiahs of the Marxist dialectic, at once providing a new socialist realm of access to the production and reception of mass media for more people than ever before, while at the same time that anonymous access obliterates the connections between producers and products, and between receivers and what is received. These media are also a prime site of the reification that Jameson observes in mass culture. The heart of the dilemma, like much of Jameson's criticism, is economic. Colin McCabe describes Jameson's perspective on cinema as such: "a cultural form permeated at every level by the practices and paradoxes of marketing — a postmodern practice which oscillates between the passive reproduction and the active remodelling of audiences" (1992: xiii).

This assessment is evinced throughout *The Geopolitical Aesthetic*, where Jameson has developed an engrossing examination of commodification and representation in various movies. Cinema remains a postmodern phenomenon, but Jameson is interested in its particular use of landscape and allegory as a means of understanding the "geopolitical aesthetic" engendered by film styles and languages. In terms of genre, for instance, he says that "what interests us here is the way in which the former genres (thrillers, spy films, social exposés, science fiction, and so on) now conflate in a movement that re-enacts the dedifferentiation of the social levels, and by way of their own allegorization: so that the new post-generic genre films are allegories of each other, and of the impossible representation of the social totality itself" (1992: 5). His examples of this conflation include the 1970s films *All the President's Men* and *The Parallax View*; my examples are the youth films discussed below, which are so self-consciously postmodern that they could herald a new 1990s genre of "postmodern puberty."

American Youth Movies

If ever there was a film that questioned the loss of history and demonstrated a mania for a certain form of cognitive mapping, it is *Bill and Ted's Excellent Adventure* (Steven Herek, 1989), in which two teenage boys travel back in time to meet important historical figures who help them with a high school project. While on the surface this teen fantasy seems like a simple spoof on Wells's time machine, with protagonists literally attempting to regather various great people of the past, the narrative is not built on what these people did but rather on what they represent in today's context. Perhaps the filmmakers rightly felt that their young audience would not know or remember the specific achievements of Joan of Arc, Beethoven, or Abraham Lincoln, but when such "revisions" take place as Socrates summing up his discourses on the human condition by reciting the soap opera mantra, "Like sands through the hour glass, so are the days of our lives," the characters function both as a hip joke and a more dramatic displacement of historical relevance. Thus, Napoleon is remembered as a French conqueror dude, Genghis Khan is an angry barbarian with bad manners, and Billy the Kid is a kindly chivalrous cowboy.

Again, the film is foremost catering to what is obviously assumed to be a rather ignorant audience, although one scene in particular speaks with an unmistakable postmodern perspective, when Bill and Ted lose their historical friends in a shopping mall. Jameson's writings on the nature of postmodern architecture and space find dramatic realization in this scene; as Anne Friedberg has noted, the mall is a site of postmodernism made manifest (1993: 111). With such irresistable temptations as having Beethoven visit a music store and Joan of Arc lead an aerobics class, the film freely participates in reducing these characters to the commercial stereotypes that Jameson sees throughout contemporary culture. Genghis Khan's violent attack on a sporting-goods store mannequin is humorous only as racist condescension; Sigmund Freud's appearance with a hot dog is a phallic gag indicative of a simplified pop mentality; and Lincoln's ultimate re-delivery of the Gettysburg Address, replacing "our forefathers" with "Bill and Ted" and concluding, "Be excellent to each other," demonstrates the central fantasy that history can somehow be reconfigured for yourself. Indeed, as we find out at the film's end, Bill and Ted turn out to be the saviors of humankind, as their history project systematically brings about universal harmony and communication. Yes, this is all in good fun, but Bill and Ted are symbols of a postmodern young adult ideal, living in a world where history is literally removed (and limited) to the present, and as available as products in a convenience store.

To parallel this style of humor with its social implications, I refer to Jameson's notion of postmodernism as a "cultural dominant" (1991: 56). Friedberg has explained, "The idea of a 'cultural dominant' requires a dialectical imagination of history, where the coupure is not temporal but discursive and epistemological" (1993: 170). The representation of history in *Bill and Ted's Excellent Adventure* enforces such a dialectical imagination of history, appropriating historical figures for their iconographic "laugh value" to the young audience. In other words, viewers are not sold visions of history in terms of fidelity, but rather in terms of the social discourse that has reduced history to "clips" of memory that can be reconfigured to fit a present context, in this case humor.

Wayne's World (Penelope Spheeris, 1992) is perhaps a better example of postmodern pastiche and nostalgia for the present. The film is loaded with dozens of pop-culture references and in-jokes, forming the basis of the characters' cable access television show. Wayne and Garth are our teen tour guides on a journey through suburbia very similar to the environs of Bill and Ted, whose slang they also share. This film clearly demonstrates the reification process that Jameson has discussed: while Wayne and Garth can be seen as potentially radical revolutionaries of the cable waves, their diegetic reality is supported by — and is humorous because of — the familiar commodities of contemporary consumer culture. There is no better statement of this than a scene in which product promotions are wryly criticized and simultaneously endorsed.

While Wayne and Garth insist to their manager that they will not promote their new network sponsor on the air (in what is presumably a defense of commercial-free public television), the characters are seen eating, drinking, and wearing a number of brand-name products, which are prominently displayed on screen. Even the form of the product presentations matches their popular commercial association, as Wayne literally pauses and poses to exhibit each product, and at one point even asks for a brand of analgesic that is filmed in the recognizable style of its television commercials (i.e., colorizing the pills against a black-and-white background).

Wayne's World *(Paramount, 1992) Penelope Spheeris*
Wayne Campbell (Mike Meyers) and Garth Algar (Dana Carvey) are our tour guides in a
postmodern pastiche of pop culture. Still courtesy of Jerry Ohlinger's Movie Materials.

As Ben Stiller, the director of *Reality Bites*, has said, "Irony is the only defense this generation has against the commodification of their culture" (Appelo 1994: 30). But this scene in *Wayne's World* implies that even irony has been commodified, since its unsubtle quality is not nearly as ironic as the actual *selling* of these products. A similar phenomenon would take place by mentioning the products in this essay. To articulate the commodity is to utilize its commercial value, and that is exactly what *Wayne's World* (and any other product placement film) does, even when there is a supposedly sarcastic or resistant presentation of those products.[2]

With further ironic attitude, Wayne addresses the audience in the end credits and says of the film, "We hope you found it entertaining, whimsical, and yet relevant, with an underlying revisionist conceit that belied the film's emotional attachments to the subject matter." Wayne's rhetoric is not an attempt to win over high-brow critics, but is rather a concluding acknowledgement that for young adult audiences, self-conscious recognition of the reification around them — whether they realize it or not — is easier to laugh at than to understand. The use of irony as critique in postmodern texts no longer has defensive potential since the critical device itself has been appropriated for commodity consumption, especially in a multi-commercial medium such as Hollywood cinema.

The romantic comedies I address here are somewhat more slippery targets. For instance, *Singles* (Cameron Crowe, 1992) has such good intentions that its criticism may be misplaced frustration with the narrative's sanguine handling of its young couples and their trials of love. To be sure, *Singles* is a film that attempts to appeal to a wide range of ages, and thereby overlaps younger Baby Boomers and the emergent Generation X population, although this does not prevent the film from exposing the fundamental postmodern challenges presented to its characters. Love for Steve, the wistful protagonist, is summed up by the famous Robert Doisneau photograph, "Kiss at the Hotel d'Ville," for this image captures — according to him — all that he has desired in his romantic experiences. Linda, another wistful protagonist, sees her love symbolized in a garage door opener, which she gives to a suitor early in the film only to find that he has deceived her; her ability to maintain control over her new garage door opener becomes a metaphor for her authority in her ensuing relationship with Steve. Thus these characters' notions of love and devotion find reification in both aesthetic and practical commodities, a staged simulation of emotion in the photograph and an exaggerated (if not unrealistic) sense of power provided by the remote control.

Other "twenty-something" singles in the film proceed within a realm of similar simple signifiers, including a woman who searches for a man who appreciates her gaudy earrings, a rocker whose band is called "Citizen Dick," and his girlfriend who spends much of the film contemplating a computer-aided breast enlargement. All of these rather peculiar conditions are summed up best when Steve tries to sentimentally explain his lost love: "We had good times and bad times, but we had times." Such a declaration of indifference supports Friedberg's argument that the "cultural shifts resulting from the organization of the look in the service of consumption, and the gradual incorporation of the commodified experience into everyday life, has... profoundly altered the subjective role of memory and history" (1993: 3). This is certainly the case in *Singles*, as images and other commodities simultaneously help the characters define themselves and situate those definitions in relation to a subjective experience of the commodities. (Another fine example is when Steve begins to propose marriage to Linda over lunch and she responds, "Don't make me remember this chili dog forever.") Perhaps as in all romantic comedies, the characters in *Singles* try to find lovers to complete

Singles *(Warner Bros, 1992) Cameroon Crowe*
Linda Powell (Kyra Sedwick) and Steve Dunne (Campbell Scott) are one of Seattle's twenty-somethings' couples on a "water date." Still courtesy of Jerry Ohlinger's Movie Materials.

their insecure identities, only here that insecurity is not based on some delirious concept of destiny or fate, but rather on how one's identity is always already insecure due to its constant need for external referents. Any "cognitive mapping" that these characters perform would reveal that their notions of love are reducible to commodity acquistion.

My concluding example is *Reality Bites* (Ben Stiller, 1994), a film that was aimed more specifically at the Generation X crowd, those graduating from college with no jobs and many anxieties. Here the characters' identities are similarly incomplete without a significant other, only the postmodern construction of identity is more pervasive. The characters sing commercial slogans and make many references to old movies and television shows, and they lament the dysfunctional qualities of *all* their families in talk-show style and lingo. One character, Lelaina, even spends much time pontificating the "profound and important" influence of a particular convenience store fountain soda in her life.

Lelaina has also been attempting to define herself through a somewhat *verité* video documentary she has been making about her friends, though when she gives her footage to her boyfriend Michael (played by the director), who happens to work at a very MTV-like station, his producers re-edit it into a postmodern melange of easy meanings. Suddenly the lengthy interviews and slow pace of Lelaina's footage are digested down to sound-bite snips of dialogue ultimately reconfigured to state that the "answer" to the world's problems is… pizza. We then see the main characters' faces superimposed as toppings on a pizza, with its brand name clearly visible. Missing as well are the very questions and backgrounds of these characters, who are seen only as responses to their conditions. The fact that all of these young people have sexual problems is thus reduced to an animal documentary image of rhinoceroses mating while the soundtrack plays "Let's Talk About Sex." Of course, this packaging of their lives will not allow for personalized discourse, only displaced commercial simulation.

The double meaning of the film's title is also brought out in this scene, as these "bites" of "reality" are reduced to constituent signifiers for commercial consumption by the diegetic television station *and* the cinema industry that produced *Reality Bites*. Since the visuals in this video-within-the-film are essentially all that we have been given of these characters, the *entire* film serves as a self-conscious testament to the reification process of these characters' lives. This produces yet another postmodern testament, what Jean-Francois Lyotard has called a "crisis of narratives" (1984: xxiii). After witnessing the disappointing

Reality Bites (*Universal, 1994*) *Ben Stiller*
Troy Dyer (Ethan Hawke) tries to console Lelaina Pierce (Winona Ryder) after she has been fired. Still courtesy of Jerry Ohlinger's Movie Materials.

transformation of her work, Lelaina says to her rebellious roommate Troy, "I don't understand why things can't go back to normal at the end of the half-hour, like *The Brady Bunch*."

I am not sure then if it is irony or conformity that Stiller wanted to display by closing the film with the joyous union of the film's inevitable couple, Lelaina and Troy, who are last seen in the idyllic setting of an empty apartment devoid of brand-name products, although his message about the commodification of experience is clear in the end credits, wherein we see that his character has turned his romance into a *faux-verité* project just like he was trying to buy from Lelaina. If you cannot achieve your desires, you can at least have simulated access to them through electronic media. Or, as Friedberg has written, "In contemporary culture, the marketing of 'commodity-experiences' has almost surpassed the marketing of goods" (1993: 115).

Conclusion

More and more media products about youth remind us of the themes and conditions elaborated here: the films *Slacker, S.F.W., Clueless, Kicking and Screaming, Romy and Michele's High School Reunion*; the television shows *Melrose Place, Beverly Hills 90210, Saved by the Bell, USA High, Dawson's Creek*; and of course, *The Real World* on MTV, which is an example of postmodern puberty *par excellence*. If the viewers of these films and shows are assumed to be as dislocated from their social and personal experiences as the characters they watch, young people face a special paradoxical dilemma when they view these dramas, for they are meant to identify with familiar but incomplete characters. The only level of completion seems to come from an assimilation of consumer culture into one's sense of self, whereby young people can be identified in comparison to the commodities around them.

Fredric Jameson's polemics on postmodernism still provide a potentially empowering — and arguably optimistic — perspective through which we can examine and even avert the ongoing cultural commodifications that result in the reification of identity and loss of self, which form the very process that otherwise ensures that "Generation X" will remain nothing more than a marketable label for a supposedly vapid population. Yet youth themselves will need a massive amount of critical skills, be they in some form of cognitive mapping or a sheer revolt against their own (mis)representation, to be able to challenge the postmodern nature of the contemporary media, which convince youth that to escape their mediated state would mean to cease existing altogether. Thus, at least in terms of the current youth generation of which many of us are still members, the films discussed here have problematized the *us* in us.

References

Appelo, Tim. 1994. "Ben Stiller's X Factor." *Entertainment Weekly* (March 4): 29-31.

Donougho, Martin. 1988. "Fredric Jameson." *Dictionary of Literary Biographies* 67: 176-188.

Easthope, Antony. 1990. "Eliot, Pound, and the Subject of Postmodernism." *After the Future: Postmodern Times and Places*, edited by Gary Shapiro. Albany: State University of New York Press: 53-66.

Friedberg, Anne. 1993. *Window Shopping: Cinema and the Postmodern*. Berkeley, CA: University of California Press.

Green, Leonard. 1982. "Interview with Jameson." *Diacritics* 12: 72-91.

Jameson, Fredric. 1983a. "Pleasure: A Political Issue." *Formations of Pleasure*, Formation Series, vol. 1. London: Routledge and Kegan Paul: 1-14.

———— 1983b. "Postmodernism and Consumer Society." *The Anti-Aesthetic: Essays on Postmodern Culture*, edited by Hal Foster. Port Townsend, WA: Bay Press: 111-125.

———— 1984a. "The Politics of Theory: Ideological Positions in the Postmodernism Debate." *New German Critique* 33: 53-65.

———— 1984b. "Postmodernism, or The Cultural Logic of Late Capitalism." *New Left Review* 146: 52-92.

———— 1985. "Architecture and the Critique of Ideology." *Architecture, Criticism, Ideology*, edited by J. Ockham. Princeton, N.J.: Princeton Architectural Press: 51-87.

———— 1989. "Nostalgia for the Present." *South Atlantic Quarterly* 88: 517-537.

———— 1990. *Signatures of the Visible*. New York: Routledge.

———— 1991. *Postmodernism, or The Cultural Logic of Late Capitalism*. Durham, N.C.: Duke University Press.

———— 1992. *The Geopolitical Aesthetic: Cinema and Space in the World System*. Bloomington, IN: Indiana University Press.

Lyotard, Jean-François. 1984. *The Postmodern Condition: A Report on Knowledge*. Minneapolis: University of Minnesota Press.

McCabe, Colin. 1992. Preface to *The Geopolitical Aesthetic: Cinema and Space in the World System*, by Fredric Jameson. Bloomington, IN: Indiana University Press.

McGowan, John. 1991. *Postmodernism and Its Critics*. Ithaca, N.Y.: Cornell University Press.

O'Neill, John. 1990. "Religion and Postmodernism: The Durkheimian Bond in Bell and Jameson." In *After the Future: Postmodern Times and Places*, edited by Gary Shapiro. Albany: State University of New York Press: 285-299.

NOTES

1. For an interesting criticism of Jameson's work on film, see "Class and Allegory in Jameson's Film Criticism" by Kathleen K. Rowe in the *Quarterly Review of Film and Video*, vol. 12, no. 4 (1991: 2). Rowe argues quite convincingly that Jameson's ideas about such totalizing theories as postmodernism are marred by "elitist and masculinist biases." While I recognize some of these biases in Jameson's writings, I maintain that his opinions about consumer culture and his claims of nostalgia for the present — a position which Anne Friedberg has critiqued in relation to cinema (see references) — are nonetheless valuable to a current understanding of the emotional and historical bankruptcy and reification of identity represented by characters in many recent youth films.

2. See "Hollywood: The Ad," *The Atlantic Monthly* (April 1990). Mark Crispin Miller offers a detailed analysis of product placement in movies that supports this argument.

Part II

Issues of Cross-Cultural Identity
and National Cinemas

Tampopo (Itami Production/Fox-Lorber, 1987) Juzo Itami
In a parody of American Westerns and Japanese Samurai films, a young widow (Nobuko Miyamoto) and Goro (Tsutomu Yamazaki) share food in Itami's "noodle wester." Still courtesy of Jerry Ohlinger's Movie Materials

CHAPTER 5

REFIGURING PLEASURE
Itami and the Postmodern Japanese Film
John Bruns

I wonder why I have to make films now that industrial society's dreams of prosperity and unending progress have shattered. You, in the light green suit. Do I have to make films in spite of that? What thoughts do you have about films and me? The most that I can create is a reverse utopia. And I don't want to lead you there. Hey, you. Still, do I...?

Nagisa Oshima, *Cinema, Censorship and the State* (1974)

When a Japanese wants to dream, they see Western films or animated films, not Japanese films.

Juzo Itami (1992)

These two quotations suggest, I believe, a dramatic (or dramatize a suggestive) shift in Japanese cinema. The first comes from the personal writings of Nagisa Oshima, the second, from a public statement by Juzo Itami. We might consider the different ways in which these two directors imagine the postindustrial Japanese subject as a starting point for an examination of the precise nature of the postmodern Japanese film. The first quotation is distinctly modern: one is left with a stronger impression of the personality of the artist than with the postindustrial Japanese subject. The second quotation seems distinctly post-modern: Itami recognizes that the postindustrial Japanese subject is always in the process of speaking itself; negotiating through cross-cultural, pan-generic discursive formations. Itami's postmodern suggests, in short, a dramatic refiguration of subjectivity. The Japanese subject is no longer that which must be spoken *for.* Identity politics are no longer at the mercy of a suffocating binary rhetoric that characterizes Oshima's writings. I would like to suggest that Itami's refiguration of subjectivity is largely the result of a process that we call *bricolage.* But Itami's application of the term derives as much from Cultural Studies as it does from postmodern aesthetics. That is, we experience the practice of *bricolage* not simply as a style of cultural *production*, or as a general "tone" of postmodernity (as some postmodern studies have characterized it), but as a mode of cultural *consumption* as well.

Using the work of Michel de Certeau, I will show how Itami's 1987 film *Tampopo* envisions the practice of consumption in postmodern Japan. Throughout the film, Itami stresses the priority of pleasure as the necessary reward for creative consumption. The concept of "pleasure," however, is not a particularly recent topic of interest for the Japanese filmmaker; as the above quotation demonstrates, the concept of pleasure seems to haunt the New Wave — the generation of filmmakers preceding Itami. What I would like to argue is that the postmodern film differs dramatically from the New Wave in its figuration of subjectivity, consumption, and pleasure. Yet this refiguration of subjectivity necessarily demands a reworking of narrative strategies, and here is where I feel the work of de Certeau is particularly useful. Itami's films are not simply stories of postmodern subjects "making do." Rather, they recognize that practices are always already stories, always already in the process of "speaking themselves." Consequently, Itami tends to show us (in de Certeau's terms) how a theory of practice is indissociable from a theory of narration (1984: 78).

Itami's film arises from a period of Japanese film that reworks classical Hollywood and Japanese conventions and appropriates contemporary cultures, although "appropriates" might not adequately describe the tone of the postmodern Japanese film, which *consumes* cultures voraciously as would an eager but discriminating omnivore. *Tampopo* is emblematic of these trends. It borrows conventions, quite liberally, from Samurai films as well as American genre films such as the gangster film and the Western. *Tampopo* garnered such success as to become Japanese cinema's number one export to the United States in 1987. And while the film is over a decade old, it remains as important a film as Ridley Scott's *Blade*

Runner in the study of postmodernism, though the two have markedly
different visions. The mise-en-scène of Scott's film is undoubtedly the
supreme example of the postmodern vision in film; it is saturated with
"successive layers of urban history" through juxtaposition (Collins, 133),
the imaginative landscape of *Blade Runner* is primarily one of bricolage —
but a bricolage that is practiced as a stylistic code. That is, the postmodern
aesthetic mimics the disparate elements of our contemporary landscape.
Consequently, we may imagine Scott's application of bricolage as an
attempt to represent postmodern cultural production: the objects we
encounter, the architecture that surrounds us.

The importance of architectural discourse in understanding the
modern/postmodern polemic cannot be understated, thus the discourse
of postmodernism is often saturated with architectural terms like "neo-
vernacular," "radical eclecticism," and "pastiche." These stylistic features
of postmodern cultural production are emblematic of a response to the
unfulfilled promise of modernity and the goals of the Enlightenment: that
rationality and freedom will progress. It is in this context that Lyotard
introduces a new connotation of the word "bricolage" understood as "the
multiple quotation of elements taken from earlier styles or periods,
classical and modern; disregard for the environment; and so on" (1993:
47). Emphasis, consequently, shifts from *identity construction* in Lévi-
Strauss's or Derrida's terms, and *cultural consumption* in de Certeau's
terms, to *cultural production*. It becomes the *mise-en-scène* of *Blade Runner*,
as well as the performance art of Laurie Anderson. Bricolage, according
to Lyotard, is the attempt of cultural producers (artists and architects
alike) to cope with postmodernity. These cultural producers recognize
the inability of one master discourse to liberate the subject (whether this
master discourse be avant-garde film or the International Style of modern
architecture) and progress through history toward the enlightened goal of
freedom and equality. As Charles Jencks writes in *The Language of Post-
Modern Architecture*: "[t]hese claims, that architecture can radically
change behavior, are Modernist ones, although attention to 'user-
reactions' and actual social research are postmodern. Indeed, the great
emphasis on the *language* of architecture and the codes of the various
groups that might use the building is precisely the postmodernism being
advocated" (1981: 99). In short, postmodern architecture is involved, as
de Certeau might phrase it, in a grand project of speaking about what
someone else (the "various groups" to which Jencks refers) says about the
practice of everyday life. The problem faced by de Certeau in his study of
the culture of everyday life is this: How does one "narrate" practices that

are themselves narrations or "enunciations"? How does one avoid speaking for practices that are already speaking themselves? What does one do with practices once alerted to one's own theoretical reflections? How does one think them?

The solution, for de Certeau, is to locate a model "in which the theory of practices takes precisely the form of a way of narrating them" and an illustration might very well be Itami's *Tampopo*. Itami's film, I argue, is indeed involved in the game of narrating postmodern bricolage; but we might consider Itami's application of the term as borrowing much more from the work of Lévi-Strauss than from architecture. In his essay, "Structure, Sign and Play in the Discourse of the Human Sciences," Jacques Derrida (summarizing Lévi-Strauss), suggests that

> [t]he *bricoleur*, says Levi-Strauss, is someone who uses the 'means at hand,' that is, the instruments he finds at his disposition around him, those which are already there, which had not been especially conceived with an eye to the operation for which they are to be used and to which one tries by trial an error to adapt them, not hesitating to change them whenever it appears necessary, or to try several of them at once, even if their form and their origin are heterogeneous (1988: 114-115).

What one encounters in Itami's film is precisely this fuller application of the term "bricolage": it is, for Derrida and de Certeau, a kind of "trickery." That is, we cannot dissociate the concept of bricolage from anti-disciplinarian operations any more than we should dissociate it from our understanding of the postmodern style. What may appear at first to be a film simply about food, *Tampopo* carries with it, I think, more profound implications than those offered to us by the idea of bricolage as mere cultural production. Primarily, Itami imagines a subject that constructs itself by utilizing the means at hand; all of his characters are *bricoleurs*. Itami's postmodern narrative seems to satisfy, quite adequately, the work of de Certeau, who has tried to "trace the intricate forms of the operations proper...to the tactics of the art of cooking, which, simultaneously organizes a network of relations, poetic ways of 'making do' (bricolage) and a re-use of marketing structures" (1984: xv). Doing just this, Itami's film utilizes Japanese cuisine as a sort of crucible within which networks of bricolage speak themselves. But Itami likewise recognizes that the materials with which these *bricoleurs* construct their identities are never those of a homogeneous culture, but instead are products of disparate cultures.

The hero of Itami's *Tampopo* (a milk-truck driver named Goro) finds himself living in a movie best described as a cross between a Samurai film and an American Western. Itami's film is intriguing because it of its polylogical examination of postmodern identity, or more precisely, bricolage as it exists in postindustrial Japan. Clearly the most intriguing scene in the film is the fight between Goro (a hybrid of "the man with no name" in *A Fistful of Dollars* and Kambei from *Seven Samurai*) and the jealous rival, Pisken. The scenario is this: a wandering loner comes to town and catches the attention of the young heroine. This establishes the opposition: the man who had previously held the attention of the young lady becomes jealous, and thus becomes the villain. The Lai Lai Restaurant operates as the "local saloon," and Tampopo as the pretty proprietress (she is, in one scene, dressed with her hair up, wearing a green checkered shirt and scarf). Goro and his sidekick Gun (short for "shotgun") drive a shiny milk truck in place of cattle (if the connection isn't immediate, Itami makes it more obvious by placing a set of bull horns on the roof of the truck). Just as Goro is about to mount his truck, Pisken pulls him aside commanding a fair fight between them. They begin their fight beneath a bridge, and Itami frames their silhouettes against the skyline which is visible in the extreme background. Yet the very next shot is of a reverse angle, which shows Goro and Pisken moving out from under the bridge toward a patch of ground. This would be the classic Western setting, with the wooden fence and the dust kicking up as they stagger toward one another (the fence and dust contributing to what Marc Vernet calls the "general atmosphere" of the Western, with its "emphasis on basic elements, such as earth, dust, water and leather") (in Altman 1986: 30-31). But again in the extreme background is the skyline of Tokyo and the bridge of a major highway. This shot is followed by an extreme high angle shot: in the bottom left hand corner of the frame, Goro and Pisken continue their fight as the camera zooms out to reveal their patch of fighting ground to be surrounded by the ever-present city, a network of highway intersections, caravans of industrial-sized trucks, and the skyline.

It would appear that the landscape of the Western is gone — eradicated by over-industrialization — but this is not the case. Itami has his characters tactically create this fictional moment; or, rather, his characters display a practice of *enunciating*, which de Certeau describes as "a process of *appropriation* of the topographical system on the part of the pedestrian...it is a spatial acting out of the place" (1984: 97-98). This process of "making *coups*" into fictional space is given an almost literal translation in Itami's film with the "blows" each character directs toward the other throughout the fist-fight. Thus the "atmospheric space" of the classical American Western

— an imaginary space within which the traditional code of honor can be fulfilled — is not so much swallowed up by the ever-present cityscape as it is in narrated into existence; the barroom brawl takes on an enunciative function in order to reconcile differentiated positions (those of Pisken and Goro). The spatial-temporal nature of this scene does not emphasize the longing for a landscape forever lost, where "men were men" or where naked Kevin Costners cavorted with wolves. Nor does it emphasize a critique of industrialized civilization, where authentic identities are alienated by ever-expanding technocracy. It works, rather, as an imaginary space in which numerous otherwise competing discourses can be reconciled.

After Goro and Pisken finish fighting, they collapse into a field of tall green grass, again with the large cityscape in the left background and the highway to the right. This shot is followed by an extreme low angle shot of the open sky (recalling the excessive headroom shots of Ford's *Monument Valley*). To the left and right of the open sky are the blades of grass and the wooden fence. The next shot reveals this as a perspective shot: the two, Pisken and Goro, in close-up, lie on the grass, complimenting each other's fighting skills. As this reconciliation continues, there follows another perspective shot of the open sky, this time with a wider angle, which reveals the highway bridge on the left, the open sky in the middle, and the grass and wooden fence to the right. The fictional spaces are put into harmony as Goro and Pisken become fully reconciled:

Pisken: Are you sweet on Tampopo?
Goro: I just want to make her place a good one.
Pisken: Let me help.
Goro: What can you do?
Pisken: I'm a contractor. I do interiors, too. Bars and nightclubs mostly.
Goro: Okay, you do the interior.

This reconciliation between Goro and Pisken is marked by a humorous combination of the slang associated with Westerns ("are you sweet on so-and-so?") and the language characteristic of rapidly industrialized cities ("I'm a contractor. I do interiors, too. Bars and nightclubs mostly"). A number of reconciliations take place in this scene: that of spaces, both rural and urban; that of histories, both past and present; that of a traditional Japanese code of honor with a code of commodification; and, lastly, that of labor forces engaged in both agriculture (Goro, the milk-truck driver) and services (Pisken, the contractor). It is perhaps in this scene as much any other in Itami's film that we see the characters so involved in appropriating topographical forms. This, for de Certeau, is precisely what distinguishes the "tactic" from the "strategic": whereas "strategic" operations construct the actual space of political, economic, and scientific rationality (the city, for instance), "tactics" are appropriations of these spaces, and thus have no "proper" place of their own (1984: xix). *Bricolage*, in Itami's film, is indeed a form of mise-en-scène — but one that answers to the logic of action of the characters. That is, the characters in Itami's film *se mettent-en-scène* before our very eyes — they are literally "making a scene."

All this, of course, is for the benefit of Tampopo's success. Success for Tampopo means developing the perfect noodle recipe, which demands a certain amount of culinary literacy on behalf of all the characters — each of whom represent a different social type. This is why Tampopo is first attracted to Goro: he is wise in the ways of noodles and has the ability to reconcile individuals in order to help construct her perfect recipe. Knowing how to prepare noodles involves research, the advice of master chefs, street gourmets, rich gourmands, and not a small amount of underhandedness. In fact, nothing could more accurately illustrate "using the means at hand" than the process by which the noodle ramen create their perfect recipe; it is bricolage in all its plurality of forms. These practices are precisely what unite all of Tampopo's ramen samurai. As in Kurosawa's *Seven Samurai*, each hired gun in *Tampopo* is very different in background, but all are reconciled in their common mission. The samurai in this case are: Goro, an experienced, hard-bitten, Clint Eastwood-like grimacing truck driver; Gun his young outspoken sidekick; an old master of ramen making, who now lives as a vagabond with a group of devoted followers; Pisken, a chef/chauffeur of a well-to-do gourmand; and Shohei, the rich, resourceful contractor. Though they all come from very different social strata, they can all agree, with similar verbosity, on noodles. What is most important, however, is the means by which each character adds to the recipe, the ways in which they make do: the ways in which they display their *culinary* literacy.

Itami, like certain Western theorists such as Barthes and de Certeau, has chosen the art of cooking as a means of expressing bricolage as a characteristically artisanlike inventiveness, a kind of creative consumption. These operations, which are "proper to the art of cooking," writes de Certeau, "simultaneously organizes a network of relations, poetic ways of 'making do' (bricolage)…" (1984: xv). It is this "network of relations" that constitutes postmodern space. And it is for this reason that Roland Barthes, in *Empire of Signs*, sees Japanese food as necessarily "de-centered"; there is no point of origin of Japanese identity. For just as "food is never anything but a collection of fragments, none of which appears privileged by an order of ingestion," no single ramen samurai is privileged in Itami's film, nor is each addition to the final recipe that accompanies them (1972: 22). Thus, Itami gives us a look at Japanese culture in its plurality of forms, a culture which is rapidly changing under influences from the industrialized West, including Hollywood (one of the many reasons Itami chose to make a *Western*). In so doing, he is able to account for a postmodern semiotics of pleasure.

It is a culture of radical eclecticism: of "stores and temples, large boulevards of expensive shops and itinerant vendors, the most bizarre western youth-culture fashion next to ceremonial kimonos on the subway" (Clammer 1992: 196). Itami recognizes the Japanese consumer as always defined as "relational." This is certainly a shift away from the preceding tradition in Japanese film, known as the New Wave. The films of this period (from about 1964 with *Woman in the Dunes* to 1982 with *Merry Christmas, Mr. Lawrence*) are films that reflect distrust, disenchantment, and disillusion with changing traditions — all of which threaten any sense of a coherent "self."[1] Many of the New Wave directors, most notably Nagisa Oshima, reject Japan's cinematic as well as historical past by presenting dystopic themes of constraint, weakness, and despair, of traditions either annihilated or annihilating. Oshima, whose films include *Japanese Summer: Double Suicide* (1967), *Death by Hanging* (1968), *A Secret Post-Tokyo War Story, or The Man Who Left his Will on Film* (1970), *In the Realm of the Senses* (1976) and, more recently, *Merry Christmas, Mr. Lawrence* (1982), and *Max, Mon Amour* (1986), has, more than any other director in his time, dealt explicitly with the issue of sexuality and politics. Oshima attempts to criticize the delusions of Japanese society regarding its sexuality, particularly in *In the Realm of the Senses*. For Oshima, "one becomes an eternal prisoner of the societal structure" when one believes sexuality is, in essence, exclusive. "For nearly every moment of our daily lives," continues Oshima,

> we are that sort of pathetic prisoner. Instinctively, however, people try to escape the fetters of such a delusion. Anticipating that, society creates purely technical escape routes, such as swapping partners and sex outside marriage. Insofar as these escape routes do not aspire to break through the myth of sexual exclusiveness and possessiveness, however, they have no essential power (1992: 247).

Thus the impossibility of genuine movement in the New Wave films of Japan. Power structures are imagined as so all-pervasive that even seemingly subversive activities are rendered useless. Such themes are unique to modern aesthetics — particularly with directors such as Oshima and Jean-Luc Godard. The artist, however, struggles to maintain aesthetic detachment from the work, and in this way, avoids the fate suffered by its characters. The modern artist, then, positions him or herself in the realm of "transcendent critique." The quotations from Oshima and Itami thus serve well to illustrate both their attitudes toward the postindustrial Japanese as well as their attitudes toward their art. I would like to suggest that Itami's quotation differs from Oshima's in two mutually dependent ways: Itami narrates identity construction in postmodern Japan, and in so doing, necessarily subordinates his own voice, silences his own interpretative agency that is, for Oshima and his contemporaries, governed by modern aesthetics. Oshima, and many of his contemporaries (Teshigawara Hiroshi and Shinoda Masahiro, for instance) examine the pleasure of consumption in terms of predominantly modernist paradigms. That is, their films apply narratives that *speak for* their subjects.

Shinoda Masahiro's *Double Suicide* (1969), for instance, is a particularly intriguing film that very clearly establishes the modern binaries within which subjects are trapped — are, in short, predetermined. The very first image of *Double Suicide* is the appearance of life-size puppets — and precisely the sort of imagery upon which Masahiro's film operates, as it examines the centuries-old tradition of the double suicide. Masahiro's film likewise utilizes radical signifying practices associated with avant-garde work, such as freeze-frame and slow-motion. What is more striking, however, is the mise-en-scène of Masahiro's film. At one point in *Double Suicide*, the husband and his courtesan rest motionless, blending in with the classical Japanese figures that decorate the floor on which they lie; the two become indistinguishable. Set in opposition against the classical figures of Japanese are the chaotic splashes of paint resembling less the Abstract Expressionist paintings of Jackson Pollock than expressing an overall tone of death and spilt blood. Both styles decorate the interiors of Masahiro's film, each asserting itself at various critical points in the narrative, sometimes appearing simultaneously in order to set up a distinct binary: one either conforms with age-old traditions (suggested by the classical figures of Japanese art), or sentences oneself to death (symbolized by the violent, chaotic splashes of paint). *Fate* carries them through their story like so many puppet strings. These directors fear a society "in which massive industrialization, urbanization, and technocratization have accelerated social change and caused the disintegration of traditional (and, in Japan's case, centuries-old) values without offering anything in their place" (Cook 1990: 805). Whereas these "values" could once speak for the subject in useful ways, their eradication has, supposedly, left the subject without a mentor. That the mise-en-scène of Shinoda's film so aggressively speaks for its subjects, administers to them, and denies them any enunciative function except death, illustrates what Annette Michelson argues is classical to the Japanese narrative, i.e., "a specific method of *storytelling* in which the narrator governs the voices of the characters" (in Oshima 1992: 30n). That such totalitarian applications of narration should be disregarded by Itami and his contemporaries is no surprise, given the changing attitudes toward self-location and identity-construction in postmodern Japan.

This seeming loss of the coherent, autonomous "self" is precisely what postmodernism struggles with; and it is from this obsolete polemic (of *either* conforming *or* death) that the ironic in postmodernism arises. Itami's film examines cultural identity without relying on impossible pretenses either to the nostalgic space of purity and harmony, or to the pessimistic space of silence and death, as the only authentic and therefore the only viable alternatives to conformity. Part of Itami's vision of postmodernism, and certainly part of the postmodern aesthetic in general, is the recognition of cross-cultural, pan-generic influences. In so doing, he likewise imagines a subject who is able to "make do" in such a milieu, whose pleasure is by no means uniformly administered by the structures within which it is hopelessly trapped. Consequently, Itami's film re-writes Japanese narrative, allowing subjects to speak themselves — each exhibiting his and her tactical operations in all their unlimited diversity.

Roland Barthes, in *The Pleasure of the Text*, tries to predict a kind of aesthetic that speaks to the later half of the twentieth century (and is not Itami's film, at crucial moments, undeniably and simply this?):

> Imagine an aesthetic (if the word has not become too deprecated) based entirely (completely, radically, in every sense of the word) on the *pleasure of the consumer*, whoever he may be, to whatever class, whatever group he may belong, without respect to cultures or languages: the consequences would be huge, perhaps even harrowing (1972: 59).

Cinematically, Itami privileges the illustration of the pleasure to any traditional narrative illustration. The plot, which is itself an ironic exposition of generic constructs, is consistently interrupted by short vignettes. The disruptions are neither superfluous, nor are they excessive.

Itami freely skips over the narrative or Tampopo, dropping the spectator into numerous sketches involving the sensual, hedonistic aromas of Japanese cuisine; and just as quickly, just as seamlessly, drops the spectator back into the "story." The narrative logic of the film, and the illustration of pleasure *within* the vignettes that upset it, manifest certain striking parallels of Itami's vision with Barthes's meditations on narrative pleasure. He strikes a consistent and delicate balance in Itami's film between an almost Zenlike respect of cuisine, and a more gluttonous, unrestrained hedonism. "We resemble a spectator in a nightclub," writes Barthes in *The Pleasure of the Text*, "who climbs onto the stage and speeds up the dancer's striptease, tearing off her clothing, *but in the same order*, that is: on the one hand respecting and on the other hastening the episodes of the ritual (like a priest *gulping down* his Mass)" (1972: 11). Itami expresses this same fascination with narrative pleasure in the very beginning of the film, when Gun reads from a book about a noodle master teaching his student the rituals of eating noodles. Gun stops in the middle of the text complaining of hunger, to which Goro hastily replies "keep reading!" Similar to this is a short episode in which Tampopo saves a rich gourmand from choking. The old man is warned not to indulge himself — to eat slowly, and to stay away from the particularly rich dishes. The gourmand begins to follow this advice, and begins to eat slowly, carefully, with almost as much respect as that demonstrated by the noodle master in Gun's book. The gourmand, however, cannot contain himself and launches into his feast with fierce gluttony, only to be saved from death by a vacuum inserted into his throat — proving, once again, the utility of using objects for purposes other than those for which they are intended.

A particularly telling excerpt from Roland Barthes's *The Pleasure of the Text* provides a useful way of thinking of these humorous vignettes in terms of the overall structure of the film. The will to pleasure is not strictly an ideological phenomenon, nor one strictly associated with a single, homogeneous mass: "Pleasure...does not depend on a logic of understanding and on sensation; it is adrift, something both revolutionary and asocial, and it cannot be taken over by any collectivity, any mentality, any ideolect" (1972: 23). The corporate "take-over" of all forms of pleasure is certainly an important issue for any director in a country that has traditionally invested so heavily in conformity. Many of the vignettes give voice to the various procedures that attempt to thwart this stifling ideology — particularly the vignette in which the connoisseurship of a young man embarrasses the stuffed shirts at a high powered business lunch. As the waiter circles the table, each businessman, with mock particularity so as not to offend one another, orders the same dish: *sole meunière*, "consommé," and a Heineken. The waiter approaches the end of the table, and finds the young man, seated next to his father, deeply engrossed in his menu and its possibilities. With each item carefully selected (and with a disapproving kick underneath the table from his father), the young man orders himself *quenelle* prepared *boudin*-style, a waldorf salad, and *Corton Charlemagne*, 1981. The waiter, after applauding the young man's culinary literacy, leaves the businessmen twitching with embarrassment. What is clear in this scene is that Japanese identity need not be expressed in terms of *either* a modern sensibility of conformity or a nostalgic sense of purity and authenticity (for the menu is obviously European). In short, Itami celebrates both "*kokusaijin*" (a person of diverse cultural influences) and "*haragei*" (thinking with one's stomach) as necessarily interrelated features of postmodern subjectivity (Clammer 1992: 205, 211).

Unlike his predecessors in Japanese film, Itami avoids the modernist notion of "subjugation" by locating moments of enunciation and empowerment on behalf of the subject. The modernist critique of the "culture industry" as a subjugating force is perhaps best illustrated by Herbert Marcuse's analogy of the road map:

> Let us take a simple example. A man who travels by automobile to a distant place chooses his route from the highway maps. Towns, lakes and mountains appear as obstacles to be bypassed. The countryside is shaped and organized by the highway. Numerous signs and posters tell the traveler what to do and think; they even request his attention to the beauties of nature or the hallmarks of history. Others have done the thinking for him, and perhaps for the better. Convenient parking spaces have been constructed where the broadest and most surprising view is open. Giant advertisements tell him when to stop and find the pause that refreshes. And all this is indeed for his benefit, safety and comfort; he receives what he wants. Business, techniques, human needs and nature are welded together into one rational and expedient mechanism. He will fare best who follows his directions, subordinating his spontaneity to the anonymous wisdom which ordered everything for him (1982: 143).

Culture as a "road map," an all pervasive sign system that rationalizes its subjugating force, relegates even "choice" as dependent on a predetermined logic. Pleasure is always already administered. A subject may be free to choose what she pleases, but those options which are open to her are necessarily preselected by the authoritarian state — to the extent that options that exist elsewhere (choosing, say, to drive off the road and into the hills) are rendered *irrational.* For Oshima, the myth of sexual exclusiveness is inescapable; society bestows "purely technical escape routes" which lack real power. Similarly, in Oshima's *Double Suicide,* the characters are reduced to puppets, unable to escape their own traditions or break from the strings that bind them to the state.

What occurs then, in Itami's films, is a proliferation of alternatives to the narratives with which critics such as Marcuse and Oshima assert their authority. Such narratives privilege the strategic operations of subjects upon which technological rationality depends; Marcuse's narrative of the "road map," as charming as it is, sacrifices "tactical" operations for the benefit of, what Jim Collins, in *Architectures of Excess,* calls an "aggregate narrative." Itami subordinates the critical position of "negative tour guide" in order to tell how pleasure is garnered in "tactical," rather than "strategic" ways. Writes de Certeau,

> [i]n the wake of many remarkable works that have analyzed "cultural products," the system of their production, the geography of their distribution and the situation of consumers in that geography, it seems possible to consider these products no longer merely as data on the basis of which statistical tabulations of their circulation can be drawn up or the economic functioning of their diffusion understood, but also as parts of the repertory with which users carry out operations of their own. Henceforth, these facts are no longer the data of our calculations, but rather the lexicon of users' practices (1984: 31).

Rather than situating pleasure as either the reward for being reconciled to the dominant ideology or a necessarily futile form of resistance against the state, Itami instead situates pleasure as the rewards for creative consumption and enunciation. Itami's characters indulge in a particularly "inclusive" sexuality exhibiting more than anything the Japanese subject's resourcefulness — a characteristic that derives from an awareness of how disparate cultural objects can be reworked, how cultural narratives can be respoken, how cultural influences can be renegotiated.

One vignette, in particular, illustrates this "lexicon of user practices" to which de Certeau refers. In the hopes of bringing yet another ingredient to what will be the perfect noodle recipe, Tampopo and Goro turn to an old master of ramen, who now lives on the streets with a group of vagabond disciples, all of whom are culinary *bricoleurs*: a vagabond soliloquizes on the near-perfection of a 1980 Bordeaux he found in the garbage outside a restaurant; another vagabond offers to cook a meal by sneaking into the kitchen of a restaurant, thwarting the confused trajectory of a security guard. Aside from the most obvious observation that these characters are engaged in a de Certeauean act of "poaching" (the latter gourmet/vagrant, in an uncanny coincidence of metaphors, literally poaches an egg for the purposes of making an omelet), we are likewise presented an illustration of how Marcuse's critique of the culture industry fails to recognize the possibility of user-practices and the "enunciative function" of appropriating topographical systems (de Certeau 1984: 97). Because bricolage is always a form of mediation with ideology (that is, bricolage is the use of cultural goods for reasons other than that for which they are produced), the pleasure it garners is necessarily without ideolect.[2] Pleasure finds its source in "the tactical and joyful dexterity of the mastery of technique."

This is perhaps why Itami presents us with yet another vignette in which an old woman dashes around a grocery store, eluding the clerk at every turn, in order to poke, squeeze, and fondle every soft item she can get her hands on. Just as the security guard in the omelet vignette is unable to account for the movement of the *bricoleur*, so is the grocery clerk one step behind the food fetishist. The "road map" metaphor is certainly useful in examining the all-pervasiveness of totalitarian regimes, but it fails to account for those operations that manage to escape ideal subjectivity. The geography of the culture industry, as Marcuse defines it, cannot trace user-practices other than those of ideal subjects who operate within it. Such a vision of the culture industry lacks peripheral vision; it is a scope too narrow, like that of cameras installed in convenient stores, department stores and banks, for which only the user-practices of ideal subjects make any sense, for which only those subjects already uniformly interpellated become visible.

I return once again to the question of representation, however, as I must make clear that Itami's narrative is as dramatically refigured as his postmodern Japanese subjects. Itami does not utilize the stylistic disruption of narrative flow for the purposes of radical signification (as is the case in numerous "anti-narrative" films of the avant-garde and New Wave), nor to illustrate how topographical space administers to the subject, eradicating its ability to speak anything but violent death. What vignettes such as those mentioned above tend to do is illustrate the randomness of tactical opportunities — so much so that it often seems as if Itami's camera is hovering patiently, waiting to seize an opportunity to surf the networks of tactical operations that constitute life in the postmodern city. These user-practices are always in the process of asserting themselves, never subordinated to authoritative "genius." That is, these practices are not objects with which Itami creates a position for himself as an authoritative interpreter, a modern genius, or an *auteur*. Rather than being governed by a higher authority, each tactic literally "makes a scene." Now, the focus of de Certeau's criticism of theoretical procedures is directed toward the art of professionals (Foucault, Bourdieu, Lévi-Strauss) who, by careful yet charismatic rhetorical gestures, create positions of authority for themselves. But if you will forgive this intercontextual exercise, I would like to address the potential parallels to the art of cinema.

"The ways of operating do not merely designate activities that a theory might take as its objects" writes de Certeau, "[t]hey also organize its construction. Far from remaining external to theoretical creation or at its threshold, Foucault's 'procedures,' Bourdieu's 'strategies,' and tactics in general form *a field of operations within which the production of theory takes place*" (1984: 78). These observations have had profound effects on postcolonial literature and Cultural Studies. Scholars have been forced to reexamine their positions within their fields and reformulate previous assumptions about *authority* — which, for de Certeau, constitutes an abuse of knowledge. For de Certeau it is a process by which one *speaks for* other cultures and assumes that one knows the culture's objects and images even better than its members do. This kind of *authority*, as we encounter it in cinema, is best described by Oshima himself:

"Adventurers" are people who head for unexplored regions and unknown territory. The world's popular "adventurers" are people who challenge the remote corners of the earth, the unexplored regions. If I were to qualify as an "adventurer," it would be only on the basis of my being a person who challenges unexplored psychological territories (1992: 206).

One can imagine Oshima's "filmmaker as adventurer" armed only with his 16mm Éclair and a pith helmet, mastering the maelstrom of adiscursive territory — a sort of Manichean *auteur* seeking to map out the seeming uncharted regions of the "self." It is for this reason that Oshima's attempts to speak *for* the Japanese subject are necessarily frustrating ones. The remarkable heterogeneity of practices that already "speak themselves" will always frustrate the authority of totalizing narratives, as well as the totalitarian narratives of *auteurs*. The solution for de Certeau, as noted above, is to let the practices "speak themselves." But what, exactly, is practiced in *Tampopo*? Quite simply, sex and eating. Itami even suggests that the most enjoyable experiences involve the sweet simultaneity of intercourse and eating. But sex and eating are likewise the subjects of the New Wave films of Oshima and Shinoda. What I have attempted to show, however, is the way the directors of the New Wave and post-New Wave approach the representation of consumption in radically different ways: in so doing, I have tried to illustrate, and thus elaborate, on the phenomenon of bricolage.

The two quotations that open this essay demonstrate Oshima's and Itami's concern with the everyday Japanese subject, though the former's words seem profoundly entangled in fanatic self-doubt. What Oshima describes is not so much the crisis of the postindustrial subject, but, perhaps more importantly, the profound ambiguity about his personal position within his field of work — the crisis of his own art. At the mercy of useless binary rhetoric and erroneous notions of "cognitive mapping," the previous wave of Japanese filmmakers found themselves suffocated, stymied by conventions no longer applicable in decentered cultures such as postindustrial Japan. Perhaps this is why Oshima felt he could only create a "reverse Utopia" — a sphere of imagination perhaps more administered than the pleasure that is celebrated by Itami. Rather than being threatened by a need to reclaim the "true" or "pure" Japanese identity, Itami's characters exploit, in all efforts, their own cross-cultural, pan-generic influences. Rather than seeing no way out, we see, in the postmodern films of Itami, a million ways to get things done, a million ways to move, and a million ways to eat a noodle. Itami proves that instances of pleasure occur not for the strict purpose of containment and homogeneity, but arise from an aspiration to creative consumption, or bricolage. In Itami's postmodern Japan, sensual pleasure is not strictly a subjugating force — it is also the exquisite fruit of bricolage.

On the Political Implications of "Tactics"

Jean-Luc Godard, in his film *Masculin/Feminin* (1966), interrupts the narrative with this intertitle: "this film could be called...the children of Marx and Coca-Cola." More than thirty years has passed since Godard made this claim, and with the failure of subjects to recognize their own alienation, and the proletariat's failure to fulfill its own role as the revolutionary agent, the slogan is even more intriguing. Are we now, simply, the children of Coca-Cola? This would certainly ring true for some cultural theorists such as David Harvey who fear that a "direct surrender to commodification, commercialization, and the market" permeates contemporary culture (1990: 59). This is tragic for some.

Many critical theorists turned to art as the last hope for instigating radical, or at least progressive, change. It seems imperative, then, to re-examine the cultural debate of the last fifty years.

In so doing, Frederic Jameson takes up where the critical theorists of the Frankfurt School left off and argues that "every position on postmodernism in culture — whether apologia or stigmatization — is also at one and the same time, and *necessarily*, an implicitly or explicitly political stance on the nature of multinational capitalism today" (1993: 64). The semiotic bombardment that characterizes postmodernity may seem to fit neatly into "free market" ideology, but, as Jim Collins points out in *Uncommon Cultures*, not only is this sadly reductive, but "it only brackets the central issue — what is the subject to do in such a context?" (1989: 146). This is an extremely troubling issue for it would seem that any attempt to look at user-practices would, for Jameson and others like him, simply be resorting to the bourgeois philosophy of instrumental rationality, and it is for this reason that Jameson is determined to authorize the mapping of the postmodern terrain himself. Yet this idea of "cognitive mapping," as Collins suggests, achieves little in its attempt to interpret postmodern space, given that this very space is "itself a proliferation of maps" and that these maps "don't coalesce into one big picture but rather a composite of overlapping views that visualize the terrain of contemporary life in reference to its specific uses" (1992: 340). Through the work of de Certeau, and perhaps with films like those of Itami, we can achieve a greater understanding of the postmodern social nexus upon which a logic of political change can be re-evaluated. One might well ask what use "tactical" operations might have, what *effect* such meager anarchy could have on actually instigating social change? If one is not openly oppositional, what political strategies does one employ most effectively?

What most postmodern critics agree upon is that *irony* is the most common, if not the most effective, political strategy. Given that the social nexus is comprised of disparate voices that have "already spoken," postmodern subjectivity seems to demand ironic distance. Indeed, it is as if one could not possibly *function* in society without a sense of irony. It keeps us from getting too caught up in the muddle and melee. But irony, as the work of many literary and cultural critics have shown, is always "double coded"; it both legitimates and subverts — in the way that bricolage both uses and abuses objects and institutions. Most critics who describe the functions of irony will be careful not to stray from this knowledge. Invariably, critics understand that irony's subversive potential is not only coupled by its conservative potential, it is perhaps even dampened by it. For instance, Linda Hutcheon reminds us that "while irony can be used to reinforce authority, it can also be used to oppositional and subversive ends — *and it can be suspect for that very reason* (italics mine; 1995: 29). Even if irony were to be understood as genuinely subversive, the question would remain: subversive for whom? Those who do experience irony are primarily cultural elites who are already "in-the-know." In this way, irony is a much more a form of symbolic exclusion than a subversive style or practice. Furthermore, irony can also be understood as far more private and exclusive than this if we acknowledge how the tradition of satire functions as refuge for individuals who altogether dissociate themselves from the social (and therefore the political).

This final, and perhaps most conservative, definition of irony is perhaps best deployed by Baudelaire in his treatise "The Essence of Laughter." For Baudelaire, laughter is a mistaken belief in the superiority over the world. We modernists know, however, that the world is no laughing matter. Even today, Baudelaire is thought to have given us the final word on the matter: "the wise man laughs only with fear and trembling" (1972a: 141). In other words, laughter is secondary to something far more important, far more serious than anything as trivial and temporary as laughter. Such a belief invades not just our sense of humor, but our sense of modernity. Here is Baudelaire on the modern man:

> And so, walking or quickening his pace, he goes his way, for ever in search. In search of what? We may rest assured that this man, such as I have described him, this solitary mortal endowed with an active imagination, always roaming the great desert of men, has a nobler aim than that of the pure idler, a more general aim, other than the fleeting pleasure of circumstance. He is looking for that indefinable something we may be allowed to call "modernity," for want of a better term to express the idea in question. The aim for him is to extract from fashion the poetry that resides in its historical envelope, to distill the eternal from the transitory (1972b: 402).

One can hardly see the characters of *Tampopo* entertaining such ideas. Still the question remains: what about these fleeting pleasures of circumstance? Well, de Certeau believes that tactics are effective precisely *because* they are fleeting, circumstantial, and enjoyable. We would never know this, however, since current theoretical writing is so resolutely committed to more "serious" concerns, so carefully structured according to strategies of power.

Perhaps it is more useful to think of Itami's work as far more comic than ironic. Comic narratives are narratives of escape, not of opposition.

The basic comic plot is one of movement, of getting out of tight situations, of freedom. Comedy understands that, in any situation and at any moment, the rules do not apply. Like the vagrants in *Tampopo* who move in and out of spaces secured by power, the comic knows he will not be caught because to him, the playing field simply looks *different*. His strength is his ability to live by circumstance, to seize fleeting opportunities, to mock "wisdom." The comic will say to the modern ironist: "if wisdom means fear and trembling, who the hell wants to be wise?" Comedy's politics are quite content with "trivial" matters. One must remember that it was the "trivial" comedy of his 1992 film *Minbo No Onma* that got Itami's face disfigured by the mob in 1992. Itami's comedy must be thought of as an indispensable element of anti-disciplinarian tactics, of "poetic ways of making do" in the postmodern terrain. Such practices are surely among Itami's deepest concerns.

REFERENCES

Altman, Rick. 1986. "A Semantic/Syntactic Approach to Film Genre." *Cinema Journal* 23, (Spring 1984): 6-18. Reprinted in *Film Genre Reader*, edited by Barry Keith Grant.Austin: University of Texas.

Barthes, Roland. 1972. *Empire of Signs*, translated by Richard Howard. New York: Hill and Wang.

———— 1972. *The Pleasure of the Text*, translated by Richard Miller. New York: Hill and Wang.

Baudelaire, Charles. 1972a. "The Essence of Laughter." *Selected Writings on Art and Literature*, translated by P. E. Chavret. New York: Penguin.

———— 1972b. "The Painter of Modern Life." *Selected Writings on Art and Literature*.

Buehrer, Beverly Bare. 1990. *Japanese Films: A Filmography and Commentary, 1921-1989*. Jefferson, NC: McFarland.

Clammer, John. 1992. "Aesthetics of the Self: Shopping and Social Being in Contemporary Japan." *Lifestyle Shopping*, edited by Rob Shields. New York: Routledge.

Collins, Jim. 1989. *Uncommon Cultures*. New York: Routledge.

———— 1992. "Postmodernism and Television." *Channels of Discourse, Reassembled*, edited by Robert C. Allen. Chapel Hill: University of North Carolina.

———— 1995. *Architectures of Excess*. New York: Routledge.

Cook, David. 1990. *A History of Narrative Film*, second edition. New York: W.W. Norton & Company.

de Certeau, Michel. 1984. *The Practice of Everyday Life*, translated by Steven Rendall. Berkeley: University of California Press.

Derrida, Jacques. 1988. "Structure, Sign and Play in the Discourse of the Human Sciences." *Writing and Difference*, translated by Alan Bass. Chicago: Univeristy of Illinois Press, 1978. Reprinted in *Modern Criticism and Theory: A Reader*, edited by David Lodge. New York: Longman.

Harvey, David. 1990. *The Condition of Postmodernity*. Cambridge: Blackwell.

Hutcheon, Linda. 1995. *Irony's Edge*. New York: Routledge.

Jameson, Frederic. 1993. "Postmodernism, or the Cultural Logic of Late-Capitalism." *Postmodernism, or the Cultural Logic of Late Capitalism*. London: Verso, 1991.Reprinted in Postmodernism: A Reader, edited by Thomas Docherty. New York: Columbia University Press.

Jencks, Charles. 1981. *The Language of Post-modern Architecture*, third edition. London: Academy Editions.

Lyotard, Jean-François. 1993. "Note on the Meaning of 'Post-'." *The Postmodern Explained: Correspondent 1982-1985*, translated by Julian Pefanis and Morgan Thomas. Minneapolis: University of Minnesota Press, 1992. Reprinted in *Postmodernism: A Reader*, edited by Thomas Docherty. New York: Columbia University Press.

Marcuse, Herbert. 1982. "Some Social Implications of Modern Technology." *Studies in Philosophy and Social Science* Vol. 9 (1941). Reprinted in *The Essential Frankfurt School Reader*, edited by Andrew Arato and Eike Gebhardt. New York: Continuum.

Oshima, Nagisa. 1992. *Cinema, Censorship, and the State*, edited by Annette Michelson, translated by Dawn Lawson. Cambridge: MIT Press.

Sterngold, James. 1992. "A Director Boasts of His Scars, and Says He Is Right about the Mob." *New York Times* 30 August, national. edition, section 4: 7.

Notes

1. Making approximations about when a tradition in film starts and another stops is always problematic, as there are always films that overlap. I am merely trying to situate *Tampopo* in the context of basic Japanese film history. The dates and film titles that loosely mark the Japanese New Wave are taken from Cook's *A History of Narrative Film* (1990: 801-806) and Buehrer (1990: 181-184 ; 206-209 ; 243-247).

2. Though ideology itself is a mediation, it masks itself with a pretense to the natural or the universal. I understand that *ideolect*, a term borrowed from Barthes suggests the language or tongue by which ideology expresses itself. For the Frankfurt School, mass culture is the hub of ideology, and therefore no commodity is without ideolect. Bricolage, however, suggests not an *ideal* subject (who is defined by Marcuse as "those who fare best by following...directions,") but a subject who is *heretical*.

CHAPTER 6

DE-AUTHORIZING THE *AUTEUR*

Postmodern Politics of Interpellation in Contemporary European Cinema

Rosanna Maule

Postmodernism is not something we can settle once and for all and then use with clear conscience. The concept, if there is one, has to come at the end, and not at the beginning of our discussions of it.

(Jameson, *Postmodernism*, xxii)

Established particularly during the postwar consolidation of European art film as a marketing strategy to counterpart Hollywood, authorship today invests those operations intertwining creative expression and commercial reception in the technically and stylistically heterogeneous context of the audiovisual. Current discussions in postmodern film theory are exploring its enduring appeal as an alternative form of cultural agency, located in shifting patterns of meaning formation (Corrigan 1991; Jameson 1992). As Timothy Corrigan argues, in its latest manifestation as a commercial strategy of enunciation authorship is undermining its aesthetic authority to the advantage of a more varied reception (1991: 136). In this framework, the practice involves tactics of enunciation and appropriation whose political effectiveness derives from a "constant double encoding-inscribing and subverting prevailing conventions" (Hutcheon 1989: 117).

The attention of postmodern criticism to issues of social agency leads to theoretical and methodological interrogations on how to place authorial interpellation in textual mechanisms of signification. I intend to explore some of these queries by analyzing instances of authorial inscription in *A nos amours* by Maurice Pialat (1983), *La messa è finita* by Nanni Moretti (1985), and *¿Que he hecho yo para merecer esto?* by Pedro Almodóvar (1984). The films were produced respectively in France, Italy, and Spain — countries where the film industry has, since the 1950s, been monitoring authorship as a marketing appeal, alternative to Hollywood both in national and international contexts. These films relate to a period when the diffusion of postmodernism in popular culture was orienting the commercial transition of authorship in the global film system. In this scenario, authorship also recovered some of its cultural prestige as a film mode, something it had lost following the crisis of cinema as a specific medium and form of expression. I mean to demonstrate how in these films some enunciative marks of authorial self-reference invalidate their interpellative authority, thus resisting being incorporated into institutionalized modes of postmodern perception.[1] The examples I individuate consist of a discursive displacement of authorship as source of expressive and narrative legitimation,[2] suggested through the physical "appearance" of the filmmakers as diegetic characters. While deflecting its traditional alignment with high art, political engagement, and national culture, this specific type of authorial performance disavows its certification also as an intentional mark of denaturalizing critique. This resistance illustrates Fredric Jameson's point (1992: 155) that the use of aesthetic concepts for periodizing should take into account the cultural estrangement that this operation involves:

> The cultural component...must be conceived as a "dominant" but not a "determinant"; it must be grasped, not as a set of stylistic features alone, but as a designation of culture, and its logic as a whole (including the proposition that culture itself and its sphere and social function undergo radical and dialectical modifications from one historical moment to another).

My general claim is that in postmodern culture film authorship indicates a type of filmmaking where agency is positioned *from within* the norms and styles of dominant and institutional cinema. This is especially true for Western Europe, where film authorship has traditionally claimed its expressive distinction from commercial production, although operating in the same predicament. The exploration of this institutional "in-betweenness" should begin with a radical reconceptualization of authorship into cultural practices aimed at dismantling its essentialist configuration in patterns of "high art" or expressive subjectivity. Nataša Ďurovičová has recently tackled this issue, questioning the validity of methods that include authorship in a "foreign-art-unpopular" cluster, as opposed to a "national-popular" cluster, while she asks for "a more conceptual definition of cinema in relation to the dynamics of a national culture as a whole" (1994: 4). As Michèle Lagny, Marie-Claire Ropars, and Pierre Sorlin stress, the arbitrariness implicit in assimilating authorship to subjective expression appears more distinctively in cinema because of the collective nature of this medium. Introducing a special issue of *Hors Cadre* on "l'état d'auteur" (1990: 6) in various art forms, they underline how cinema displays the coexistence of unitary and multiple determinants in the notion of authorship. While noting how film offers a "privileged terrain of observation" for scrutinizing the unresolved ambivalence of the author between creation and fruition, they illustrate its mediating position between unity and subjectivity, concluding that *"Dans ce dernier cas, l'état d'auteur est une composante d'un processus esthétique, dans le premier il en est une condition, porteuse de légitimité"* [In this latter case, the status of the author is a component of the aesthetic process, in the former case it is one of its conditions, conveyer of legitimacy].

In investigating the mechanisms through which postmodern authorship may claim interpellative effectiveness, I intend also to give a contribution to the theorization of its agency from non-oppositional perspectives. To this purpose, I will analyze some of its contemporary manifestations through the conceptual model of nomadism, a term that for Gilles Deleuze and Félix Guattari (1987: 360) connotes an alternative relation to a milieu, characterized by multiple, immediate, and vectorial tactics of orientation and appropriation, and engaged "in a perpetual field of interaction" with dominant apparatuses.

The Politics of Postmodernism in Film Studies

Death metaphors have dominated the European discourse on cinema for the past twenty years, depicting the crisis of the modernist medium par excellence, particularly its art form. This trope has revived old questions on the ontology of the film apparatus, in the effort less to reconstitute cinema as a defined object than to question its historical and aesthetic function, faced with the impending event of its extinction. Overdetermined by the collapse of Europe's cultural hegemony at the international level, this mournful attitude has envisaged in authorship both the phantom and the vestige of film forms that retain their aura in the postmodern homogenization of styles and contexts.

The death of cinema has also prompted a theoretical exploration at the fringes of authorial signification, examining the shifting structures that regulate its contemporary address to underline their readiness to multiple meaning formations. From this perspective, the emergence of postmodernism as a distinctive paradigm in 1980s and 1990s cinema inserts itself in poststructuralist and Marxist-derived investigations on power relations implicated in film practices. Insofar as it localizes the radical potentialities of authorship in this framework, this discourse touches upon the controversial debate about whether postmodernism can claim a political theory of its own. The 1990s' revisionism on authorship shares a preoccupation with analyzing power relations at the interface of structures of feeling and global commercial strategies. In this context of reception-based critiques, Corrigan claims that in their latest commercial version, auteurs "begin to communicate as simply figures within the commerce of [their] image," and viewers find new pleasure in "engaging and adopting one more text that surrounds a movie without the pretenses of its traditional authorities and mystifications" (1991: 136).

As Tom Conley (1990: 78) stresses, for contemporary criticism the postideological integration of authorship in institutional film practices constitutes a premise for activating tactics of cultural resistance, so:

> *De nos jours, l'auteur serait, à l'intérieur d'une industrie "stratégique", l'exemple d'une "tactique"….Le cinéaste-auteur serait pour ainsi dire un site problématique, composé de stratégies de massification et de tactiques, variables, menant à une prise de conscience des idéologies de masse.*

> [In our days, the author would be, inside a "strategic" industry, the example of a "tactic"….The filmmaker would be, so to speak, a problematic site, composed of strategies of massification and of variable tactics, leading to a conscious realization of mass ideologies].

Explicitly situating film authorship between modernist and postmodernist aesthetics, James Naremore locates its emergence in the conjunction of institutional and ideological determinants, including the decline of the studio-system and the diffusion of television and video images. According to Naremore, since 1950s' auteurism had cut across popular and elitist film traditions, its symptomatic persistence nowadays would reveal a political force in the film text that marks cultural production (1990: 22).

These approaches individuate modes of critical recognition that prevent authorship from being the mere reflection of subjective hermeneutics. On the other hand, though, they also reinstate its authoritative role as enunciative presence, interpellating an "expert" audience prefigured in multimedial and global reception practices. One way to prevent restoring authorship as an implicit component of postmodern aesthetic or economy is to evidence its complicity with and critique of the ideology that founds the notion of author in Western culture. The analysis of how this ambivalence interacts with the mechanisms of film enunciation lets us perceive new possibilities of authorial interpellation.

European Film Authorship as a Local Tactic of Enunciation

The potential of European film authorship to maintain its counter-hegemonic role within the progressive blurring of standards in postmodern aesthetics finds origin in its dialectic construction with dominant film structures. Highlighting this circumstance in the local/global configuration of contemporary cinema presupposes the foregrounding of the discursive boundaries and contradictions of European national identity, particularly in a period when political and ideological changes are radically undermining its foundation in the modern nation-state (Petrie: 1992). This undertaking is now at the center of film inquiries concerned with cultural specificity in national film systems. Stephen Crofts, for instance, inserts authorship among other postmodern strategies that define the "disaggregated" status of national cinemas today, together with national labels and "censorial liberties" (1993: 50-2). Recent overviews of the national cinemas I have taken into consideration also contextualize authorship in this direction, analyzing its role in the articulation of ideology and consensus which inform cultural identity through their appeal to national master narratives. Susan Hayward's survey of French cinema moves away from the traditional

117

focus of film historiography, adopting a methodological approach that she defines as "a synchronic and diachronic filling of the gaps between the auteurs and movements" (1993a: xi). Angela Dalle Vacche's reading of Italian postwar cinema concentrates on national representation as a reflection of an intellectual obssession with dialectical historicism, thus linking Italian film authorship's penchant for this discursive formation to the patriarchal structure of the nation's political unconscious. Marsha Kinder's analysis of modern Spanish cinema interprets its authorial expression as the idiosyncratic development of cultural motifs that metaphorize the traumatic heritage of the nation's modern history (1993).

As these studies remind us, in the international film market European authorship counts in measure of its capability to make aesthetic distinctiveness viable and to uphold cultural and industrial strategies in a dialectic relation to each other. As Kinder comments apropos, while the North American and Japanese film styles tend to eradicate difference to suit international audiences, "the European Community is developing a strategy that retains and highlights cultural diversity" (1993: 400).

The variety of configurations representing European national cinemas in the present cultural and political scenario finds echo in the heterogeneity of practices characterizing contemporary audiovisuals and complicates the analysis of their interrelations in the global economic system. Marcia Butzel and Ana López (1993) stress this point with reference to the intrinsically ambivalent notion of the nation:

> The exploration of the interrelationship between nationalism, internationalism, and audio-visual production is, then, like nationalism itself, "Janus-faced,"... addressing both the impossibility of the national as a space for unitary transcendent representation/identity and its persistent presence/political necessity (3).

In *What Is an Author?* Michel Foucault defines authorship as an "ideological figure" that regulates discourse according to the exigencies of a given context, by marking "the manner in which we fear proliferation of meaning" (Rabinow 1984: 119). In the cultural history of modern Europe, the notion of authorship pertains to a bourgeois-nationalist attempt to sanction the social function of creation with subjective categories of hierarchization. The *politique des auteurs* betrayed this intention by infusing criteria of judgment generally reserved to high art into a popular means of entertainment. From a commercial viewpoint, French auteurism promoted a marketing rationale that in the 1960s and 1970s consolidated the export of art film and led European national cinemas in their efforts to break into the international film market.[3] As Crofts (1993) reminds us, the purpose of European cinema in that period was:

> To differentiate itself textually from Hollywood, to assert explicitly or implicitly an indigenous product, and to reach domestic and export markets through those specialist distribution channels and exhibition venues usually called "arthouse" (50).

The dialectic relation that this European mode of production entertains with dominant film structures retains cultural specificity in measure of its capability to activate its national heritage. Introducing the *Autorenfilm* in New German cinema in the context of European art film, Thomas Elsaesser (1989: 40) argues that in France and Italy, for instance, art cinema

> ... often succeeded in being nationally specific by capitalizing on intellectual or literary traditions. It gained international recognition and hard currency where the films addressed themselves to an audience which most probably regarded cinema as a "vulgar" form of mass entertainment, yet looked to film for a representation of modernist cultural themes.

The same conviction informs Kinder's interpretation of the 1950s' Spanish film renaissance as a critically aware combination of neorealist and Hollywood conventions, by filmmakers who used dialectically opposed languages to destabilize the mythological construction of Spanish unity imposed by the Franco regime (1993: 38).

The dialectic constitution of Western European film authorship with dominant film forms and institutions is particularly evident because of its financial dependence on government and state or national television subsidies and its progressive involvement in large production networks. Public financing and audiovisual monopolies are modifying the modes of circulation of film authorship by means of appealing to a vaster audience, with the intent to counteract the parallel effort of Hollywood to diversify its production style for a more select typology of spectatorship. However, because of the hierarchical structure of the film market, the commercial enhancement of authorship has also created the counter-effect of limiting the expansion of independent projects, both in commercial channels of distribution and exhibition and in specialized circuits such as arthouse theaters, film festivals, and cineclubs.

French cinema holds the lead in this regard, especially since the early 1980s' mandate of the minister of culture Jack Lang. Lang's policies to introduce protectionist laws on domestic film production, distribution, and exhibition only partially reached their goals to keep pace with the shifting international market and to promote domestic production (Hayward 1993b: 388-89). Yet, they have effectively inserted a new generation of commercial auteurs in the international circuit, whose combination of technical sophistication with high production value has often raised questions about its actual distinction from commercial cinema. In Italy the limited, albeit consistent, contribution of government and state television funding for small and medium film projects encourages many authorial debuts, which however lack adequate subsidy and distribution and rarely result in further achievements. Since the mid-1970s, the crisis of the domestic film industry and especially the drastic reduction of theater attendance has aggravated this situation, relegating authorial projects into independent and often marginal areas of production and circulation. As Piero Spila argues, *"il problema del giovane cinema italiano non sta quindi nel poter esordire, ma nel poter continuare; non sta tanto nella difficoltà di proporsi, ma nell'impossibilità oggettiva di esprimersi al meglio"* [the problem of young Italian cinema is therefore located less in the possibility of starting out than of continuing; less in the possibility of proposing itself, than in the objective impossibility of expressing itself at its best] (Montini 1988: 31). In this context, independent film authorship represents an exception and marks fortuitous trajectories of enterpreneurish initiative, symptomatic of the fragmentary condition characterizing the Italian film industry. Only a few filmmakers (including Nanni Moretti and Pupi Avati) have successfully adopted alternative strategies of production and distribution. Even the appreciation that Italian film authorship has recently had in international film festivals and awards has not concretely reinstated its commercial prestige in the film market.

Spanish contemporary authorship has been dominated by the phenomenon of decentralization, paradigmed by the juxtaposition between Madrid and Barcelona as competitive centers of cultural reference, both participating in the growth of "macro-regional" film coproductions. This local/global dialectic, complicated by a parallel evolution in television broadcasting, has encouraged what Kinder calls "the reinscription of the marginal as the center," that is, the reappropriation of dominant circuits on the part of filmmakers, film styles, and areas of film production that had been restrained during the Franco regime. This movement has also proved successful in appealing to the international market, especially through those films Crofts links to the promotion of "censorial liberties," while the government's several attempts to protect and promote Spanish domestic production with subsidies and laws establishing screening quotas on foreign films have proved rather ineffective in contrasting the monopoly of Hollywood in the domestic market and reviving the international prestige of Spanish New Cinema.

The various outcomes in which result the dialectic implication of authorship in the global film system call for approaches to avoiding its essentialist assumption as a cultural practice. The concept of nomadism as a radically resistant model of social organization, yet constructed within state apparatuses seems suitable for this type of analysis. Nomadism may account for authorship in contemporary cinema in two respects: by undermining its conceptualization as a structuring principle and by helping conceive the discontinuity of its manifestations in the film market as a potential displacement of dominant circuits. Positing authorship as a nomadic tactic of enunciation in *A nos amours, La messa è finita,* and *¿Que he hecho yo para merecer esto?* transforms the appearance of the filmmaker-author into a shifting vector of meaning that relieves the spectator from perceiving it as an authoritative mark of enunciation.

Nomadism also conceptualizes the relations established between authorial, national, and global film practices as instances of institutional deterritorialization. Deleuze and Guattari describe this kind of spatial perception in terms of "local absolute," that is, "an absolute that is manifested locally, and engendered in a series of local operations of varying orientations" (1987: 382). They claim that this type of locality always remains external to the "relative-global" space of the state, which is limited, oriented in its directions, and divisible by boundaries. This geo-political antinomy applies to the de-authorizing idea of authorship as an intersubjective monitoring of cultural identity in institutional film practices. The local absolute describes the situation of commercial auteurism that Corrigan contextualizes in a "cinema without walls," an imaginary open-museum, where series of aesthetic instances are appropriated by boundless social formations. According to Corrigan, in the international landscape of cinema, multiplied by reproductive technology and democratized by commercial marketing, the role of national cinema is that of complicating the process of deinstitutionalization of borderlines and distinctions. I would add that in the global film market, national cinemas demarcate meaning formations also insofar as they provide the cultural and material conditions for authorship to survive as a local practice and circulate as an absolute cultural currency.

Authorial Performance and Enunciative Displacement

Enunciation connotes a series of linguistic operations that manifest a film text as such, bringing to the foreground its instances of constitution, contextualization, and self-reference (Casetti 1993: 263). Its normative role of prefiguring and justifying film as a coherent form of communication finds articulation in a complex structure of traces, more or less made explicit in the text. When foregrounded with marks of interpellation, enunciation installs a particular mode of narrative and discursive address, whose modality and degree of perception vary according to subjective and contextual conditions of reception. These types of *"énonciation énoncée"* [enunciated enunciation] (Casetti 1983: 84) unveil the mechanisms of narrative and representational mimesis,[4] violating the rule of cinematic address and transparency. As François Jost remarks, they install the spectator in a circuit of communication and make the spectator aware of being addressed (1983: 200).

The enunciative marks of authorial appeal in *A nos amours, La messa è finita,* and *¿Que he hecho yo para merecer esto?* relate to extratextual references belonging to the author's body of work as well as to a domestic tradition of film representation and criticism. In the case of Pialat's film, this framework concerns the pursuit of a film style that escapes any critical categorization and sets the ontologic nature of filmmaking as its own limit. Playing the "problematic" father in *A nos amours,* Pialat engenders a narrative and a mise-en-scène that metaphorize the troubled search for the perfect correlation between formal and immediate expression typical of his style and his central issue with the "fathers" of the *nouvelle vague*. Moretti's film refers to a body of work illustrating a radically "autarchic"[5] conception of filmmaking — coherently sustained even after achieving international recognition — and representing a commercial and stylistic exception in a panorama of inconsistent and insignificant debuts. In *La messa è finita* the "autarchic" Moretti assumes the role of a priest, who fails his mission once confronted with his social milieu. The priest's self-referential quest metaphorizes the author's trajectory throughout the topoi of his previous films and screen characters, reinstating also Moretti's critical view of Italian society. Almodóvar's cameo appearance in *¿Que he hecho yo para merecer esto?* asserts authorial identity as a self-conscious display of postmodern strategies of representation. The film constructs an inextricable *mise-en-abyme* of transgressive appropriations of Spanish modern cinema, including the spatial and figurative representation of the opposition between city and country (D'Lugo: 1991), the stylistic clash of inferences from Hollywood melodrama and neorealist drama (Kinder: 1993), and the use of narrative and mise-en-scène to metaphorize national history and tradition (Kóvacs: 1991). The parodic function of this reinscription is made explicit by the overtly camp performance provided by Almodóvar, singing an old Spanish love song with a transvestite as his romantic partner.

As a structuring principle of enunciation, authorship has informed various strategies of film marketing, linked to the historical and cultural requirements of specific film systems and discourses. Denoting the attempt of the film industry to create cultural demand by means of promoting the stylistic and aesthetic distinctiveness of the medium, this form of enunciation derives its ideological premises from artistic and particularly literary conventions of representation. Jean-Paul Simon has underlined how authorship serves as an ultimate strategy of mimetic reinforcement, representing an authoritative source of legitimation in the moment when the self-reflexive presence of enunciative marks seems to undermine narrative credibility (1983: 184-85).

The examples of authorial interpellation present in *A nos amours, La messa è finita,* and *¿Que he hecho yo para merecer esto?* concern a peculiar mode of narrative reinforcement, interpellating the spectator as a vicarious narrator, substituting the "absent narrator." Simon describes this authorial strategy as a move that may block the spectator in an "impossible position" between enunciation and narration (1983: 185). I suggest that it may also provide an "opening" to those appropriative strategies that constitute the basis of postmodern film reception. According to François Jost (1983: 200) the anchorage of the film text to enunciative marks produces a sudden perception of the narrative act, detached from mimetic illusion and analogous to a "visually subjective narration." Together with Jost, Christian Metz (1991) stresses the impersonality of this narration, arguing that enunciation is a textual construction that excludes any anthropomorphism and manifests less a subjective address than a self-reflexive contextualization. In these three films, however, authorial interpellation calls also for an anthropomorphic recognition, depending on the spectator's awareness of the physical presence of the "real" author in the film's diegesis. This type of interpellation establishes authorial agency at the threshold of the formal organization and commercial promotion that characterizes postmodern auteurism. From this perspective, the presence of the filmmaker as a character reinforces the structuring function of authorship as "an active and monitored engagement with its own conditions as the subjective expresses itself through the socially symbolic," to use Corrigan's words (1991: 104-5). This mode of interpellation is both overdetermined and neutralized by postmodern conditions of reception and determined by the spectator's approach to authorial discourse and its engagement with the author's narrative performance.

The father embodied by Pialat in *A nos amours* narratively metaphorizes an authoritative model of authorship, based on a hierarchical concept of textual organization and creative expression. As a fictional character, the "authoritative father" rules the family *tout court*, including its business, schedule, and living style. His strongest ascendancy in this sense is exercised on his daughter Suzanne, the protagonist of the film, whose Electra complex also frames the structure of the narrative. The film narrative in fact outlines Suzanne's sentimental search for a father figure, in an endless carousel of sexual experiences that are also explicitly linked to psychological mechanisms of identity processes in some instances of the dialogue. From this perspective, the father-daughter relationship regulates the balance of all the other family members, inspiring the mother's hysterical and the brother's incestuous reactions to Suzanne's sexual exuberance. The effort to substitute for the missing father becomes an even more explicit element of psychological motivation when the father actually abandons the family, reappearing only at the end of the film. In his new function of structuring absence, the father provides the family story with the extreme tones of ancient tragedy. Similarly, his return transforms the narrative resolution into a moment of recognition that reveals the precariousness of the situation established among the members of the seemingly recomposed family. Instead of resolving the existing conflicts, his breaking of the narrative *qua Deus-ex-machina* brings the characters' structure back to the original unbalance, thus reinstating the privileged relationship between father and daughter and indirectly making the daughter start her sexual wandering all over again, after her brief matrimonial parenthesis.

Pialat's diegetic character represents the postmodern deflection of the author's structuring role defined by David Bordwell as "the real-world parallel to the narrational presence" (1985: 211). In this respect, he figuratively and discursively denaturalizes the enunciative context and narrative outline of the film. This displacement of diegetic and discursive authority through the filmmaker's screen persona does not actually correspond to the author's enunciative position, which is instead conveyed in the diegesis through the nomadic figure of the daughter, symbolizing authorial creation dispossessed of a father, or endlessly looking for one. Hence the actual force of Pialat's authorial self-inscription in the film concerns the unresolved dialectic between author and work, and follows the rhizomatic rules of heterogeneity and discontinuity. This relation results in an ultimate means of disruption of narrative continuity and psychological justification. The spectator is constantly confronted with the detours of Suzanne's erratic conduct, the family's bursts of violence, and the temporal ellipses of the narration. At the end of the film, the bus taking the father back from the airport where he has accompanied his daughter leaving for San Diego with her latest lover enters a tunnel. The fade-to-black of the final shot obscures him, relieving also the author from the control and the responsibility of the narrative.

In *La messa è finita* the character embodied by Moretti is overdetermined by the filmmaker's appearance as the protagonist of all his films, mostly in the role of a screen alter-ego named Michele. The psychological traits of this recurrent character include an inquisitory attitude toward the surrounding environment, a maniacal obsession with some objects and words (an instance being the *Sacher torte*, also the name of Moretti's own production company established in 1987), and an idiosynchratic contempt toward other characters' behaviors and beliefs. Because of its repetitive and individual connotations, Moretti's self-inscription in his films seems to suggest an authorial intent to interfere with the diegesis. A film critic has compared this intention to the compulsory reenactment of the *fort/da* experience — the translation of the vocal emission accompanying a child's experience of distance and closeness from an object that Sigmund Freud interprets as a strategy to cope with the trauma of separation from the mother — linked to the necessity to simulate a discomforting experience of relationship (de Bernardinis 1991: 11-12). Another critic interprets it as a narcissistic-masochist symptomatology (Tesson 1987: 6). As a character, Moretti betrays the effort to reconnect his environment to a unitary worldview, unfailingly reinstating his ultimate alienation from it. Ultimately, Michele's narrative experiences represent attempts at human interaction within self-enclosed social milieus that reflect Moretti's eccentric position in the Italian film industry.

In this film, however, the character played by Moretti, the priest Don Giulio, takes the autarchic premises of this authorial inscription to their extreme consequences, provoking an implosive reaction that brings them to new patterns of nomadic (dis)order. The character's local range of action and personal aim as a priest grow to reach "Society" and "Good" as absolute terms of confrontation and lead to a defeat on all fronts that opens uniquely to his absolute isolation. Don Giulio ends his last mass in fact by announcing his departure for a place close to the polar circle. This radicalization of intent and failure marks a shift in attitude implied in the vocation of priesthood, that also introduces a filter between the author and Moretti's screen character. In entrusting the performance of authorship in the metaphorical figure of a priest, the film both multiplies and circumscribes the possibilities of its intervention. Don Giulio's quest thus epitomizes the nomadic challenge implicit in any (autarchic) authorial practice: embracing a potentially infinite space of action, although possessing actually limited resources. In the church, immediately following his good-bye speech, Don Giulio announces that *"la messa è finita"* [the mass is over] and turns his back to his diegetic and extradiegetic audiences, the notes of a popular song he had previously danced to at his home making him turn and smile, as he looks at the dancing spouses and wedding guests. The character Moretti's smile in the camera reconciles the author less with his self-reflexive obsessions than with his social mission. In the moment when the author looks benevolently at the same diegetic scene that the extra-diegetic audience sees in the theater (or at home), he places his authority and agency within spectatorial authority and agency, ideally opening the self-enclosed milieu of film representation to the indefinite scope of its reception.

Finally, in *¿Que he hecho yo para merecer esto?* the physical presence of the author-filmmaker is limited to a short appearance, almost indirectly inserted in the diegesis, intruding on the characters at home and on the film's sequence by breaking both narrative and editing continuity with a 180-degree turn into the "transgressive" perspective of the frontal off-screen space. Suddenly cutting through an ordinary scene of a working-class Spanish family watching television while having supper, Almódovar's intrusion comes from a program that the film audience has just before been listening to from a television set ideally positioned in the place of the camera and, by extension, other viewing spaces (the movie theater, other homes). The uncanny effect of these insertions is enhanced by the unrelatedness of the family's commentary on the song and the way the song is actually performed. The spectatorial expectations coming from listening to the song and witnessing to the nostalgic appreciation and evocative lip-synching of the old grandmother, are immediately overthrown by the images of the program. The performance takes place on a gaudy studio stage, whose camp mise-en-scène includes vivid operetta costumes, excessive make-up, and stylized overacting, and contributes, together with the presence of a transvestite actor in the role of the singer's counterpart, to the creation of a slippage not only between sound and image, but also between the narrative and the performative levels of representation. This gap also continues in the editing structure of the sequence establishing another perverse relationship between viewing and performing circumstances. The song lyrics, stating the lover's loss of affection for a woman, address a grandmother trapped in her son's city apartment longing for her native country-town, her stoned teenager grandson just back from his drug-dealing job which enables him to eventually raise the money to take her back to the barrio, and the constantly quarrelling parents, dispassionately making love in the next-door bedroom. This scene concentrates the typical motifs of Almodóvar's parodic subversion of Spanish cultural traditions, family values, and aesthetic hierarchies that constitute the authorial marks through which the filmmaker has become the "commercial auteur" par excellence of post-Franco Spanish cinema during the 1980s. In one of his rare appearances on screen, Almodóvar thus places his authorial agency in the regulation of a mise-en-scène that shifts spectatorial expectations and pleasures in a series of eccentric positions with respect to traditional patterns and rules of film representation and reception. From this perspective, his authorial authority is here reinforced in virtue of its postmodern function of subverting the established order, placing agency at the antipodes of any structuring principle of meaning.

Another aspect of this authorial self-inscription eludes its identification as a mechanism of the characteristics celebrated in Almodóvar's acclamation as postmodern auteur: the *mise-en-abyme* of enunciative posts activated by his diegetic appearance, through various sources and modes of cinematic interpellation. In placing his parody of Spanish popular culture and reception from within a popular medium (television) and in popular reinterpretations of popular genres (the cabaret parody of a love song), Almodóvar demystifies not only the identification of authorship with high culture and tradition, but also its postmodern appropriation as an item of commercial consumption. In this sequence, the "nomadic spectacle" of Almodóvar's sketch displaces the author's physical and enunciative authority from inside the very apparatuses of its commercial monitoring.

Conclusions

The recent return to authorial concerns in film theory and criticism expressed also in literary theory after a long period of critical boycott brings some issues relative to the meaning and purpose of anti-authorialism to the foreground. In both fields, the resistance to authorship coincides with a self-reflexive questioning about the role of criticism in this respect. Seán Burke has argued that the poststructuralist and deconstructivist anti-authorial movement betrays "defensive strategies against the essentially overdetermined nature of the text" (1992: 173). Despite its reductive inference that anti-authorialism would be a reaction to the theoretical failure of accounting for authorial subjectivity, Burke's reading focuses on how any debate on authorship ultimately addresses a methodological and epistemological inquiry into the standing of theory *per se* and into the standing of subject-centered approaches in particular.

The role of authorship in European cinema is inextricably linked to that of a film discourse that has made of subjective film categories internalized objects of mourning in light of the death of cinema. In claiming a presence of its own, film authorship is now exploring strategies of self-reflexive address that call for transparency in representation insofar as they are constantly displacing their modalities of critical contextualization and reception. As I have illustrated in my analyses, in the context of postmodern address, authorship may disengage the interplay between narrative instances, implicit author, and real author that has traditionally founded its authoritative address in the film text.

REFERENCES

Bordwell, David. 1985. *Narration in the Fiction Film*. Madison: University of Wisconsin Press.

Burke, Seán. 1992. *The Death and the Return of the Author: Criticism and Subjectivity in Barthes, Foucault, and Derrida*. Edinburgh: Edinburgh University Press.

Butzel, Marcia and Ana López. 1993. "Mediating the National." *Quarterly Review of Film and Video* 14, no. 3: 1-8.

Casetti, Francesco. 1983. *"Les yeux dans les yeux." Communications* 38: 78-97.

———— 1993. *Teorie del cinema: 1945-1990*. Milano: Bompiani.

Conley, Tom. 1990. *"L'auteur énucléé." Hors Cadre* 8 (Spring): 77-95.

Corrigan, Timothy. 1991. *A Cinema without Walls: Movies and Culture after Vietnam*. New Brunswick, New Jersey: Rutgers University Press.

Crofts, Stephen. 1993. "Reconceptualizing National Cinemas." *Quarterly Review of Film and Video* 14, no. 3: 49-68.

Dalle Vacche, Angela. 1992. *The Body in the Mirror: Shapes of History in Italian Cinema*. Princeton: Princeton University Press.

de Bernardinis, Flavio. 1991. *Nanni Moretti.* Milano: Il Castoro.

Deleuze, Gilles and Félix Guattari. 1987. Trans. Brian Massumi. *A Thousand Plateaus: Capitalism and Schizophrenia.* Minneapolis and London: University of Minnesota Press.

D'Lugo, Marvin. 1991. "Almodóvar's City of Desire." *Quarterly Review of Film and Video* 14, no. 3: 47-65.

Ďurovičová, Nataša. 1994. "Some Thoughts at an Intersection." *Velvet Light Trap* 34: 3-9.

Elsaesser, Thomas. 1989. *New German Cinema: A History.* New Brunswick, New Jersey: Rutgers University Press.

Hayward, Susan. 1993a. *French National Cinema.* London and New York: Routledge.

——— 1993b. "State, Culture, and the Cinema: Jack Lang's Strategies for the French Film Industry." *Screen* 34, no. 4: 380-91.

Hutcheon, Linda. 1989. *The Politics of Postmodernism.* London and New York: Routledge.

Jameson, Fredric. 1991. *Postmodernism, or the Cultural Logic of Late Capitalism.* Durham: Duke University Press.

——— 1992. *Signatures of the Visible.* New York and London: Routledge.

Jost, François. 1983. "Narration(s): en deçà et au-delà." *Communications* 38: 192-212.

Kinder, Marsha. 1993. *Blood Cinema: The Reconstruction of National Identity in Spain.* Berkeley, Los Angeles, London: The University of California Press.

Kovács, Katherine. 1991. "The Plain in Spain." *Quarterly Review of Film and Video* 14, no. 3: 17-46.

Lagny, Michèle, Marie-Claire Ropars, and Pierre Sorlin, eds. 1990. "L'état d'auteur." *Hors Cadre* 8 (Spring): 5-7.

Metz, Christian. 1991. *L'énonciation impersonnelle ou le site du film.* Paris: Klincksieck.

Montini, Franco, ed. 1988. *Una generazione in cinema. Esordi ed esordienti italiani: 1975-1988.* Venezia: Marsilio Editori.

Naremore, James. 1990. "Authorship and the Cultural Politics of Film Criticism." *Film Quarterly* 44, no. 1: 14-22.

Petrie, Duncan, ed. 1992. *Screening Europe: Image and Identity in Contemporary European Cinema.* London: BFI.

Rabinow, Paul, ed. 1984. *The Foucault Reader.* New York: Pantheon Books.

Ross, Andrew, ed. 1988. *Universal Abandon?: The Politics of Postmodernism.* Minneapolis: University of Minnesota Press.

Simon, Jean-Paul. 1983. "Enonciation et narration: Gnarus, auctor et Protée." *Communications* 38: 155-191.

Tesson, Charles. 1987. "Mission impossible." *Cahiers du cinéma* 391 (January): 4-7.

All translations are those of the author.

NOTES

1. Lawrence Grossberg argues that in postmodern culture " ... we appropriate events and practices....using them not as representations or interpretations but simply as empowering signposts — billboards — that mark, perhaps even celebrate, the gap itself" (Ross 1988: 187).

2. David Bordwell notes how in auteurism this type of certification establishes a parallelism between the foregrounding of narrative self-consciousness and the "extratextual emphasis on the filmmaker as source" (1985: 211). Jean-Paul Simon traces the authoritative role of authorship back to its etymologic meaning of promoter (1983: 184-85).

3. Jameson (1992: 200) makes an insightful distinction between the concept and the practice of auteurism. According to him the concept describes " ... a method whereby the former genre films are now rewritten in terms of the new reorganization of the category of the auteur," the practice of a "... new specifically auteur type of production," responding to criteria of aesthetic autonomy typical of high modernism and traditionally identified with the 1950s and 1960s art cinema.

4. François Jost (1983: 200) remarks that *"... l'acte narratif n'est réellement sensible qu'au moment où l'image se détache de l'illusion mimétique ... c'est à dire lorsque, à travers les énoncés visuels, sont perçues des marques d'énonciation."*

   [... the narrative act is not actually perceptible until the moment when the image moves away from mimetic illusion ... that is to say, as soon as the marks of enunciation are perceived through visual enunciations].

5. *Io sono un autarchico* [I am an Autarchic], 1976, is the title of Moretti's first feature film. Shot in Super 8mm on an extremely low budget, the film was initially shown in a Roman cineclub, got good reviews, and unexpectedly became a local success. Blown into 16mm and distributed by the communist cultural association *ARCI* in the cineclubs and art theaters of the main Italian cities, *Io sono un autarchico* was eventually programmed by Italian state television and sanctioned Moretti's investiture as the best auteur of his generation, as well as his lasting reputation as an irredeemably independent filmmaker.

CHAPTER 7

THE POSTMODERNIST CONDITION IN POST-SOCIALIST EASTERN EUROPEAN FILMS

The Case of a Political Pastiche and the Socialist-Hollywood Thriller in Recent Films of Polish Filmmakers

Janina Falkowska

A t a recent conference of The International Society for the Study of European Ideas (ISSEI), "The European Legacy: Toward New Paradigms" in Graz, Austria,[1] the political and cultural theoreticians pondered the question of the European character in the context of European unity and the collapse of Socialism in the countries of Eastern Europe. Two full sessions were devoted to a postmodernist turn in the study of European unity. Barrie Axford of Oxford Brookes University, for instance, in his paper entitled "Multiple Truths and Postmodern Imaginings: New Ways of Reading European Unity," (1994) suggested that Europe is now in the midst of a period of epistemic transition, in which its making, both political and cultural, is seen as an active and contingent process. Axford proposed that recent events in the European arena indicate "a burgeoning disorder, most notably the

The Pigs (Zespol "zebra", *IFDF Helios, Film Polski, IMP, 1993*)
Wladyslaw Pasikowski

process of systemic transformation set in train by the collapse of the
Soviet Union and the states of actually existing Socialism along with the
local impact of the disappearance of bipolarity as a global institution"
(Axford 1994: 2) This burgeoning disorder reveals multiple continuums,
influences, or traits, which together form what Frederic Jameson
(1984: 83) called a "postmodern hyperspace." Hyperspace, which can be
physical, discursive, or epistemological, is a realm of transformative
potential in which concepts like "local" and "global" have little meaning
because the truth of experience no longer coincides with the place
in which it takes place (Jameson 1984:89-92). Instead, there are
economic and cultural flows and communication networks in which
agents are involved, and in which, through processes of invention
and reinvention (both cognitively and aesthetically), they can establish
new identities.

This postmodernist scenario implies that the process of creation of a
new Europe is perceived as the fluctuation of an amalgam of diverse
traits — an attitude that accurately reflects the cultural situation of
contemporary Eastern European film in which Western and Eastern
influences, Slavic and Germanic idiosyncrasies, European and American
voices, along with other semantic elements form an intricate mélange.

There are no longer texts defined by a particular cultural and political orientation, but texts in which a variety of influences appear on the textual stage as if they were actors who, through processes of invention and reinvention, establish new identities. So, as Norman Denzin argues, the postmodern is interpreted as "the force field in which very different kinds of cultural impulses — what Raymond Williams has usefully termed 'residual' and 'emergent' forms of cultural production — must make their way" (1991: 43). In this sense, culture emerges as a fluctuating space of flows and meanings as opposed to a fixed territory to be governed. In Poland, for example, the cinema no longer is a domain dictatorially regulated by the principles of Socialist Realism of the Stalinist period, or by the Socialist trends apparent in the cinema of the 1970s, but becomes a realm encompassing a free flow of ideologies, cultural influences, and attitudes. Whether this political and cultural freedom will produce artistic masterpieces is difficult to judge at present. Most certainly, the new European (un)reality creates original aesthetic values in contemporary Polish film.

Two kinds of combinations of voices characteristic of this new postmodern (un)reality in Poland will be presented in this paper. The first interfusion of voices constitutes a mingling of the Western and the Eastern, the commercial and the idealistic; the second is a pastiche of political voices both from the past and the present. Illustrating the first trend in Polish cinema, *The Pigs* (1993) by Wladyslaw Pasikowski represents a new action-packed cinema where Hollywood influences and Polish idiosyncrasies combine to produce an intricate blend of voices. *The Man From* (1992) by Konrad Szolajski, a film representative of the second trend, is a political pastiche which alludes to the most important political film of Andrzej Wajda, *Man of Marble* (1977). In *The Man From* the political struggle of the Solidarity Movement is questioned and ridiculed. The film plays with the political icons of Wajda's film, finally making irrelevant any meaning they might once have possessed.

This paper will analyze these two films as examples of a postmodern scenario in Eastern European film. In recent Polish cinema this combination of voices became especially striking when Poland changed its political orientation and mode of film production after 1989. Until then Polish film production was heavily subsidized by the state. The Film Committee at the Ministry of Culture dictated every facet of a film's content and form. After the official abolition of the Socialist system in 1989, Polish cinema went through a period of radical change. As Maria

Kornatowska explains in her article "Polish Cinema" (1993: 47), what was once a director-oriented cinema has turned into a producer-oriented cinema. Profit and commercial success have become the most important considerations in the decision-making process as far as the production of films is concerned.

The Pigs

Wladyslaw Pasikowski, a film director of the younger generation, easily embraced the new capitalist process and started directing films that satisfied the requirements of the new producers in post-Socialist Poland. His film *The Pigs*, considered the best Polish film of 1993, broke all box-office records in Poland. The film tells a story of former secret police agents, Frantz and Olo, who, following the abolition of the Socialist system in Poland, have to find their place in the new system. Frantz, who works for the new government, is delegated to solve an especially nasty murder which, the police suppose, has been committed by the mafia whose criminal activities include the smuggling of amphetamines from Poland to Germany. In an attempt to solve this case, Frantz asks his friend Olo to help him in the investigation. He soon realizes, however, that Olo is a member of the mafia and has to be arrested. The two friends meet in an abandoned warehouse where they engage in a chase sequence typical of American thrillers. Finally Frantz confronts Olo and when he sees that his former colleague is armed and dangerous decides to kill him. The presentation of this act is wonderfully paced, as the director slows the movement of the sequence as though revelling in the aesthetic effect of splattering body parts, streams of blood, and the overall carnage.

The Polish audience, especially the younger contingent, was fascinated by the violence and brutality presented in this and other scenes of the film. Usually violence in Eastern European film is shown only when it is fully justified in the story. Either historical events cause its outbreak — whether the incident be an insurrection, a war, or another noble cause — or it is perpetrated by a sick criminal who acts irrationally. Never before has violence been presented on the Polish screen in this highly artistic fashion: glamorized and beautified. The fascinated spectators watch the whole grisly spectacle in a postmodern manner, desiring "to see evil while being repulsed by it" (Denzin 1991: 74). Beyond the message of death with all its moral and cultural meanings, there is in this scene another force at work, not really reducible to a message, not completely codified as a signified, a force that exceeds the denotative significations of the scene. This force is the sheer energy of the act of killing seen as spectacle. Change, movement, and energy characteristic of spectacle here take the form of a repulsive act in which the shots present the unrepresentable in the ensuing stages of carnage. As in Hieronymus Bosch's *The Last Judgement* (1505), Wladyslaw Pasikowski's film realistically portrays the unrepresentable. Horrific representations of tortured and decaying corpses exhibit the loathsome in an aesthetically fascinating way. The splattered body parts are displayed in a playfully ludic manner, ironically parodying the carnage usually taking place in American gangster films (Hutcheon 1989: 93-101). In this, the film replicates the carnivalesque dismemberment of the protagonists of the comic plays, amusingly analyzed by Bakhtin in *Rabelais and His World* (1984: 200-220). The grotesque mingles with the horrific in a postmodern bloodshed.

Violent acts are scattered throughout the film culminating in the final act of killing. However, the justification of the final scene is unsatisfactory. The grotesque final scene is perceived as problematic when Frantz explains to the stunned Olo that the primary reason he is going to kill him is the fact that he has betrayed him on a personal level. Frantz blames Olo for the loss of his girlfriend, Angela. Thus, Frantz is not presented as a criminal but as a person fully justified in murdering a close friend according to the code of honor which Olo has broken. Betrayal on both the personal and the professional levels justifies the gore and violence presented on the screen. This peculiar justification somehow does not work in view of the misogynist presentation of Angela earlier in the film, portrayed as "a cheap little tart," as one of the characters in the film calls her, not worthy of any respect. She hops from one bed to another in hope of a better life; for Angela a change of partners is another step on the social ladder. To kill out of love falls within a Slavic Romanticism with its ideas of honor and reverence for women, but this romantic code clashes with her negative presentation earlier in *The Pigs*.

This particular solution to the story fully satisfies the convention of an American thriller genre in one sense. After all, in almost all of them blatant or disguised misogyny is rampant. The openly misogynist presentation of a woman is a new ingredient in Polish film, however, a surprising twist in the country which represents its women as strong mother figures or romantic lovers, but rarely as "cheap little tarts."

This surprising turn in the film's crucial scene illustrates a postmodernist scenario of clashing values. On the one hand, the thriller genre with its fast-paced action and simplicity of motives is juxtaposed with a naive Slavic longing for Romantic values. Conditioned by years of indoctrination in a Socialist Poland that espoused both a high regard for family values and a Romantic view of women, Frantz cannot stand Olo's betrayal in this area. On the other hand, the Romantic call for revenge stands in opposition to the scenes earlier in the film in which Angela is presented in a negative way. The contrast in these presentations is so striking that it creates a moment of rupture that distances the Polish spectator from the events presented in the film. The meticulously copied American thriller collapses and is replaced by a hybrid of the grotesque, the unreal, and the controversial.

In this destabilization of the symbolic order through the deconstruction of signs, Pasikowski betrays "a basic ground of meaning: that belief in a fundamental psycho-spiritual truth that transcends institutional assumptions and socio-historical circumstance" (Risatti 1990: 257). Truth is no longer an important or valid concept in the postmodernist discourse of *The Pigs*, illustrating Risatti's statement that

> Perhaps because of the Modernist obsession with the idea of discovering absolute, verifiable truth, the realization that this is not possible, that truth is culturally contingent, has had the effect of causing a crippling doubt to enter the Western psyche, undermining the sense of direction and purpose of contemporary life (1990:257).

Risatti quotes the words of the critic Suzi Gablik who notes that the inability to give credence to meaning is a widespread symptom of postmodern society. "We are experiencing in our culture a sudden radical break with the will-to-meaning which until now has always been understood as a fundamental drive of human life" (cited by Risatti 1990: 257).

In a formal sense, the chase film becomes a splatter film, a B movie with special effects crudely assembled. This simplistic presentation of violence in a thriller film, so different from sleek Hollywood film images, provokes a response of laughter and cynical detachment. The film no longer can be perceived as an American-like thriller or a social film showing the reality of crime in contemporary Poland but as an amusing, postmodern collage composed of elements of gore, slavic Romanticism, misogyny, and youthful bravado.

It is interesting to note that the responses of Western and Eastern audiences to *The Pigs* differed greatly. During the presentation of the film at Toronto's International Film Festival in September 1993, I observed that while North Americans watched with disgust as the same old tricks performed almost every day on Western screens were inexpertly executed by an Eastern European film director, the Eastern Europeans reacted to them with a burst of laughter. The crude attempts to imitate a Hollywood action-packed film were so hilarious in the context of contemporary Poland that these members of the audience felt completely distanced. At the same time such humourous attempts concealed the gravity of the social reality presented in *The Pigs*: the unhampered rise of the local and international mafia; the inadequacy of Polish police forces to deal with them; and, in general, a complete loss of control on the part of the Polish authorities. The film turned into a postmodern site of signs, representations, and simulations of the real in Baudrillard's sense (1981). The representation became the real, and while it was interpreted as such by the Western audience, it was completely rejected by the Polish one. Polish spectators know that spectacular car chases and duels in abandoned warehouses do not often happen in their country, and that mafia accounts in Poland are usually settled in a less bloody manner.

Wladyslaw Pasikowski himself admits that he is fascinated by American film, especially by Scorsese's *Taxi Driver* and *GoodFellas*, Spike Lee's films, Quentin Tarantino's *Reservoir Dogs,* and Roman Polanski's *Rosemary's Baby* (Czartoszewska-Retmaniak 1994: 15). In his attempt to introduce the elements of horror, he nevertheless upsets the delicate balance between surrealism and the real. The film brims with a subversive humour present in the dialogues and sometimes impossible scenes. Humour functions here as a shield behind which the protagonists must hide to overcome their powerlessness in view of the rising crime in Poland and to distance themselves from the events in which gore meets the surrealist macabre. At the same time, *The Pigs*, like the American film *Blue Velvet*, locates the viewer in the perpetual present. Such films which Denzin calls examples of "late-postmodern nostalgia, bring the unrepresentable (rotting cut-off ears, sexual violence, brutality, insanity, homosexuality, the degradation of women, sado-masochistic rituals, drug and alcohol abuse) in front of the viewer in ways that challenge the boundaries that ordinarily separate the public and private life (Baudrillard 1983: 130). The wild sexuality and violence that these films represent signify, in the Bataille sense (1982), modes of freedom and self-expression that the late postmodern period is both fearful of, and drawn to at the same time" (Denzin 1991: 68).

The Man From

A different mixture of postmodern voices is present in the second film, *The Man From* (1992) by Konrad Szolajski, a political pastiche that closely refers to the famous film by Andrzej Wajda, *Man of Marble* (1977). *Man of Marble* inaugurated the cinema of moral concern in Poland and contributed greatly to the political debate before Solidarity came to power. The film deals with sensitive subjects: the 1950s, Stalinism, overwhelming ideology, repression. In watching the film, the spectator follows two stories at once, the story of a bricklayer set in the 1950s, and the story of a contemporary young filmmaker making her diploma film about the 1950s. Scibor-Rylski's script was based on the texture of genuine events, as Michalek and Turaj note in their book about Polish film (1988: 156). In the early fifties, bricklayers, miners, weavers, and others, with a rate of productivity exceeding five hundred percent of the norm, became part of the propaganda landscape. The so-called work-emulation movement, based on the Soviet Stakhanovite phenomenon, was cultivated, and chosen workers were exploited for the purpose of publicity, to inspire or pressure their peers toward greater efforts.

The story within a story of the film is about just such a young Stakhanovite, Mateusz Birkut, a simple, good-natured bricklayer who becomes the subject of rampant propaganda and is hailed as a national hero. Then comes the turning point: he is passed the hot brick. At this point the plot turns and so does the character of Birkut. He takes the side of a fellow worker who is accused of sabotage in the incident, and so aggressively does he pursue the defence of his friend that he too finds himself in the courtroom as a defendant and is sent to prison. Immediately, the huge posters of him are taken down, the press drops any mention of him, and a marble statue of him, a work of art typical of the period, disappears into the basement of a museum.

Agnieszka, the second protagonist in the film, is a young filmmaker who lives in contemporary Poland. She wants to base her diploma film on a period during the fifties. As she tries to find out what reality was at the time the bricklayer worked, the people and circumstances of the worker's life emerge in rough contours. The more she learns, the more resistance she encounters among those who were originally involved in the process of producing and later destroying the myth of the Stalinist worker. Agnieszka does not complete her film; her project is aborted, ostensibly because it is not complete, but really because the person whose approval is necessary is himself not willing to take the risk involved in giving the green light to this controversial work.

Based on this narrative, Konrad Szolajski creates an amusing pastiche of *Man of Marble* that challenges every aspect of its content and form. The character who corresponds to Agnieszka, Anna, is a young woman who has nothing to do with filmmaking. When asked to make a film about a member of the Solidarity underground she reluctantly agrees. Everything is ready for her — the studio, the cameramen, and the producer. While Agnieszka has to fight for every piece of filmstock and suffer deprivations while making her film, Anna gets what she wants and is guided through the process of filmmaking itself. The principal protagonist, Mikrut (the name is an anagram of Birkut in *Man of Marble* and means someone small and unimportant), is not a courageous leader of the underground movement but a man accidentally caught by the police during martial law with some Solidarity leaflets in his possession. He is arrested and held at a special internment center where he befriends a security police officer. While in *Man of Marble* the security men are presented as a frightening force, in *The Man From* they are portrayed as human beings interested in art. Mikrut becomes a model for the police officer, an artist, and greatly stimulates the officer's artistic career. When Mikrut leaves the prison, the former police officer greets him warmly and takes him to his home.

Produced in 1992, *The Man From* appears in a different political context than *Man of Marble,* produced in 1977. Solidarity, the courageous revolutionary organization that brought about the collapse of Socialism in 1980, is now fighting for positions in the government. That which was great and noble in *Man of Marble* is grotesque and shallow in *The Man From.* The film reveals the corruption of Solidarity and the superficial nature of revolutionary motives; it shatters the myths surrounding the Solidarity movement and the Solidarity activists; and it questions the ways security police are presented in the media. The protagonists in *The Man From* are no longer heroes of the silent revolution in Poland; they are but caricatures. While Agnieszka and Maciek in *Man of Marble* are romantic heroes, so characteristic of the Romantic tradition in Polish literature and film, Anna and Mikrut are opportunists who join the political movement by accident.

This deconstruction of myths, and subversion of the political ideology so dear to Poles are carried out on another plane as well. The film *Man of Marble* deals with the ethical problems of the creation of reality in art. Burski, a successful filmmaker in the 1970s, recalls the Stalinist times in the 1950s when he had to produce propaganda films for the Ministry of

Culture. The films he produced were sheer fabrications for political purposes. *Man of Marble* shows the process of production of such a film in the 1950s, in which light and camera positions were manipulated and the film was carefully edited to portray revolutionary heroes as invincible and courageous people. The same subplot is presented differently in *The Man From*. The film director here is a police officer who, after a successful production of a propaganda sequence for television (the purpose of which was the denunciation of Mikrut, the pseudoactivist of Solidarity), decides to produce an entire film about his capture and trial. The police officer, fascinated by the process of filmmaking itself, indulges in the pleasures of sign production. Content becomes irrelevant, the economy of signs gains an upper hand. While in *Man of Marble* the purpose of editing and lighting is to enhance the overall content of the film — a belief in the importance of hard work in order to rebuild the country after the second world war — in *The Man From* the police officer's film experiments are merely self-indulgent.

In *Man of Marble* historical truth is meticulously uncovered by Agnieszka. In *The Man From* the historical truth is only a part of a hilarious story that questions the past, the present, the fictive, and the factual. In this transgression of the borders of a conventional film narrative, the film becomes an example of postmodern fiction that stresses the tensions existing, on the one hand, between "the pastness (and absence) of the past and the presentness (and presence) of the present, and on the other, between the actual events of the past and the historian's act of processing them into facts" (Hutcheon 1989: 73).

The Man From ridicules the political icons and political struggle in general, and forces the spectator to engage in a wonderful intertextual game, an endeavour that in the end erupts in hysterics. The political becomes

> an object of laughter, an object which is close at hand, drawn into a zone of crude contact where one can finger it familiarly on all sides, turn it upside down, inside out, peer at it from above, break open its external shell, look into its centre, doubt it, take it apart, dismember it, lay it bare and expose it, examine it freely and experiment with it (Bakhtin 1981: 23).

The grand tradition of the cinema of moral concern is openly mocked in an intelligent and sometimes cruel manner. All the political traits in Wajda's mythical films are mercilessly exposed: the frightening world of security forces is replaced by a congenial world of police officers who befriend their prisoners and cooperate with them after their release. Socialist Realism art, so exposed in *Man of Marble,* is questioned and openly undermined in *The Man From.* For instance, a sequence presenting the creation of a Socialist Realist presentation of Birkut in Wajda's film is paralleled with a sequence in which Anna discovers a similar sculpture in the basement of the National Museum in Warsaw. In *Man of Marble*, the sequence that shows a marble figure of Birkut is made in the convention of Socialist Realist films — with low-angle shots presenting the marble figure in a serious and even pompous manner. Clearly, the purpose of the sequence is to display the glorious figure of the worker who seriously considers himself a hero of the Socialist work ethic. The marble figure looms above the artist who polishes it in all its glory and solemnity. The representation of Mikrut in *The Man From* is made from clay; it is small and resembles the figure of a child. The sculpture is shot from a high-angle position of the camera in a dark, dingy basement of the National Museum in Warsaw. Anna and her film crew attempt to raise the clay figure from the ground. When they put it on a makeshift pedestal, the figure falls to pieces. The metaphor of the clay figure contrasts obviously with the metaphor of the marble figure, thus undermining the value of the superhuman (excessive) effort of the Stalinist workers in the 1950s. The formless clay figure also mercilessly ridicules the value of the Stalinist Realist representations in art and questions their simplistic system of signification.

In Szolajski's *The Man From*, irony supersedes the martyrdom of suffering political activists. It presents them now, in post-Socialist Poland, and reveals their commercialism, nihilism, and ideological and moral confusion. In this sense, the postmodern impulse in *The Man From* is playful and paradoxical. It mocks and absorbs historical forms, always having it both ways, always modern and postmodern. The political struggle presented in *Man of Marble* becomes a modernist source for the postmodernist *The Man From* that playfully subverts the essence and validity of its ideals. In this, the 1992 film epitomizes a postmodernist text in which, as described by Sherrie Levine regarding the post-modernist painting,

> Every word, every image, is leased and mortgaged. We know that a picture is but a space in which a variety of images, none of them original, blend and clash. A picture is a tissue of quotations drawn from the innumerable centers of culture… The viewer is the tablet on which all the quotations that make up a painting are inscribed without any of them being lost (1987: 92).

While the modernist *Man of Marble* creates a fusion of the personal and the political in the sense that politics constitutes the essence of the life of the protagonists in the film, *The Man From* ridicules these idealistic notions and questions both the political and the personal. The film shows the opportunism of the leaders of Solidarity, their self-interest and egoism. Everybody is immoral in the film, but the immorality of all the protagonists, both members of Solidarity and its opponents is playful and inconsequential. The film celebrates the banality of evil, the superficiality of ideals and shows them all as clownish participants of a ridiculous spectacle. In this manner, the film is an important political statement using parody to critique the myths surrounding new ideologies, and irony "to engage the history of art and the memory of the viewer in the re-evaluation of aesthetic forms and contents through a reconsideration of their usually unacknowledged politics of representation" (Hutcheon 1989: 100). In the film parody functions not as an ahistorical and apolitical statement, but rather plays an important role in the revealing of new truths and new histories. As Dominick La Capra puts it:

> Irony and parody are themselves not unequivocal signs of disengagement on the part of an apolitical, transcendental ego that floats above historical reality or flounders in the abysmal pull of aporia. Rather a certain use of irony and parody may play a role both in the critique of ideology and in the anticipation of polity wherein commitment does not exclude but accompanies an ability to achieve critical distance on one's deepest commitments and desires (1987: 128).

To recapitulate, both *The Pigs* and *The Man From* show a new, postmodernist face of post-Socialist Poland. On the one hand, a nostalgia for every facet of Western culture makes the spectator accept and enjoy a capitalistic collage of Western brutality and an unscrupulous show of violence. On the other hand, the disillusionment with the political reality of 1992 allows for films that question every moment of the political struggle responsible for the collapse of Socialism. Cynicism and nihilism reign, as one of the Eastern European participants of the ISSEI conference concluded. In consequence, the new culture emerging from the ruins of Socialism in Poland is a postmodernist spectacle where old and new values are playfully engaged in creating a postmodern hyperspace in recent Polish cinema.

REFERENCES

Axford, Barrie. 1994. "Multiple Truths and Postmodern Imaginings: New Ways of Reading European Unity." Paper presented at The Fourth Conference of The International Society for the Study of European Ideas, *European Unity and Europeanism Workshop*. Graz, Austria. Unpublished.

Bakhtin, Mikhail. 1981. *The Dialogic Imagination: Four Essays*. Austin: University of Texas Press.

———— 1984. *Rabelais and His World*. Bloomington: Indiana University Press.

Bataille, George. 1982. *The Story of the Eye*. New York: Berkeley Books.

Baudrillard, Jean. 1981. *For a Critique of the Political Economy of Signs*. St. Louis, MO: Telos Press.

———— 1983. *Simulations*. New York: Semiotext.

Czartoszewska-Retmaniak, Ewa. 1994. "W jego kinie nie jest miło" ("Things are not nice in his films"), *Kobieta i Zycie*, no. 21/2238, 21 May: 15-16.

Denzin, Norman K. 1991. *Images of Postmodern Society: Social Theory and Contemporary Cinema*. London: Sage Publications.

Hutcheon, Linda. 1989. *The Politics of Postmodernism*. London: Routledge.

Jameson, Frederic. 1984. "Postmodernism or the Cultural Logic of Late Capitalism." *New Left Review* 146 (July-August): 53-92.

Kornatowska, Maria. 1993. "Polish Cinema." *Cineaste* 19, no. 4: 47-50.

La Capra, Dominick. 1987. *History, Politics, and the Novel*. Ithaca, New York: Cornell University Press.

Levine, Sherrie. 1987. "Five Comments" in *Blasted Allegories: An Anthology of Writings by Contemporary Artists*, ed. Brian Wallis. Cambridge, MA: MIT Press.

Michalek, Boleslaw, and Frank Turaj. 1988. *The Modern Cinema of Poland*. Bloomington and Indianapolis: Indiana University Press.

Risatti, Howard. 1990. "Introduction to Part Five: Psychoanalytical Criticism and Art." In *Postmodern Perspectives*, ed. Howard Risatti. Englewood Cliffs, New Jersey: Prentice Hall Inc.

NOTES

1. The Fourth Conference organized by The International Society for the Study of European Ideas took place 22-27 August 1994 at Karl-Franzens-Universität in Graz, Austria. Over 800 scholars from five continents registered to present papers in 102 workshops. At these workshops cultural, political, and historical implications of the European unification were discussed at length.

Part III

Postmodernism as Tourism, (Post)History, and Colonization

A Room with a View (*Cinecom International Films, 1986*) *James Ivory*
Lucy Honeychurch (Helena Bonham-Carter) and George Emerson (Julian Sands) in a story of
anti-touristic tourism. Still courtesy of Jerry Ohlinger's Movie Materials.

CHAPTER 8

E.M. FORSTER'S ANTI-TOURISTIC TOURISM AND THE SIGHTSEEING GAZE OF CINEMA

Ellen Strain

Postmodern theory moves toward a new phenomenology in its exploration of fluctuations in the very nature of experience, fluctuations that appear to be hinged upon structural shifts in our economy. This chapter contributes to that body of scholarship in its investigation of postmodernism in relationship to one particular type of experience. In fact, this inquiry isolates a form of interaction with reality that one theorist has labeled the paradigmatic experience. In this assertion, Eric J. Leed refers to travel (1991: 5). To support his point, Leed excavates the word roots of "travel" and "experience" in various Indo-European languages and declares the two words to be "intimately wedded terms." In another book on travel, sociologist Dean MacCannell focuses on the nature of experience. Using tourism as his primary example, he postulates that our continued economic development has been marked by the commodification of experience. He writes, "Increasingly, pure experience, which leaves no material trace, is manufactured and sold like a commodity" (1989: 21).

Adding to the equation the other central concern of this anthology — cinema — this examination of postmodern experience becomes in many

147

ways a bifocal analysis. The ostensible subject of this chapter is tourism as seen through the eyes of British novelist E.M. Forster and the film directors who have adapted his work for the screen. Yet, with the addition of this filter for examining travel as a mode of experience, the study expands from a closely circumscribed look at travel practices as depicted in film and literature to a study of the filmic medium's contribution to the postmodern mediation of reality. Essentially, the use of film as an analytical lens creates a double layer of touristic practice to be examined: the travel experience of the fictional character at the center of the novel or film in question and the "virtual tourism" of the reader or spectator positioned as armchair traveler.

Within the dialectic of these two layers of tourism lies an essential irony. As I explore in the first section of this chapter, the touristic gaze of the cinematic apparatus and its delivery of a simulated reality has been a dominant force in the heralding of a manufactured reality which, in its superb mimesis, goes so far as to question the relevance of any original pro-filmic reality. The meticulously constructed spectacle of Classical Hollywood Cinema exemplifies simulation in a heightened, postmodern form that takes on a life of its own separate from any conception of an original. However, despite cinema's collective contribution to postmodernism's frenetic mediation of reality, the individual film does not necessarily integrate a knowing recognition of its participation in the loss of faith in a pure and immediate reality. In fact, it is through their masterful artifice that many films seem to insist upon the accessibility of some form of authenticity and real experience. Certainly, this is true of the adaptations of E.M. Forster's work, which submerge any questioning of the image's mediation of reality by conflating the experience of the fictional traveler with that of the filmic spectator.

In the end, Forster's novels far more closely approximate the theoretical position of postmodern scholars who have postulated on the fading of a tangible, reliable, and unmanufactured reality than do the filmic adaptations. His novels' insights echo sophisticated analyses of tourism and cultural commodification by scholars who post-date Forster by well over half a century. For Forster, travel entails the fruitless search for cultural authenticity and an unmediated reality, a search ultimately played out upon the body and frequently in violent terms. Yet, Forster's critique of the traveler's quest is submerged within the filmic versions which appear to be more invested in delivering touristic pleasures to spectators than in translating into filmic form Forster's analysis of the collapse between tourism and a kind of anti-tourism.

Postmodern Travels

The issues of tourism, simulated travel, and the tourist's gaze target many of the central questions up for debate within the discussion of postmodernism. For instance, idealist talk of "multiculturalism," colliding with the more ambivalent dialogue on postmodernism, has brought the question of how individuals see across cultural difference to the forefront in an era of globalized culture. Interestingly, many of the various theoretical concepts developed to grapple with this question and others have evoked the metaphor of travel. For instance, both Gilles Deleuze and Lawrence Grossberg have theorized the passing of modernism using the idea of "nomadism" and speculating on the "nomadic subjectivity" required by postmodernism (Grossberg 1987). Maria Lugones seeks a solution to the postmodern political conundrum in a pluralistic feminism that "world-travels" or identifies across cultures without erasing difference (1990: 390). Even Elspeth Probyn warns against the potential epistemic violence of the postmodern by comparing the contemporary touting of diversity to the superficiality and Western ontologies associated with tourism (1990: 184).

Despite the popularity of tourism and traveling subjectivities as metaphors for speaking about postmodernism, sociological and anthropological studies of touristic behavior have yet to be imported into scholarship on postmodernism. Written in 1976 before academic discussion of postmodernism reached a feverish state, MacCannell's sociology text *The Tourist*, still the most influential book on the subject of tourism to date, explores the cultural activity of sightseeing in relation to modernism. However, in the 1989 revision of *The Tourist*, MacCannell is compelled to remark on tourism's role in the postmodern movement. In the new edition's introduction, he writes, "Perhaps 'the tourist' was really an early postmodern figure, alienated but seeking fulfillment in his own alienation — nomadic, placeless, a kind of subjectivity without spirit, a 'dead subject'" (x). Although such comments could be interpreted as a contrived attempt to update his explication of tourism and modernism, MacCannell's tourist can undoubtedly be seen as a figure situated in the transition from modernity to postmodernity. Many anecdotes from his description of modern culture — Australian aborigines who dress in a modified "Beachboy" look and play Hawaiian ballads, sightseeing bus tours of "The Top Ten Polluters in Action" — seem more postmodern than modern (1989: 31, 40). Additionally, his primary contribution to the theory of tourism, the concept of staged authenticity, can be viewed as a postmodern oxymoron that questions the Benjaminian "aura" of the tourist attraction and looks forward to the postmodern "post-tourist" who delights in the game of sightseeing artifice. In fact, as the article moves on to examine the implications of postmodernism for cultural authenticity, MacCannell's thoughts become quite useful.

Although drawing on little of the sociological work on tourism that has been conducted by MacCannell and others, Anne Friedberg draws out connections between tourism, cinema, and postmodernism, bringing us closer to a notion of the tourist's gaze appearing in cinematic texts. In her book *Window Shopping: Cinema and the Postmodern*, Friedberg locates the onslaught of postmodernism in the commodification of a mobile and "virtual" gaze, a form of visuality intimately connected with both cinema and tourism (1993: 2). The mobility of the gaze seems quite clear in reference to the tourist; the sightseer exits everyday life and travels to a liminal space defined by its geographical separation from work, home, and other realms of day-to-day experience. Cinema's mobility, on the other hand, involves the immobility of the spectator; yet, the cinematic gaze reaches across space via the linked apparatuses of camera and projector to bring distant sights to the movie theater sightseer.

To continue with Friedberg's model, the postmodern touristic/ cinematic gaze is also defined by its "virtuality." Initially, the definition of virtual — reproducing the illusion of reality — may appear to be more appropriate to film. Tourism, on the other hand, would seem to be rooted in the realm of the real rather than the virtual. However, an amalgam of ideas from anthropologists, sociologists, and media theorists suggest ways of positing a continuum or at least a pronounced similarity in distanced perspective and "derealized" space between tourism and media travel.

The term "environmental bubble" suggests one way of seeing tourism and cinema as similar visual practices. Mass tourism has only grown through the expansion of the environmental bubble or the physical boundaries between tourists and the foreign environment. With air-conditioned tour buses, Western-owned hotels, and purified water supplies, travel no longer involves physical hardship or significant risk to corporeal well-being. Not only does the environmental bubble provide a safer, more disembodied journey, but it alters perception in such a way that it becomes more akin to the visual practices associated with media experiences. Both Susan Sontag and Wolfgang Schivelbusch bring attention to the framing mechanisms associated with travel that separate tourists from the locales which they visit. As Schivelbusch argues, both the framing of the landscape by the train window and the train's velocity removes the traveler from the space through which she travels by blurring the foreground (1980: 65). In her work, Sontag discusses not the frame of the train window but that of the camera viewfinder. Taking photographs is another way of distancing oneself from an environment, recording and appropriating an image at the same time as refusing direct experience (1990: 9-11). A number of other scholars including Mary Ann Doane, Lynne Kirby, and Margaret Morse have also commented on the similarities between the distanced, framed vision of cinema and television and the viewing strategies associated with train or automobile travel. The space on the other side of the window becomes less real and less enterable, like a painted canvas, a televisual depiction, or a movie screen.

The Un-Real Objects of Tourism

Another way of questioning the directness of the tourist's experience is to suggest that the sights witnessed by tourists may not be any less "authored" or more authentic than film images. One school of thought on this issue has been led by Daniel Boorstin, who not only derides the inauthentic nature of the tourist attraction but suggests that tourists prefer the inauthentic, commercialized tourist site, flocking to the "pseudo-event" in droves, trampling the "real thing" in their path (1964: 77-117).

MacCannell's theory on touristic motivations differs significantly from Boorstin's and rings more true. According to MacCannell, a fading of reality and the lost sense of oneness with the world around her impels the tourist out into the world seeking exactly what Boorstin says she eschews. As MacCannell writes, "For moderns, reality and authenticity are thought to be elsewhere: in other historical periods and other cultures, in purer, simpler life-styles" (1989: 3). The tourist as modern individual thus embarks on a journey, traipsing through foreign landscapes in search of some truth, simplicity, or sense of nature which is missing from her daily life. Thus, rather than being content with superficiality and artificiality, MacCannell argues, the tourist is motivated by a desire for involvement and understanding.

Unfortunately, such goals are rarely reached. The desire to satisfy tourists' search for authenticity can lead to staged authenticity or "an infinite regression of stage-sets," i.e., a series of front regions designed to look like back regions with the "true" back region lost in the regression (1989: 105). Davydd J. Greenwood (1977) similarly suggests that indigenous culture loses any authentic meaning as soon as it is

151

commodified, or turned into a stage set, by the tourist industry. Thus, like King Midas's touch, the tourist's search for the heartbeat of local culture reaches out but, with its transformative touch, contacts only culture as lifeless commodity. While defining authenticity may be more complex than suggested by the above statements, such quandaries have elicited references to "the vanishing horizon of authenticity" to which the tourist endlessly defers (Frow 1991: 128).

Although MacCannell was the first to connect the tourist's quest to the alienation of modernity, he was certainly not the first to comment on the diminished authenticity of modern society. In fact, to say that modern life, its bureaucracy, capitalist system, and technological production brings about a widespread alienation and anomie is almost a truism. It also seems worthy to mention that many of the ways in which modernism has been described — the loss of the real, the mediation of image and language, and the slipping away of direct contact with the phenomenological world — are not unlike some descriptions of postmodernism, a movement which seems to primarily be an intensification of modernist consciousness. The following passage on postmodernism (Connor 1989: 56) could even provide an introduction to a theory of tourism's compensatory function not unlike MacCannell's theory:

> Alongside [postmodernism's incessant production of images with no attempt to ground them in reality], as though in response to the awareness of the fading out of the real, is a compensatory attempt to manufacture it, in an escalation of the true, of the lived experience; in other words, the cult of immediate experience, of raw, tense reality, is not the contradiction of the regime of the simulacrum, but its simulated effect.

Tourism may provide the illusion of immediate experience and intense reality missing from a postmodern world; yet, as the passage suggests, this cult is similarly manufactured or simulated.

MacCannell's notion of staged authenticity also approaches postmodern theories of simulation. Noting that with the loss of distinctions between front region and back region, representation and reality begin to merge, John Frow (1991) repositions MacCannell's work within a postmodern context:

> MacCannell thus elaborates something like Baudrillard's theory of a historical regime of simulation in which the difference between original and copy falls away, and indeed where the very existence of an "original" is a function of the copy (128).

152

Although MacCannell primarily deals with the tourist attraction as stage set or as a "copy" of the real thing, it is also true that the practice of tourism often involves confronting various copies of the original in the form of postcards, tourist brochures, snapshots, and images delivered by film and television. With this flooding of images, the tourist may read the original, whether it be the Parthenon or Stone Henge, through the filter of these previous images, judging the sight according to its adherence to the copies. Experience of the tourist object is also accompanied by its translation into image through the practice of amateur travel photography; the object is thereby read in comparison to previous images and as possible future image. In the process, the image begins to subsume the original which in turn is only valued for its ability to be represented in yet another copy.

Two additional concepts, a semiotics of tourism and the ideology of perception, further deny a notion of travel as accessing an unauthored, authentic reality. According to Jonathan Culler's explication of the semiotics of tourism (1981), rather than experiencing the reality of a new environment, the tourist reduces aspects of culture to signs of themselves. Another semiotician clarifies, "A place, a gesture, a use of language are understood not as given bits of the real but as suffused with ideality, giving on to the *type* of the beautiful, the extraordinary, or the culturally authentic" (Frow 1991: 125). So the kissing couple becomes a sign of the romance of Paris, just as the arguing merchants are seen as a sign of 'Greekness.' What we might call the ideology of perception also comes into play in the analysis of touristic vision. Bill Nichols argues that unmediated, nonideological perception of any environment is impossible. Like the viewing of visual media, "our perception of the physical world is...based on codes involving iconic signs," thus "the environment becomes a text to be read like any other text" (Nichols 1981: 11, 26). Consequently, tourism can no more provide direct interaction with the real than any other form of perception.

In short, seeing is a form of "reading," and in tourism this reading involves interpreting aspects of a culture as essentialized types. The tourist attraction as a sign of itself is also perceived as an image previously seen in films and on postcards or as a potential image to be captured on film or videotape. And the landscape or monument is judged according to standards of picturesqueness, framed by the tourist's viewfinder, and separated from its context and placement in a real world by the act of recording. This interpretive mediation of the real, or of a staged reality as MacCannell might add, is perhaps a different type of virtuality than the cinematic version, but in both cases the staged reality of the pro-filmic or of the tourist attraction is reduced to a series of framed signs interpreted in a socially constructed manner.

Cinema, Tourism, and the Myth of Direct Experience

Despite the critique of tourism's claim to direct experience, the mythology of tourism still puts forth the promise of travel in terms of what Leed calls "direct and genuine experience." Thus, the tourist's gaze seeks out authenticity or what sightseers might call the "real India" or the "true Italy." As MacCannell writes, the tourist "has been condemned to look elsewhere, everywhere, for his [sic] authenticity, to see if he can catch a glimpse of it reflected in the simplicity, poverty, chastity or purity of others" (1989: 41). These words are echoed by less theoretically minded writers like Michael Crichton who writes, "Stripped of your ordinary surroundings, your friends, your daily routines . . . You are forced into direct experience" (in Leed 1991: 5). Other authors have suggested some type of recovered ability to fully experience reality by way of a return to an earlier stage of life. T.S. Eliot wrote that to visit Greece is "to arrive where we started and know the place for the first time" (in Eisner 1991: 7). Also in reference to visiting Greece, Robert Eisner rhapsodizes, "Perhaps the greatest benefit is the sight of things once more as you saw them in childhood, fresh and bright and exciting and alien" (1991: 7). This supposed reaccess to the real is reminiscent of the way cinema has been theorized as the illusion of a return to the imaginary where the presymbolic plenitude of the real can be recovered. In the case of cinema, however, this plenitude is revealed to be a fetish disavowing cinema's structuring lack, i.e., the very absence of the pro-filmic reality (Silverman 1988: 27). And as we have seen in the case of actual tourism, the myth of direct experience through travel may be equally fictional.

With film as a medium celebrated for its realism and for its ability to make the spectator feel as if she were in the midst of the action, filmmakers are often judged according to their capacity for extending this illusion of direct experience. Directors of location-shot and/or epic films are lauded to the extent that they realize film's potential for visual plenitude and grant spectators access to the diegetic world. And films depicting an exotic locale may be evaluated in accordance to their overlay of both cinema's and tourism's myth of direct experience; in other words, a good filmic depiction of an exotic locale is deemed to be one that places the spectator on the scene as a tourist viewing the environment with a renewed vision that sees an unfamiliar world as "fresh and bright and exciting and alien."

We are thus confronted with an interesting predicament when we view a collection of films by filmmakers considered to be masters of location shooting and of cinematic illusion in general, and when these same films are adaptations of literary works that attempt to critique tourism's myth of direct experience and question the extent to which the tourist has access to cultural authenticity. While the films deliver the visual pleasures of tourism through cinematic plenitude, through their narratives they are also assigned the task of convincing the viewers of the impossibility of any authentic access to the culture depicted, a fact which seems to be denied by cinema's ability to deliver an illusion of materiality, of place rendered in elaborate detail, scale, and spectacle. Indeed this is the tug of war that characterizes David Lean's and Merchant-Ivory's filmic adaptations of E.M. Forster's travel literature.

Forster and the Collapse of Anti-Tourism

One might call E.M. Forster's stance toward the tourist's overseas search for genuine experience conflicted and ironic. Forster was himself a traveler, yet had unusual and critical insight into the practice of tourism. Long before his time, the distinction had been made between the traveler and the tourist — the traveler seeks meaningful, authentic interaction with the inhabitants of her destination and the superficial tourist seals in her environmental bubble eschewing contact with the foreign space unless recommended by her guidebook. Forster's attitude toward this discourse of anti-tourism, however, approaches the sophistication of contemporary scholars who recognize the negligibility of difference between tourist and traveler. The attempt to recognize your own travel experience as distinctively meaningful and authentic has become part of the phenomenon of tourism. As Jonathan Culler explains, the tourist/traveler distinction has functioned primarily "to convince oneself that one is not a tourist . . . the desire to distinguish between tourists and real travelers [being] a part of tourism — integral to it rather than outside or beyond it" (1981: 156).

Through the figures of the sheltered mass tourist and the romantic tourist, who in the spirit of anti-tourism call themselves travelers, Forster first evokes the anti-tourist position and then shows the collapse of difference between tourist and anti-tourist. He uses the well-known stereotype of the uptight, upper-class spinster traveling abroad on an extended museum tour. This is the tourist who returns from her tour of classical ruins remarking that the main problem with Turkey is the Turks. She demands English food, English standards of comfort, English company, and all the rituals of home. Her tourism is distanced, sterile, and permeated with class discourse. And, of course, she spends most of her voyage complaining.

Two women from Forster's novels stand out in their conformity to this early stereotype. Harriet Herriton in *Where Angels Fear to Tread* travels to Italy to retrieve the baby of her deceased sister-in-law. Harriet is perpetually miffed at the inconveniences of her surroundings and would probably barely emerge from her hotel room were it not for the exigency of her mission. The similar character of Charlotte Bartlett from *A Room with a View* views her expeditions in Italy as a chance to get to know other Brits of her social class. As a chaperone for her young cousin, Charlotte considers herself responsible for keeping the maximum distance between all Italians and her impressionable, young companion.

Within each of these texts, the stereotypical tourist is gently ridiculed through humor or through a generally unsympathetic depiction. Forster's critique of this brand of tourism also surfaces through the juxtaposition of another tourist type — the self-declared traveler. Unlike the sheltered tourist who despises the crude materiality of an "uncivilized land," this romantic tourist searches for authenticity and spiritual transformation. In *Where Angels Fear to Tread*, Philip Herriton tells Lilia, "Don't, let me beg you, go with that awful tourist idea that Italy's only a museum of antiquities and art. Love and understand the Italians, for the people are more marvelous than the land" (1). He urges Lilia to get off the beaten path and allow the romance of Italy to seep into her spirit. She takes his advice to heart, eventually sending her family notice of her engagement to Gino, a young Italian she met in the town of Monteriano. In *A Passage to India*, Adela Quested and Mrs. Moore are also interested in more than the sheltered tourist's role. They are eager to see "the real India" and rub shoulders with real Indians, a discouraged practice in colonialist India.

Within Forster's novels, however, even the romantic tourist fails to encounter the real, or at least not the one she expects. In *A Room with a View*, the comical character of Miss Lavish demands that Charlotte put away her guidebook and experience the true Italy. In an amusing scene, she drags Charlotte around the back streets of Florence, insisting that they breathe in the smells of Italy and quickly getting the two of them lost. Miss Lavish later reappears as the author of a poorly written romance novel that uses Florence as a backdrop. As one of Lawrence Durrell's characters in *The Dark Labyrinth* observed about Southern Europe, "I think it is only in the south that they warm themselves at life instead of transforming it into bad literature," but as Miss Lavish's trashy novel proves, this does not stop the British from pretending to live life and then turning it into bad literature.

In *Where Angels Fear to Tread*, Philip's romantic view of Italy also proves to be the stuff of bad literature. His idealist fabrications crumble when he hears that Gino's father is a dentist:

> A dentist in fairyland! False teeth and laughing-gas and the tilting chair at a place which knew the Etruscan League, and the Pax Romana, and Alaric himself, and the Countess Matilda, and the Middle Ages, all fighting and holiness, and the Renaissance, all fighting and beauty! He thought of Lilia no longer. He was anxious for himself: he feared that Romance might die (26).

The collapse of romance hits Lilia even harder. She tries to marry a specimen of Italian simplicity and charm while still living and entertaining like an English lady. Instead she wakes up next to a chauvinistic, unfaithful, and often violent husband and a culture which can only accommodate her British customs with difficulty.

In this way, the anti-tourist or the romantic tourist craves experience in an explicit rejection of sheltered tourism that refuses involvement with an unfamiliar environment. Ironically, however, in trying to get off the beaten path the romantic tourist follows a well-trodden route. And what the romantic tourist holds up as authentic experience dissipates into mirage. According to James Buzard, the real emerges on only one front within Forster's work: "The representation of foreign cultural authenticity by means of an irrepressible human body is a characteristic Forsterian metonym: bodies assert themselves and their materiality throughout Forster's work, in opposition to the falsely spiritual and romanticized experience that is tourism's stock-in-trade" (1993: 310). Through the insistence of the body, Forster returns to the fantasy of the Other and the linkage of desire and difference; yet he maintains that a price must be paid for this fantasy and that it be paid in corporeal terms.

Likening the journey to Victor Turner's rite of passage, the tourist passes through three phases: separation, margin or limen, and reaggregation. Although the sheltered tourist circumvents the liminality of travel, many of Forster's characters do become liminars within this margin which Turner likens "to death; to being in the womb; to invisibility, darkness, bisexuality, and the wilderness" (1978: 249). The liminar's escape from traditional social structures is both liberating and dangerous. And it is the ambivalence of this liminality that erupts on the fictional Forsterian body. Across the three mentioned novels, an unnamed Italian suffers a bloody death, a baby is crushed in a carriage accident, a British woman has a nasty run-in with a cactus, and a British man suffers various physical injuries.

Yet, there is a sexual edge to much of the violence. In fact, perhaps Forster's attraction to the eroticized marginality of tourism can be attributed at least in part to his own sexuality. Mirroring his personal life, desire in his novels comes bubbling to the surface only at a distance from the repressive atmosphere of urban England and is always linked to escape and transgression. Repeatedly, the boundaries between races, nations, and classes are crossed and the rules of English propriety broken. The tourist's voyage becomes a sexual passage racked with promise and peril played out in carnal terms.

One example of sexually inflected violence is the Piazza della Signoria scene in *A Room with a View,* which has been labeled by some literary critics as Lucy Honeychurch's "symbolic loss of virginity" (Rosecrance 1982: 92). She wanders unchaperoned into the square, gazing up at the looming Palazzo dei Medici, appearing "no longer a tower, no longer supported by earth, but some unattainable treasure throbbing in the tranquil sky." She witnesses an argument between two locals. One man assaults the other in a flurry of events with Lucy virtually caught in the middle. The one man "bent towards Lucy with a look of interest, as though he had an important message for her. He opened his lips to deliver it, and a stream of red came out between them and trickled down his unshaven chin" (40). Perhaps no experience could be more authentic than death or orgasm, or in this case, a strange cross between the two which leaves Lucy swooning. The movement toward Lucy begun by the unnamed Italian but cut short by death is completed by George Emerson instead; the chain of events initiated by the Italian reaches completion in the moment of physical contact between George and Lucy as he catches her fall. In this chain of events, the real penetrates Lucy's touristic bubble, allowing the slow transformation ending with her departure from expected roles.

The psychic violence enacted upon Lucy's delicate sensibility is symbolically represented by the blood splashed on her newly purchased postcards. Additionally, the postcards (like the broken binoculars in *A*

Passage to India) are a symbol of the tourist's attempted appropriation of the foreign destination. Thus, the epistemic violence of tourism seems to double back against Lucy, and in the process, the Italian body, Forster's sign of authenticity, is subsumed in the narrative's very wake. Nonetheless, the end effect for both Lucy and George is positive. With Italy acting as a catalyst, the symbolic loss of virginity is transformed into an actual loss of virginity by the end of the novel. Genuine cross-cultural contact thus appears to be both violent and fleeting, with the true victim consisting of an anonymous dead man left in the piazza, his life consumed in this catalytic process.

This idea of tourism's power differential becoming visible as actual violence on both sides of the host/guest encounter is but one explanation. It is also reasonable to suggest that since the Forsterian voyage is a sexual passage and since Forster's sexuality, although displaced into heterosexual forms within some of his novels, was considered to be of a taboo nature during the time of his writing, then these intertwining forces of desire and punishment are not so surprising. Other psychoanalytic investigations of homosexuality have linked homoerotic feelings and masochism. For instance, Kaja Silverman locates a linked homosexual and masochistic content in the Freudian "A Child Is Being Beaten" fantasy. The desire to be loved by the father manifests itself in a fantasy of being beaten by the oral mother. This involves a transference of power which expels the father from the symbolic order (1992: 210-211). In Forster's work, the father is connected to the homeland that is left behind by the tourist's adventure into liminality. Britain and the father are replaced by the foreign landscape that is often coded as feminine. Adela's rape by either the echo of the cave or the cactus thorns could then be read as an act of the phallic maternal power of the land. Forster's textually repressed homosexuality erupts in displaced forms across the various characters, exposing them to the effects of this sexual discourse of masochism. Such a theory remains speculative without further development but nevertheless adds support to the supposition that several forces lie behind this attack on the body within Forster's fiction.

Films with a View

The bodily attacks in Forster's literature are carried over into the filmic adaptations of each of the three novels and remain an essential part of the narrative. In fact, Charles Sturridge's *Where Angels Fear to Tread*,

Merchant-Ivory's *A Room with a View*, and David Lean's *A Passage to India* all remain fairly loyal to Forster's own words and story structure. However, it is almost inevitable that currents of meaning will shift as literature is converted into another textual system. In this case, the primary changes are brought about by filmic stylistics that position viewers as tourists at the same time as the narratives critique tourism and its complicitous partner — anti-tourism.

Various factors are in place to encourage this positioning of spectators as tourists. First of all, there is the long history of cinema's claim to capturing the real, a claim buttressed by the tradition of location shooting. Just like the tourist who seeks out the full range of perspectives from the intimate inspection of ancient craftsmanship to the commanding view from the Eiffel Tower, much of classical film and location film in particular provides a variety of visual positionings. Before the film dips into close-ups and other building blocks of a scene, an establishing shot provides a scenic panorama from an elevated position, the same position so feverishly sought by tourists.

Each of these films is ripe with such scenic moments, with lingering shots of the Florentine skyline or of the Marabar caves perched above the city of Chandrapore. Additionally, since the characters themselves are tourists, the camera occasionally takes up their position, allowing the spectator to view Italy or India through their eyes. What is more unusual is the prevalence of a number of postcard moments motivated neither by a character's gaze nor by the traditional purposes of establishing shots, i.e., the introduction of a new scene, the announcement of the arrival of daylight/nightfall, a cueing that directs as to a change of location, or some other transitional function. These are moments of omniscience for spectators who glimpse the sights even before the characters are privy to the same views or who view a location from a privileged vantage point unavailable to diegetic characters. For instance, in *A Passage to India*, Adela and Mrs. Moore are frustrated in their attempts to make contact with the "real India," only witnessing Indians as decor in a ceremony celebrating British imperialism or meeting Indians of a higher class who have in part anglicized themselves as a means of social mobility within colonial India. Their disappointing sightseeing tour led by a British tour guide includes only British sights: a war memorial, the barracks, the hospital, and a church. Yet, on the women's train ride into Chandrapore, spectators receive several unusual views of India not visible to the train passengers. One such shot depicts a number of Indians sleeping beneath the railway overpass. As one coughs with the dust kicked up by the passing train, perhaps the spectator fancies that she has seen the "back region" of Indian so eagerly sought by Adela and Mrs. Moore.

These picturesque views of tourist destinations seem to function in one of two ways, either unhinging from the narrative or endowing the landscape with a narrative function. During the times when these views unhinge from the narrative, they create the effect of a travelogue interspliced within a narrative film. In *A Room with a View*, locales such as Santa Croce and the Piazza della Signoria spark brief "slide shows" within the film. Narrative progression slows to a halt while a montage of close-ups of sculptures or frescoes ensues. In the Piazza della Signoria scene, the unhingement is visually rendered through camera movement, and the montage of images provides a brief respite before the outbreak of a quarrel. As Lucy crosses the piazza, the camera swings upward and away from her forward movement. She remains in view only thanks to the removal of her dark coat, making her a spot of color in a sea of movement. The details of the Loggia sculptures revealed in the following montage remain disassociated from Lucy's gaze and only retrospectively can any vague link be made between her disrobement, the passion and aggression of the nude figures of stone, and the following sexually nuanced violence. In a montage of fresco details in the church of Santa Croce, links between the narrative and the "slide show" are even more vague.

In *Where Angels Fear to Tread*, these moments of touristic pleasure existing outside of the narrative help to romanticize Italy despite the narrative current that attempts to deromanticize this land of dentists. For instance, at one point, the camera fails to keep up with the protagonists as it pauses to capture the quaint image of young Italian schoolboys running and giggling on the cobblestone streets of Monteriano. Similar images in *A Room with a View* are a bit more complex. In one scene, an Italian hanging out of a second floor window lowers a bucket by rope to another Italian below. On the sound track, lively Italian folk music seems to reinforce the quaintness of this scene. Again, spectators witness this image before the protagonists do, allowing it to be viewed directly rather than from a fictional character's point of view. When the comical figures of Charlotte and Miss Lavish do enter the depicted space, they are in the midst of a conversation about the "simple souls" of Italy, a nation of peasants. Perceiving the oversimplifications of Miss Lavish's proclamations, spectators could read in a retroactive critique of their own complicity in this trope of quaintness.

In the case of the Merchant-Ivory filmmaking team and David Lean, the masterful composition of images creates an appreciation of the image perhaps not unlike the sightseer's appreciation of a beautiful postcard. Lean's aesthetic sense tames the India seen in *A Passage to India* by imposing an order upon the environment, an aesthetic order that encourages the viewer to see abstract patterns within the foreign landscape. In *A Room with a View*, an alternation between an extreme symmetry in composition and more unusually balanced compositions similarly elicits an aesthetic appreciation. In this way, the alien becomes understandable through Western artistic tradition.

One such tradition is that of the picturesque. In her analysis of the "monarch-of-all-I-survey" scene in Victorian travel writing, Mary Louise Pratt describes the "relation of mastery predicated between the seer and the seen" in the perception of the picturesque (1992: 204). The landscape is apprehended from a viewpoint that imposes a symmetry between background and foreground. The scene becomes a painting to be judged, appreciated and even purchased. Buzard further comments on this trope of the picturesque transforming foreign culture into *mise-en-scène*, quite literally doing so in film. The role of the spectator is all-important as the act of seeing corrects and completes the landscape. With the discovery of the vantage point that provides this balance of foreground and background, a "sublime synthesis" occurs: "The authenticity of effect takes place in the epiphanic moment in which the unified aesthetic essence of the place shines forth" (Buzard 1993: 188). However, this essence is not a quality of the place itself. As Buzard describes,

> What occurs at the moment of sublime synthesis is a successful matching of images stored in the memory (from reading, listening to travelers' tales, viewing paintings and sketches, and otherwise preparing oneself for the object) with scenes as they are encountered. The 'original' becomes itself when the viewer perceives that it suits its representations. But to conclude this is to attribute a particular importance to the role played by the viewer in *making* the original become what it (potentially) is. The implication is that only when it comes within the purview of the properly appreciative witness does the site attain its full aesthetic value and the realization of its essence (195).

The filmmaker, as surrogate witness for the filmgoers, captures this moment of sublime synthesis in an image that conforms to audience's pre-existing conceptions of India or Italy, while differing just enough from previous representations in order to claim authenticity as just not another canned image. In *A Passage to India*, Lean even provides some of the images that would become the standards for confirming the "original." Before boarding the ship to Chandrapore, India, Adela glances at paintings of India, and of the Marabar Caves in particular, which decorate the walls of the travel office where she purchases her ticket. The narrative then carries us up the hills sheltering Chandrapore to these caves so that the viewers might glimpse the "original" perceived in all its picturesqueness.

Lean's picturesque vision is also a mobile one. With moving shots from trains, boats, automobiles, and even elephants, Lean highlights the movement of the traveler, and conversely, the stillness of the locale. Upon the protagonists' arrival in India, an automobile carries them through a marketplace. India is delivered in all its tactile glory as a market where the tourist may not only witness but purchase the exoticism of the East. India's liminality is simultaneously represented as a corpse is carried past the automobile. During this car ride, two Indian bicyclists who are knocked off their bicycles as if to enforce the Westerner's monopoly on motion occupy some kind of middle ground in terms of class and privilege between the colonial subjects on foot and the British in their cars, ships, and trains. This theme continues throughout as the mobility of one of these bike-riders, Aziz, is circumscribed by British desires and demands; he travels to accommodate British patients and tourists, getting his Tonga stolen by two English women, and eventually being immobilized through wrongful incarceration. Indians of lower status experience even more negligible movement in contrast to the incessant motion of British characters. Adela and Ronnie walk by a static gauntlet of servants which line the path into Ronnie's home. With much pomp and circumstance, the viceroy and his wife drive through a crowd of Indians assembled for their arrival. A single Indian waves goodbye as Mrs. Moore's train departs. In short, the British with the privilege of mobility construct India as an immobile stage, a place of stillness outside of time awaiting the traveler's arrival. To the extent that this construction is aestheticized and the spectator is absorbed by the beauty of the image, the critique inherent in this portrait of stillness is obscured.

Viewing the landscape as picturesque or sublime serves to personify the land. In other words, although the filmmaker's or tourist's perception is required to make the vision come to life, the land with its "authenticity of effect" becomes a narrative character affecting spectator and diegetic character alike. The spectacular landscape may have a pleasurable effect on the spectator at the same time that the land's mysterious effects are foregrounded by the narrative itself. In *A Room with a View*, Miss Lavish says to Charlotte, "I have a theory that there is something in the Italian landscape which inclines even the most stoic nature to romance." This theory is communicated through visual and sound design as one of Puccini's arias accompanies the nap of the Italian carriage driver, an individual who has already displayed his passionate temperament. If such passionate impulses are indeed a function of the landscape affecting those who are, as Miss Lavish says, "open to physical sensation," then their infectiousness is signified by the music that ceases whenever the less susceptible Charlotte and Miss Lavish come into view. The carriage driver directs Lucy to George who engages her in a long and fervent kiss in the middle of a Fiesole poppy field overlooking the city of Florence. After the kiss is broken up by the frigid Charlotte, an unusually long and static shot of the Florentine skyline is accompanied by the final bars of the aria. The extended shot endows the picturesque landscape with an assumed significance, acting as a kind of wink between filmmaker and audience. However, the degree to which the film takes entirely serious the idea of catalytic scenery is questioned by the gentle ridicule of Miss Lavish and her idea for a second-rate romance novel: "a young English girl transfigured by Italy."

In *A Passage to India*, Lean as scenarist adds a scene to Forster's tale in keeping with this notion of land as transfigurative force bringing repressed elements of the tourist's character to the surface. In a precursor to the rape scene, Adela's bicycle ride leads her to a delapidated, apparently abandoned temple strewn with erotic statues, an exotic locale seemingly frozen in time for the benefit of the tourist. Entranced by the impassioned embraces of the stone figures, Adela approaches until a troop of screeching monkeys scrambling across the temple ruins frightens her away. The incident's repercussions are soon evident as a stirred-up Adela takes back her rejection of Ronnie's marriage proposal and as her morning dreams are haunted by these same sexually entangled bodies immortalized in stone.

In Lean's film, as in *A Room with a View*, a place's authenticity of effect is communicated orally as well as visually. While much of the visual material is of a pleasurable nature, the violence of Forster's novel is cinematically rendered through sound. The monkeys' approach in the temple scene is announced first through sound effect before the actual creatures are visible. The chaos of their screeching and clawing on rock, breaking the scene's relative tranquility, is perhaps more distressing than its visual counterpart — the monochromatic tan fur of the monkeys against carved stone of the same color. Similarly, the visual paucity of the cave's interior is no match for the echo that unnerves Mrs. Moore and later incarnates Adela's rape fantasy.

In the end, it is difficult to say which filmic elements have the stronger effect — the visual touristic pleasures or the violence rendered through sound and narrative action. Andrew Higson has argued that the concern for surface detail which we see in each of these films characterizes many of Britain's heritage films. He suggests that the heritage film converts nostalgia into spectacle, thereby draining the original work of its emotional and political content and delivering the past as "a museum of sounds and images, an iconographic display" (1993: 115). Undoubtedly, the skillful "iconographic display" of these films delivers a spectacle of place endowed with the illusion of authenticity, thereby in contradiction to Forster's political critique and his suggestion of the unreachable nature of direct experience within tourism. For Forster, only the genuine expresses itself in the unpleasantness of a violent culture shock that either attacks the tourist's body or consumes the indigene in a reminder of the exploitative effects of using the foreign locale as a catalyst for the visitor's self-transformation. Within the visual splendor of these films, this critique begins to short circuit, leaving conflicted filmic texts that position spectators as tourists with only a brief questioning of touristic aims.

REFERENCES

Boorstin, Daniel. 1964. *The Image: A Guide to Pseudo-Events in America.* New York: Harper.

Buzard, James. 1993. *The Beaten Track: European Tourism, Literature, and the Ways to Culture 1800-1918.* Oxford: Clarendon Press.

Connor, Steven. 1989. *Postmodernist Culture: An Introduction to Theories of the Contemporary.* Oxford: Blackwell Publishers.

Culler, Jonathan. 1981. "Semiotics of Tourism." *American Journal of Semiotics* 1: 127–140.

Durrell, Lawrence. 1962. *The Dark Labyrinth.* New York: Dutton.

Eisner, Robert. 1991. *Travelers to an Antique Land.* Michigan: University of Michigan Press.

Forster, E.M. 1975. *Where Angels Fear to Tread* (1905). London: Edward Arnold.
——— 1988. *A Room with a View* (1908). New York: Bantam Books.

Friedberg, Anne. 1993. *Window Shopping: Cinema and the Postmodern.* Berkeley, CA: University of California Press.

Frow, John. 1991. "Tourism and the Semiotics of Nostalgia." *October* 57 (summer): 123-151.

Greenwood, Davydd J. 1977. "Culture by the Pound: Tourism as Cultural Commoditization." *Hosts and Guests: The Anthropology of Tourism,* edited by Valene L. Smith. N.p.: The University of Pennsylvania Press.

Grossberg, Lawrence. 1987. "The In-Difference of Television." *Screen* 28, 2: 28-48.

Higson, Andrew. 1993. "Re-presenting the National Past: Nostalgia and Pastiche in the Heritage Film." *Fires Were Started: British Cinema and Thatcherism*, edited by Lester Friedman. Minneapolis: University of Minnesota Press.

Leed, Eric J. 1991. *The Mind of the Traveler: From Gilgamesh to Global Tourism*. N.p.: Basic Books.

Lugones, Maria. 1990. "Playfulness, 'World'-Travelling, and Loving Perception." *Making Face, Making Soul*, edited by Gloria Anzaldua. New York: Aunt Lude Foundation.

MacCannell, Dean. 1989. *The Tourist: A New Theory of the Leisure Class* (1976). New York: Schocken Books.

Nichols, Bill. 1981. *Ideology and the Image: Social Representation in the Cinema and Other Media*. Bloomington: Indiana University Press.

Pratt, Mary Louise. 1992. *Imperial Eyes: Travel Writing and Transculturation*. London: Routledge.

Probyn, Elspeth. 1990. "Travels in the Postmodern." *Feminism/Postmodernism*, edited by Linda J. Nicholson. New York: Routledge.

Rosecrance, Barbara. 1982. *Forster's Narrative Vision*. Ithaca, NY: Cornell University Press.

Schivelbusch, Wolfgang. 1980. *The Railway Journey: Trains and Travel in the Nineteenth Century*. Translated by Anseln Hollo. New York: Urizen Books.

Silverman, Kaja. 1988. *The Acoustic Mirror: The Female Voice in Psychoanalysis and Cinema*. Bloomington: Indiana University Press.

———— 1992. *Male Subjectivity at the Margins*. New York: Routledge.

Sontag, Susan. 1990. *On Photography* (1977). New York: Doubleday.

Turner, Victor and Edith Turner. 1978. *Image and Pilgrimage in Christian Culture*. New York: Columbia University Press.

CHAPTER 9

IMAGINARY GEOGRAPHIES

The Colonial Subject in Contemporary French Cinema

Christine Bolus-Reichert

W ith this selection of three films about the colonial experience in French West Africa — *Coup de torchon* (1981), *La Victoire en chantant* (1976), and *Chocolat* (1988) — I hope to describe the *recolonizing tendency* of travel cinema. Do these films merely tell stories about the past or do they reclaim lost territory? Incorporating the conditions for the growth of colonialism and for its ultimate dissolution, such narratives recreate the complex history of imperialism, and at the same time reify its formal structures through visual material. Even as untenable positions are readily surrendered, the film as a living, usable document complicates the desires of the spectator. In his landmark work entitled *Orientalism*, Edward Said pointed to the problematic relationship between colonial rule and its justification: "To say simply that Orientalism was a rationalization of colonial rule is to ignore the extent to which colonial rule was justified in advance by Orientalism" (1979: 39).[1] This now famous statement might be recast this way: "To say that

Coup de torchon *(Home Vision, 1981) Bertrand Tavernier*
Lucien Cordier (Philippe Noiret) and his companion in crime, Rose (Isabelle Huppert) in a
complex story of the dissolution of imperialism.

Africanist discourse arose through the encounter with the peoples of the lands of Africa is to ignore the extent to which colonial rule was justified (and is rejustified) by representations of Africa."

In the first section of this chapter, I sketch some of the narratives that French travelers to Africa have exchanged in the past, and that remain current in the contemporary travel cinema. These travelers' tales form the base of our postmodern experience of the newly independent, recommodified African continent. In the second section, with the cast of characters firmly in place, I move on to an analysis of the setting in each of the films, in particular the establishing shots that problematize the viewer's postcolonial stance vis-à-vis colonized landscape. Parts three, four, and five then discuss specific details selected from the three films: the masquerade and mimicry of colonizers and colonized in Annaud, the homelessness of the *pied noir* in Denis, and the messianic decadence of the imperialist in Tavernier. Finally, I use the short, final section on *Coup de torchon* to summarize the stance of the French cinema toward its former colonies.

Colonists and Ethnographers

In some ways, colonial film might seem a more extreme form of travel film. A person emigrates from Europe to a culture assumed to be less civilized and altogether different from her own. She may have expectations about the landscape, her house, her wealth, what her life will be in the settlement. A man may view the emigration as an opportunity to prove his manhood, to have an adventure. In either case, this individual thinks very little about the natives, and a great deal of himself. The conquered land becomes a background for the performance of a fantasy, even when the emigration was not a choice. Unless the traveler is stricken with fear and unable to act, he will begin to apply preconceived narratives to these unfamiliar events and locations. The colonist may possess or be possessed. In some instances, she desires both outcomes simultaneously. But the careful script does not always meet the demands of actual experience. As André Gide recounts in *Travels in the Congo*, the less intelligent a white man is in the construction of his fantasy, the more trouble he will have with the native people, who will resist his authority:

> An unfortunate official is being tried who was sent out to the colonies too young and placed in a remote station without sufficient instructions. He needed a strength of character and a moral and intellectual quality that he was without. When these are lacking, a man tries to make the natives obey and respect him by the spasmodic, outrageous, and precarious use of brute force. He gets frightened; he loses his head; having no natural authority, he tries to reign by terror (1929: 14).

Several points of Gide's account are worth noting. First, the official had not received proper instructions; that is, he had no script to follow which would have made him less susceptible to the disorienting effects of the encounter with difference. Gide also emphasizes that the colonist needs strength of character, an internal consistency and sense of purpose necessary for the exertion of power over others. Above all, the man cannot lose control of himself and still expect to control others. The use of force to sanction one's authority cannot be sustained if it breaks with the figure of order.

Significantly, Gide does not blame the loss of control on Africa itself; such an assumption, found in *Heart of Darkness* and numerous other reports from the contact zone,[2] is the application of a false mirror. The traveler identifies with the land and its inhabitants in purely negative terms saying to himself, "Africa has made me crazy"; or the author says to the reader, "Kurtz was an ordinary man until this *place*, this Africa destroyed him." Even the seemingly progressive view offered by these contact zone stories (i.e., white men are bad, too) is suffused with the notion that Africa is irretrievably dark, unknowable, mysterious, preconscious. They say: "Africa is the unconscious."

Coup de torchon replays this narrative. It is 1938. Lucien Cordier, the "cop of Bourkassa," asserts that in Africa, where one has no use for the law, terms like "good and evil" become rusty and disused. In this way, he justifies the murders of several Europeans and one African. Like Kurtz in *Heart of Darkness*, he makes his own moral code, since Africa has none. Lucien Cordier turns himself into a Messiah, but one who is completely decadent. While *Coup de torchon* poses as a colonial revisionist film in its depiction of French colonists, it cannot overcome the force of the African myth. The myth is sustained until the final breath of the film. Two scenes convey this orientation: Cordier and Anne dancing — what he has done does not matter, since he has already been dead for such a long time (because of Africa); Cordier in the bush, watching a boy — he aims his gun, and then pulls up when other boys appear. Cordier imagines that he has control, that he can resort to order; but the implication of the film's *vision* is that Africa exerts its influence on this otherwise rational man.

The intellectual traveler is another kind of émigré. This man comes to Africa to discover the *place*. Of course, he has prepared himself with books, maps, and statistical charts. He has seen engravings in popular editions of the explorers; he has acquired a few curiosities for his room. His narrative tradition begins with Montaigne and continues with Gide, Leiris, Lévi-Strauss, and the hundreds of others who have traveled and written like them. In the sixteenth century, Montaigne used the accounts of Brazilian primitives to critique his own culture.

> All things, says Plato, are produced by nature, by fortune, or by art; the greatest and most beautiful, by one or the other of the first two, the least and most imperfect by the last. These nations, then, seem to me barbarous in this sense, that they have been fashioned very little by the human mind, and are still very close to their original naturalness. The laws of nature still rule them, very little corrupted by ours; and they are in such a state of purity that I am sometimes vexed that they were unknown earlier, in the days when there were men able to judge them better than we. I am sorry that Lycurgus and Plato did not know of them; for it seems to me that what we actually see in these nations surpasses not only all the pictures in which poets have idealized the golden age and all

their inventions imagining a happy state of man, but also the conceptions and the very desire of philosophy. They could not imagine a naturalness so pure and simple as we see by experience (1957: 153).

Montaigne's words echo through the centuries in Gide's: "Naked Negroes run about, shouting, laughing, quarreling, and showing their cannibal teeth" (1929: 7). The idea that these barbarians were superior in their manner of living was commonly repeated by travelers to both South America and Africa; *utopia* became possible with the discovery of the primitive. Susan Sontag's perceptive analysis of Lévi-Strauss uncovers a profoundly utopian mission for anthropology:

> Radically anti-historicist, he refuses to differentiate between "primitive" and "historical" societies. Primitives have a history; but it is unknown to us. And historical consciousness (which they do not have), he argues in the attack on Sartre, is not a privileged mode of consciousness. There are only what he revealingly calls "hot" and "cold" societies. The hot societies are the modern ones, driven by the demons of historical progress. The cold societies are the primitive ones, static, crystalline, harmonious. Utopia, for Lévi-Strauss, would be a great lowering of the historical temperature (1966: 81).

These descriptions of small-scale societies by French intellectuals have several points in common. The natives' emotional and physical closeness to nature, on the evolutionary ladder, makes them our ancestors. The implication is one of loss; European culture, with its pace and complexity, has distanced itself from its divine origins. Vico, in *The New Science* (1744), outlined a cyclical theory of history by which we can discover and know only what we make ourselves. This poetic wisdom proved to be the foundation of all human institutions; with imagination, the first people extended their knowledge to all realms of human experience. Since we cannot know what came before this imagination of things, even geography can be comprehended only through a *poetic* discursive structure. So for Lévi-Strauss, Gide, and Montaigne, primitive peoples only became accessible through European narrative traditions — like the noble savage, but also like the *Heart of Darkness*. In fact, André Gide dedicated his *Travels in the Congo* to the memory of Joseph Conrad, patterning his own journey on the accounts of those who traveled before him.

It is this idealist, intellectual traveler who takes up the imaginative geographies of Conrad, Buchan, Burton, Gide, Leiris and others in *La Victoire en chantant* (*Black and White in Color*). To his interpretation of events in Fort Coulais, West Africa in 1915, the character Hubert Fresnoy

171

brings numerous books, botanical specimens, and the enthusiasm of the amateur geographer. Annaud presents Fresnoy as an extremely attractive, charismatic personality. I have sympathy with him from the beginning; through his sensitive vision, the boorishness, racism, and ignorance of his fellow colonists are readily apparent. From a well-written letter I ascertain that his view of the Africans is progressive: they deserve to be called MEN, he says. It is but the *feeling* of superiority that maintains French dominance. But Fresnoy also wonders: where are the heroes of the adventure novels, and the great deeds he had expected to find in Africa? He thought that Africa would transfigure any ordinary citizen or merchant into a hero. The "marquis de la géographie" does ultimately transform himself into a hero (the villagers call him the young chief) and restructures the relations between French colonists and natives, at the same time that he wages an organized war against the Germans and "their" natives. He does the great deed he had imagined Africa would inspire.

Annaud's parodic vision of the colonial situation, which I will discuss in more detail in the third section of this essay, is undermined by contradictory desires. He presents his audience with two versions of colonialism: the first shows us crude, materialist imperialism (colonialism done badly); the second shows us an attractive *picture* of the two cultures living in harmony with the land. Colonialism, in these terms, can be done well, but it hasn't been done very often. The second picture is appealing: the colonists act responsibly and Fresnoy has become integrated into both communities. Now he possesses and is possessed — by the land. His beautiful, black mistress symbolizes his sexual liberation. Responsible and free, the colonial community has been transformed, by Fresnoy's narratives, into utopia.

Gide and Leiris expressed similar contradictions in their travels. Both ultimately advocated the end of colonialism, but could not abandon the idea that the natives would benefit from some outside assistance. Leiris, for example, wrote of the cultural work that ethnography could do: "it can be of some use to colonized peoples in the process of emancipation, who are beginning to think about the meaning of particular characteristics of their traditional cultures" (1989: 122-23). Enthusiastically, he suggests that the records of his own study could become the future history — the archives — of these preliterate people. And perhaps he could help them define their place in a postcolonial world. Leiris's writings are rife with conflicting attitudes, even in his most lucid moments. In fact, Marianna Torgovnick remarks that Leiris had a tendency to continually rewrite himself, "by rewriting his relationship to Africa." She goes on to explain that in 1950

Leiris rejects what he sees in the postwar era as his earlier fear of Africa, a fear which made him concerned (in the 1930s) more with himself than with the cultures he studied. He rejects not only colonialism but cultural contact "by which entire peoples find themselves alienated from themselves." Leiris refers to the colonized as "alienated" here, but he may be projecting outward, in Existentialist terms, his own condition onto the Africans. That projection would repeat, in a different form, the equation between his confused impressions in Africa and the nature of Africa (1990: 105-06).

Torgovnick reminds us that Leiris's original journey across Africa in the 1930s (recounted in *L'Afrique fantôme*) was commissioned by the government for the purpose of collecting African art for French museums. Hardly a mission of pure science, the activity of the *collector* is conjoined with that of the ethnographer. In *La Victoire en chantant*, Fresnoy collects plants, rocks, and human beings (to fight in his war). The entire project of naming the environment and people, bringing meaning to the unknown, and acquiring concrete knowledge is shared by European colonists and ethnographers. Both have exported narratives of discovery which do more to define themselves than their intended *objects* of study, especially since these objects are defined in terms of the collectors.

Like Leiris, Fresnoy passes through an ordeal, a psychological revolution which makes him a "new man." Claude Lévi-Strauss used exactly these terms to describe the ordeal of the anthropologist who goes into the field. Likened to primitive rituals of the passage from boy to man, the anthropologist's passage is from homebound to homeless. He can never feel at home anywhere. "He is a man in control of, and even consciously exploiting, his own intellectual alienation" (Sontag 1966: 74). For Sontag the *technique de dépaysement*, which is the anthropologist's profession, amounts to a paradigm of modern homelessness and compulsive travel. Leiris, in the insert to the 1934 edition of *L'Afrique fantôme*, states that a man *ought* to be able to fulfill his passions in his own civilization, but "he will learn here as elsewhere, man cannot escape his isolation; so that one day he will set off again, in the grip of new phantoms — though without illusion this time!" (1989: 46). Rather, it is *unceasing* illusions that will inform his every journey — the phantoms which he makes of others. Each time an ordeal, disorientation, or transfiguration: "modern sensibility moves between two seemingly contradictory but actually related impulses: surrender to the exotic, the strange, the other; and the domestication of the exotic chiefly through science" (Sontag 1966: 70). For Leiris, as for the character Fresnoy,

173

"Africa and things African are mere settings and props" in their imaginative geographies (Torgovnick 1990: 106).

Claire Denis, in her *Chocolat*, makes the issue of *dépaysement* infinitely more serious. The film is truly retrospective, and so avoids becoming immersed in its reconstruction and forgetful of the present. Already, we have met two kinds of travelers — the one dutiful, the other studious. Both may go to Africa for their country or for material gain, but they are intrinsically different characters with a different social status. Denis introduces the third kind of traveler: she is the *pied noir*, born in a colony, and now returning to it. What will she find in Africa? Maybe she will find herself as a child (Leiris proposed that one travels through space to negate time). For her, the *pied noir*, the journey is made neither for gain, nor for country, nor for science: this pilgrimage rediscovers *place* as the catalyst for memory.

The child named France embodies homelessness, but not because of any deliberate intellectual alienation. Her *dépaysement* results from being caught in the structures of colonialism like any native, while being taught that her home was always some *other place*. Kristeva's delineation of two types of expatriates does not include France. In the film, she is not shown to be nostalgic (although the return to Cameroon might suggest it) or forgetful. Quite simply she arrives, neither at home, nor away from home. In fact, she more perfectly achieves the anthropologist's vision of homelessness, except that she does not come to study or appropriate. Even the child she has come to find cannot be mentioned, because the little girl constitutes part of a history that has become unmentionable. No one speaks to her except an American. She is white; the others will have guessed her identity. For what, then, does she come to Africa? To replay the colonial experience, its visual pleasure and mortification. This traveler clearly differs from Cordier and Fresnoy. Yet she, too, brings a narrative with her — perhaps *more* fantastic because it was lived — and her father's journal containing drawings of landscapes.

Establishing Shots: Landscapes

In each of these reconstructions of the colonial period, the establishing shots of the film invite the viewer to enter the narrative through a landscape. This picture serves to introduce and initiate; it is the viewer's rite of passage. It repeats the original figuration of the colonist, the ethnographer, the adventurer. Its status as a framed object does not detract from its documentary authority; on the contrary, the limitations of the frame are overcome by imagination, by a process of focalization that automatically occurs within its borders. Its lack of historical authenticity is insignificant; an overabundance of detail would bar your entrance. No, the picture must resemble the viewer's imagination more than it does reality; for, as W.J.T. Mitchell writes, a picture of a landscape is a representation of something that is already a representation in its own right.

> Before all these secondary representations, however, landscape is itself a physical and multisensory medium (earth, stone, vegetation, water, sky, sound and silence, light and darkness, etc.) in which cultural meanings and values are encoded, whether they are *put* there by the physical transformation of a place in landscape gardening or architecture, or *found* in a placed formed, as we say, "by nature." . . . [Landscape] is already an artifice in the moment of its beholding (1994: 14).

With this distinction between what I call the *view* and the *picture*, it is possible to theorize that people can only perceive *land* as *landscape* by making it into a representation, something *like*. Landscape is always a panorama. Mitchell emphasizes that the rise of European landscape painting was contemporaneous with the rise of imperialism, emerging in the seventeenth century and peaking in the nineteenth. Of course, the implication is that visualization justifies domination *in advance*. Mary Louise Pratt analyzes the travel writings of Richard Burton in similar terms. Three rhetorical strategies are employed in the transcription of the view: aestheticization and ordering of description in pictorial terms, density of meaning derived from focalization, and mastery in the relationship between seer and seen.

> The metaphor of the painting itself is suggestive. If the scene is a painting, then Burton is both the viewer there to judge and appreciate it, and the verbal painter who produces it for others. From the painting analogy it also follows that what Burton sees is all there is, and that the landscape was intended to be viewed from where he has emerged upon it. Thus the scene is deictically ordered with reference to his vantage point, and is static (1992: 204-05).

Europeans traveling to Africa formed an image of the place in advance of their arrival, a figuration vital to their mobility. Once on foreign shores, their expectations enabled them to act, to put themselves in the picture. For explorers like Burton, the framed view was meant to convey to his readers at home the wonderment of his presence in this location, what it was like to be there; but he could only describe the place as one they would recognize. André Gide uses the same strategy in *Travels in the Congo*:

> It gives me the keenest pleasure to see Mala again. It is certainly one of the most astonishing things we have seen in our journey, and even one of the finest I ever saw. . . . The gravity of the forms, the subtlety of the colors, remind one of certain of Corot's Italian pictures. (I am thinking particularly of the view of the Forum.) This village would have charmed him. The relations of the tones and the masses, the soft blue of the sky, the grey pink of the walls of the houses, the dash of green given by a few enormous, admirably spreading trees in the open places, the greenish grey-blue expanse of the Logone, seen through a breach of the "carnak," all contribute to the enchantment (1929: 268).

Gide recreates the landscape, in his own terms. This position of mastery, underscored by his aesthetic judgment, lets Gide appropriate the place for his own actions, which he then goes on to describe to his reader. The view provides the ground, and the passage, for those who come after.

Chocolat: the credits roll over an extreme long shot of the sea. Two people advance slowly toward the camera until they reach the shore. From these dark bodies on a light background, the camera pans across the beach to a dark green line of trees where a young white woman sits watching. A boy and his father rest on the beach at the waterline, small waves washing over them. Another cut, and the white woman walks along a tree-lined road. The bathers pull up alongside her in their large car, offering the woman a ride. They ask her if she is "going native." The exploration of the landscape continues with long tracking shots taken from the car.

This opening sequence represents the journey of France — across the sea, through the coastal jungle, a town, and finally into the dry, brown landscape of her childhood. She prepares herself for re-entry by consulting the carefully preserved journal of her father. The drawing of a mountain, and a language game played by father and son, provide the necessary links to her past. Suddenly, France the little girl is riding along the same road with her father and mother and their black servant, Protée. The numerous long shots, revealing shapes of huts and hillocks and contrasts of light and dark, form a visual repertoire, a kind of gallery of Cameroon. Throughout the film, but most significantly in their establishing function, these *tableaux* cast into relief the precise structure of colonial presence.

It is the repetition of her father's sight and of her own naming of Protée that constitute France's re-admittance to the colony. In the establishing

176

sequence, the viewer is encouraged to identify with France's point of view, which makes the entire flashback into part of the viewer's memory, the viewer's revision. In the past, the child's gaze does not master what it sees, and so the remembrance seems precarious and disturbed. What began as a journey, with all the codes of a travel film, alters with the splintering of perspective. At different times, we see Aimée, France, Protée, and Marc, alone or with others, just looking at the place where they find themselves. The retrospective frame with its multiple focalizations restricts your imagination to the present (avoids submersion in the image) while enabling a subjective and selective reconstruction of history.

Bertrand Tavernier's *Coup de torchon* confines consciousness to a single mind, but without the structural distance of *Chocolat*. Its opening sequence similarly places, within a single frame, Africans in a landscape and a lone European colonist who contemplates them from afar. However, this establishing shot bears none of the complicated nostalgia of Denis's work; rather, it is infused with the pathos of the Kurtz narrative. A group of boys are standing or sitting in the sand, at a great distance from the camera. Their bodies are thin and very dark, resembling the stark black line of trees behind them. This equation of form and color naturally serves to objectify the Africans. The lack of definition in their faces and bodies dehumanizes them; the darkness of their bodies overtakes them. The pictorial abstraction of the scene increases when a white man emerges from offscreen right where he seems to have been watching the boys. It then becomes apparent that the initial picture was taken from Cordier's point of view. His continued stare, and the intercutting of a circling vulture, turns what might be recreation or a meeting into an incomprehensible, ominous vision. Tavernier's barren mise-en-scène manages to place these figures at such an emotional distance, that they might truly occupy another planet.

Cordier has come in the role of the ethnographer, or perhaps of Pavlov himself. Shots of the sky reveal an eclipse in progress. Cordier waits near the large tree as darkness covers the motionless boys. Standing, he lights a fire; the boys cautiously draw near as Cordier backs away. Although I was at first tempted to see this as an act of kindness, I have since understood that it was actually an experiment, a test of behavioral response. The mise-en-scène does not allow a more generous interpretation. The Africans were established as objects of an interested gaze, as the focus of a study. Abstraction of form and color to the point of erasing identity excludes the possibility of a humane gesture. Cordier possesses the knowledge of civilization — he knows what it means when the sky darkens at noon. Like the Connecticut Yankee, he can take the light away and give it back at will.

Another cut, and Cordier returns to town in sunlight. Viewer identification with the cop of Bourkassa increases with the liberal use of a hand-held camera. His gaze swerves amid the brightly dressed people who seem to advance very rapidly toward him or to be very close. Although his manner toward natives in subsequent scenes cannot be faulted, the opening sequence nevertheless marks Lucien Cordier's position. None of the French are abstracted in the same way, none are remade into pure matter. They are corrupt, decadent, even evil, but these are human qualities.

The opening sequence of Jean-Jacques Annaud's *Black and White in Color*[3] does not begin with a picture of a landscape, but with close-ups of various parts of soldiers' bodies: marching feet in thick leggings and low boots, guns held next to the body, ribbons on a chest, a helmet, a flag. This initial fetishization of pieces of soldiers' bodies is not exactly equal; rather, the selected items show the German officer's rank and patriotism, and the labor and obedience of the African recruits. As the soldiers are dismissed, a rousing German march commences and the camera begins a long, slow pan right, across the landscape. Leaving the German station, the camera finds the rectangular homes of the natives, a green, tree-filled landscape which dissolves into a browner landscape; the pan continues across conical African homes, to the sleepy French town. At that point, "La Marseillaise" can be heard, quite distinctly, revealing that the camera's journey was not through Africa, but across European borders and cultures. The entire joke, which is nevertheless a perceptive vision of colonial structures of power, is made with a pan, a dissolve, and nondiegetic music.

Another Masquerade

The credit sequence of *Black and White in Color* contributes an amusing element to the thematic structure of the film. "La Victoire en chantant" is heard over a montage of "period" photographs which have been hand-painted or tinted in shades of blue and red, and white. The ostensible patriotism evoked by the song and by the pictures of soldiers and missionaries is undermined by the overblown gestures and intense theatricality of the colored photographs. Multiple readings of the sequence are possible, but what I find interesting is their discursive function in relation to the rest of the film. The special value of photography, especially in the nineteenth century, was its immediacy, its capacity for the spontaneous representation of reality. It never was a matter of mistaking the daguerreotype or the gelatin print for reality, but people did assume that the photo looked like reality or that some reality which they had never seen looked like the photograph.

Annaud's manipulation of the title sequence photomontage, made up of what are presumably historical documents from the period, draws attention to the very artificiality of the photo's mise-en-scène. Instead of convincing the viewer that this story, known only through written accounts and black and white photographs, is going to be as real as the evidence is true, Annaud disrupts the truth value of the photograph and the efficacy of the song by combining them in a way that makes both instantly suspect. The photographs are posed; the backdrops are painted cloth. The song, which should make us think of heroic deeds in war, becomes hollow, a displaced vaudevillian review. The soldiers, the women, and the missionaries are transformed into stage performers whose roles are recognized by the costumes they wear. The denotative meaning of the costumes has been understood, but their connotation has been altered.

The entire historical dimension has been colorized, remade, as the photomontage so explicitly illustrates. From the opening sequence, an ironic distance is created between what is seen or heard by the viewer and what is thought or assumed by the French characters. Early in the film, we see the missionaries in the field trading Christian trinkets for the native pagan carvings. One missionary refuses to trade a statue of Mary or a crucifix with one of the "converts," because he finds the carving not to be valuable enough. The exchange of artifacts, set up like a trading post, leaves the natives no stronger in their faith, nor any wealthier. In fact, they are trading authentic cultural artifacts, both useful and beautiful, for second-hand, mass-produced, useless European objects. Several scenes later, the missionaries are burning the masks and totems offered by the natives, selecting one or two pieces that might have value but destroying the rest. The irony is apparent: the priests burn what we now consider great art (which they claim is in bad taste) and instead give the native artists tasteless factory pieces and abstract religion. On their return from the "wild," the missionaries are carried by natives who sing of how heavy the white men are and how bad they smell, while ironically the priests comment with excessive sentimentality how much the song pleases them. Annaud's ironic juxtapositions defrock these false friars.

The two priests are among those who argue most virulently for war against Germany, despite Fresnoy's reprimand, and even agree that the battle should be on a Sunday. When the others hear of the six-month-old war with Germany, they immediately take up the cause of France and break into "La Marseillaise" shouting "Vive la France!" Even the reluctant commander of the town, Bosselet, leaves the room to find his uniform and instruction manual. The urge to join the cause is irresistible, and utterly ridiculous. Thousands of miles from France, they have transplanted an entire national culture — its slogans and hatred, its symbols and costumes. The next day, all the Frenchmen wear uniforms and set about recruiting blacks to do the fighting for them. They call all the men into the square, speak to them in French about their duty to France, and offer them iron basins if they will fight. Scores volunteer and are given new, French names. The whole preparation for war has the atmosphere of a carnival.

The colonial fantasy is based on an imaginary geography: in their ignorance, people take what they know and apply it to the rest of the world. In the next scene, as the recruits are marching to German territory, the merchants and their wives arrive in their very best clothes. They approach the creek which separates the two colonies and declare that it could be the Rhine; a merchant carries the French flag across. Only Hubert Fresnoy seems to be exempt from the heavy irony leveled at the other types. In fact, he cannot stand to see the whole thing done so badly and takes over the war operations (after the first, miserable failure). In his serious, intelligent way, he gains full cooperation. The citizens are disciplined and patient, glad to let someone else direct the show; and the villagers recruit bushmen as soldiers for Fresnoy. Since Fresnoy most fully understands the narratives of colonialism, he most competently employs them.

Two scenes are crucial for understanding the young geographer's efforts at transforming the colony. When Monsieur Caprice returns from his mission and tries to see Fresnoy, he is barred from entering by the chief's man, Barthélémé. Caprice speaks rudely to the black sergeant, calls him "boy," and strikes him for his power to refuse entry, to speak perfect French, and to take charge of matters that concern the whole town. Caprice hates the black man's Frenchness, where before he hated his Otherness, his absolute difference. Caprice's racism exists on the surface; its terms are clearly discernible. Fresnoy's approach to racial difference is, in Homi Bhabha's terms, much more ambivalent, a mixture of high ideals and low mimetic effects: "colonial mimicry is the desire for a reformed, recognizable Other, as *a subject of difference that is almost the same, but not quite....* Mimicry is, thus, the sign of a double articulation; a complex strategy of reform, regulation, and discipline, which 'appropriates' the Other as it visualizes power" (1984: 126). Fresnoy bestows certain French accoutrements on his assistant, but Barthélémé can never *become* French; for such benevolent colonialism to continue, the native must always be in need of assistance, of guidance. In explaining why opposition to colonial occupation is so total, even when it has brought some benefits, Fanon says, "on the level of the whole colonized society, we always discover this reluctance to qualify opposition to the colonialist, for it so happens that every qualification is perceived by the occupier as an invitation to perpetuate the oppression, as a confession of congenital impotence" (1965: 122).

Fresnoy's intellectual, reformist colonialism does nothing to liberate the oppressed people. Instead, the internal hierarchy becomes more stratified; the French must now live up to the most heroic, most abstracted and idealized definition of the colonial mission. Fresnoy's reform is *another masquerade*. Attired in a simple white uniform, Fresnoy and his black mistress in her finest array approach the colonists. Nondiegetic music sets the scene for a royal greeting. Fresnoy honors Caprice's mission, but does not accept his hand. They approach the women so that these honored subjects may bow over the hand of the beautiful *négresse*. The couple's every gesture articulates their blessed condition, their royal status. They are seated with Bosselet, while the others stand to watch a parade at arms. The black soldiers wear matching uniforms, they march well. Fresnoy signals that the others should clap, and they do. The soldiers sing "La Victoire en chantant," and the full irony of the scene becomes apparent. Fresnoy has succeeded in turning the natives into French subjects, easily ruled. He has roused their natural abilities, appreciated their beauty, and directed it in the interest of the nation. The seemingly contradictory pattern of successful colonization has been described by Edward Said as "the struggle, first, to stimulate the Orient (lifeless, timeless, forceless) into movement; second, to impose upon that movement an essentially Western shape; third, to contain the new and aroused Orient in a personal vision . . ." (1979: 241). This *transplanting* of Western values to African soil makes Fresnoy's leadership more effective; he could have written a manual of the growth cycle of a colony. The particularity of place, Fresnoy demonstrates, can be overcome with sufficient preparation of the ground in advance.

Annaud's conclusion — the advancing British take over the German position — demonstrates that the colonists' roles are completely interchangeable across nations. Fresnoy meets the German commander and discusses philology, abandoning his native woman for more

181

stimulating conversation. Was she merely a prop in the *picture* of his fantasy? What works against Annaud's clever exposure of the colonial masquerade is *his* picture of the African landscape. Numerous stills resembling paintings are intercut with Fresnoy's rise to power; his palette is traditional within the colonial period genre, and incredibly attractive to the viewer. If the events themselves did not make the viewer nostalgic for this particular past, then the earth colors, the cool interiors, the white clothes, the exoticism would. This is the perpetual difficulty with travel films: they transform sites of oppression into desirable scenery. Fresnoy's actions are admirable, ingenious, and very difficult to critique, resulting, as they do, from a revered set of contact-zone narratives.

Proximity and Distance

In *Chocolat*, France journeys to Africa to find something she has missed. In the containment of one narrative by another, there is slippage, excesses of desire which cannot be held within the frame. One of the severe trials of colonialism, both for Europeans and Africans, was the inevitable proximity, even intimacy of the two peoples. As Edward Said confirms, "every traveler or resident in the Orient has had to protect himself from its unsettling influences.... The eccentricities of Oriental life, with its odd calendars, its exotic spatial configurations, its hopelessly strange languages, its seemingly perverse morality..." (1979: 166). Most of all, the Orient or Africa seemed to offend sexual propriety. Everything about the Orient "exuded dangerous sex, threatened hygiene and domestic seemliness with an excessive freedom of intercourse" (1979: 167). Of course, part of the attraction of travel would have been precisely these aberrations, these vertiginous glances into unexplored fantasies. In numerous encounters between Aimée and her servant, sexual tension erupts. The woman, betrayed by her proximity to Protée, cannot suppress her fantasy. The camera's visual fetishization of the black man's body represents Aimée's point of view, and imposes it on the viewer, who longs for the ultimate transgression. We locate Protée in our imaginary Africa, where the black man desires the white woman; but the real object of our desire does not exist there — he does not exist. At a distance, a man suffers the woman's degradations; he waits in her bedroom, he handles her clothes, he serves her at table, he plays father to her daughter, and now with her gaze, she asks for his body.

182

Susan Sontag wrote that "Europe seeks itself in the exotic" (1966: 69). France seeks herself in an image of Africa, which she imagines like a spring, the source of herself, her identity as *pied noir*. Bathed in these exotic waters, France cannot shed the scent of Africa. The place adheres to her, proclaiming her difference. Emily Apter explains this mutual attraction as a derivation of European fetishism:

> Just as throwing African statues and masks in with the china and *tchotchkes* of bourgeois curiosity cabinets had the effect of rubbing some of their exoticist aura off onto Western *objets d'art*, so the European literary imagination increasingly found itself attracted to a defamiliarizing Africanist idyll, whereby Europe made itself strange to itself. Africa was seen as prelinguistic, prerational, unskeptical, its "signs" naive in their simplicity and mediated by sensualism (1993: 6).

Claire Denis's interiors, the wide veranda and the spare, furnished rooms, frame and expose the spatial configuration of Aimée and Protée, how they move, what they see and feel. The natural intimacy of the house changes with Denis's careful, static compositions. Minimal use of shot/reverse shot prevents the viewer from taking a constant position. Even the fetishization attached to Aimée's gaze can be attributed to France's. France repeats her mother's narrative. Both women want intercourse with Africa, but the Africans refuse them.

So *Chocolat* is not about Africa. It is not even about the French colony that existed there for a span of fifty years. It expresses, in its visual style, a whole set of ideas about (post) colonialism. Can one have a national identity divorced from the national terrain? Is it possible for a culture to be transplanted from one location to another? Claire Denis attempts to define identity as an experiential relation to place, yet ultimately she abandons the possibility of a reconciliation. Aimée's proximity to the land depended on a distancing of its inhabitants from herself, so that they existed within her picture. Even France cannot transcend her parents' visions, but only recreates versions of their stories. She cannot exist there as an African, although she is *pied noir*; for, attached to her identity, France vies with Africa for ascendance. Denis returns us to an identity of landscapes.

Decadent Messiah

It is appropriate that my final words on this matter should concern the apocalyptic narrative of *Coup de torchon*. In the establishing sequence of the film, Cordier lit a fire during an eclipse of the sun. Throughout the entire movie, this decadent messiah burns a path to the end of the world. Tavernier depicts a society on the verge of collapse. Its members are completely corrupt. The first scenes of the film reveal incest, wife-beating, desecration, and anarchy among the French. Huguette constantly inquires when the war is coming. Ironically, the Second World War does signal the end of colonialism as the European empires disintegrate. Only Cordier remains aloof, forming a plan. He reveals that he is Jesus Christ, ridding the world of its garbage. A series of murders gradually reduces the population; others are merely humiliated. Cordier spares one woman, a teacher, whom he perceives as different. He imagines that he can make a clean start for the world. Yet Tavernier denies the viewer a visual spectacle of mythical dimensions. The colors of the mise-en-scène are completely atypical of the colonial period genre. Cordier's house is painted electric blue. No one wears white clothes, but all wallow in filth and degradation. The view into the latrine below Cordier's balcony becomes a recurring image in the film, and the site of a struggle for power among the French colonials.

French culture could not be transplanted to African soil and the clash of cultures is obvious in the mise-en-scène. But in Cordier's imagination, *Africa has done this to France*. The mystique of place is conjured as the explanation for an apocalypse. The Africans themselves are only documentary evidence, playing virtually no role in Cordier's machinations. They are static — Lévi-Strauss's cold society — and without historical consciousness. Therefore, they will not be susceptible to apocalypse. France, which has taken responsibility for history, will pay for its sins alone.

In all of these postcolonial representations of the colonial period, there is a strong tendency to revert to familiar aesthetic and cognitive patterns — an imaginary geography which still locates identity in the landscape or power relations figured in the tales of travelers. All seem to be ironically aware of their own nostalgia (even Tavernier's film foregrounds the experience of loss in the form of the Kurtz narrative) or reactionary position. It is from this precarious position that each of these postmodern directors criticizes the colonial narrative and at the same time displays that which made it so appealing and sustaining for more than five hundred years. Even as these fantasies break down in *Coup de torchon*, and narratives of expectation fail to transform either the character or his destination, a strong impression prevails that the world will end like this because nothing has arisen which could possibly take their place. The postmodern travel cinema does not invent new forms, but merely falls back upon stock figures.

REFERENCES

Apter, Emily. 1993. "Introduction." *Fetishism as Cultural Discourse*, ed. Emily Apter and William Pietz. Ithaca: Cornell University Press.

Bhabha, Homi. 1984. "Of Mimicry and Man: The Ambivalence of Colonial Discourse." *October* 28: 125-133.

Conrad, Joseph. 1963. *Heart of Darkness*. New York: W. W. Norton.

Fanon, Frantz. 1965. *A Dying Colonialism*. New York: Grove Weidenfeld.

Gide, André. 1929. *Travels in the Congo*, trans. Dorothy Bussy. New York: Knopf.

Leiris, Michel. 1989. *Brisées: Broken Branches*, trans. Lydia Davis. San Francisco: North Point Press.

Mitchell, W. J. T. 1994. "Imperial Landscape." *Landscape and Power*, ed. W. J. T. Mitchell. Chicago: University of Chicago Press.

Montaigne, Michel de. 1957. "Of Cannibals." *The Complete Essays of Montaigne*, trans. Donald M. Frame. Stanford, CA: Stanford University Press.

Pratt, Mary Louise. 1992. *Imperial Eyes: Travel Writing and Transculturation*. London: Routledge.

Said, Edward W. 1993. *Culture and Imperialism*. New York: Knopf.

———— 1979. *Orientalism*. New York: Vintage.

Sontag, Susan. 1966. "The Anthropologist as Hero." *Against Interpretation and Other Essays*. New York: Doubleday.

Torgovnick, Marianna. 1990. *Gone Primitive: Savage Intellects, Modern Lives*. Chicago: University of Chicago Press.

Vico, Giambattista. 1968. *The New Science of Giambattista Vico* (1884), third ed., trans. Thomas G. Bergin and Max H. Fisch. Ithaca, NY: Cornell University Press.

NOTES

1. Said's extensive discussion of Joseph Conrad, André Gide, and others in Africa in *Culture and Imperialism* (1993) underlies much of my thinking on Africanist discourse throughout this essay.

2. This term is offered by Mary Louise Pratt in *Imperial Eyes* (1992) as a way to talk about the spaces of colonial encounters, where there is sustained contact between the conquerors and the conquered.

3. Only one written source refers to the original title *La Victoire en chantant*; the movie seems to have been widely released in 1976 as *Black and White in Color*.

Barton Fink *(20th Century Fox, 1991) Joel Coen*
Chatty travelling insurance salesman Charlie (John Goodman) who lives next door is one
of the inhabitants of Barton Fink's (John Turturro) chaos. Still courtesy of Jerry Ohlinger's
Movie Materials.

CHAPTER 10

DECAPITATED SPECTATORS

Barton Fink, (Post)History, and Cinematic Pleasure

Barry Laga

In the last scene of *Barton Fink*, Barton can but sit on the beach with his tidy little box, apparently unwilling or unable to see what it contains. That box implies that there is no innocent knowledge to be had; whatever Barton discovers in it will necessarily taint his supposed innocence, especially if it contains Audry's head. The woman's question, "What's in the box?" verbalizes our own curiosity and suggests an impulse and desire to achieve closure, resolve dissonance, fold back any exclusion upon the body of the film.

This impulse for closure combined with the film's preoccupation with wrestling is reminiscent of Roland Barthes's essay on amateur wrestling, certainly insofar as the film's action centers on a writer's inability to write a formulaic wrestling picture. Barthes argues that wrestling is a spectacle that serves a social function, namely, to repeat a narrative or myth that is important in some way to a social system's very stability, reducing anxiety by explaining away contradictions or providing a way of living with the contradictions so that they do not become too disruptive. Wrestling becomes a kind of "resolution of dissonance." The sign must contain its own meaning, and if meaning does proliferate, it must then fold back upon itself, thus illuminating the spectacle even more clearly. Therefore, the wrestler's object is not to win, but to fulfill a role, for "it is to go exactly through the motions which are expected of him" (1972: 16). The wrestler makes excessive gestures and postures, guaranteeing that the sign is endowed with "absolute clarity"; there is no ambiguity in wrestling. Importantly, "what the public wants is the image of passion, not passion itself," not actual suffering, but the image of suffering. It is the form, the gesture, the exterior sign, the iconography that counts. Pleasure, then, comes from "seeing the moral mechanism function so perfectly" (1972: 18). The spectacle of wrestling, then, fulfills a set of expectations, and in the fulfillment creates a kind of pleasure, reproduces the social and moral order, and reinforces the very expectations it later fulfills. The result is a process of cyclical legitimization in which the artificial takes on a common-sensical, it-goes-without-saying, naturalized status.

The Coens seem keenly aware of this concept, and their film at first seems to employ the postmodern strategy that seeks to contest and parody the desire for closure in an effort to defamiliarize and implicate us in the illusion: we never do know what is in that carefully wrapped brown box. But what is constantly parodied in *Barton Fink* is not some amorphous, generalized concept of the real, but a specific moment from the past, 1941, and specific locations, New York and Hollywood. The film also asks specific questions: How did anti-Semitism play itself out in America during a heightened period of racism and xenophobia? Who embraced fascism? Why did not Americans, particularly leftist intellectuals, recognize these fascists? What role did theaters and film-making industries play during this period? *Barton Fink*, then, is not so much a reflection on a moment in time or even a representation of an era, but a postmodern reworking of history.

Articulating a postmodern poetics, Linda Hutcheon argues that

> parody is a perfect postmodernist form in some senses, for it paradoxically both incorporates and challenges that which it parodies. It also forces a reconsideration of the idea of origin or originality that is compatible with other postmodernist interrogations of liberal humanist assumptions. (1987: 17)

Hutcheon goes on to point out that postmodernism does not deny the *existence* of the past; it does question whether we can ever *know* that past other than through its textualized remains. Parody, then, functions as a mode of resistance in its ability to exploit and contest that which came before. To be more precise, parody involves a kind of dialogic doubling in which a parodic text "simultaneously destabilizes and inscribes the dominant ideology through its almost overly self-conscious 'interpellation' of the spectator as subject in and of ideology" (1990: 125). The result is not a mere nostalgic escapism, but an utter obsession with history, politics, and epistemology, for parody encourages the spectator to "accept responsibility for the fact that he or she *makes* meaning and is therefore, as Brecht saw, the only possible locus of social change through art" (1990: 130). *Barton Fink* is doubly encoded throughout, forcing us to question the real/reel, to interrogate the way we conceptualize the real/reel. The result is a dissonance that will not go away, that cannot be resolved.

But the celebration of postmodernism's challenging of the historical referent is highly problematic and suspicious for many theorists, for the obsession with epistemology is often seen as a way to trivialize and evade historical determinants. For example, Huyssen argues that the

> problem with postmodernism is that it relegates history to the dustbin of an obsolete *episteme*, arguing gleefully that history does not exist except as text, i.e., as historiography. Of course, if the 'referent' of historiography, that which historians write *about*, is eliminated, then history is up for grabs — or, to put in more trendy words, up for 'strong misreadings' (1986: 229).

Huyssen is not alone, of course, for many flinch at postmodern critiques of historical knowledge. Jameson's highly influential "Postmodernism, or, the Cultural Logic of Late Capitalism" (essay and book) and "Postmodernism and Consumer Society" take the position that "the past as 'referent' finds itself gradually bracketed, and then effaced altogether, leaving us with nothing but texts" (1991: 18). Jameson describes this situation as a "crisis of history," for there is no longer any "organic relationship" between what we read and what we experience. As a result, the postmodern historical text "can no longer set out to represent the historical past; it can only 'represent' our ideas and stereotypes about that past...." We are left then to "seek History by way of our own pop images and simulacra of that history, which itself remains forever out of reach" (1991: 25).

But this general wariness of the present status of history misdirects us to a degree, perhaps revealing a nostalgic yearning for a prelapsarian state rather than providing us with a useful framework; for the issue is no longer between "having" or "not having" access to the historical referent, but is between various forms of historical representation that are part of a larger web of intersections which include political, ideological, aesthetic, psychological, and cultural forces. The question is not, "is history obsolete?" or even "what is the most productive or emancipatory conception of history?" but instead, "in what ways do desire and ideology structure our conceptions of history?" or "in what ways are desire, identity, and enjoyment sewn together in different forms of historical representation?"

What I need to stress is that while the past has never been eliminated, different conceptualizations of that past have been made philosophically dubious, thus giving the impression that dealing with "history" is impossible and therefore a pointless affair. Jameson and Huyssen are right in that we are left only with texts, but it is not as though we can go back to a point where there was an organic relationship between text and history. There is not and there never has been a directly and unproblematically accessible past for us, but there are attempts to negotiate and make sense of our past, for we have to live with the historical signs imposed upon us. It is how we go about this process of negotiation that matters and should be the focus of our attention.

As a text that attempts to make sense of the past within a postmodern perspective, *Barton Fink* provides us with what I would call "(post)history." That is, (post)history (and its adjective, (post)historical) is less a state, period, or moment, than a cultural/political practice by which a certain social intelligibility is produced. (Post)history embodies a mode of perception and a form of representation that undermines the very conventions of history which insist on structures of significance or metanarratives. (Post)history in part redefines time as a function of position, reconceptualizing temporality in that "essence or identity is multiplied because it is always *situated*, and where the situation is always discursive, which is to say always constructed by systems of signs whose function is differential" (Ermath 1992: 11). Put in simpler terms, (post)history could be described as an attempt to acknowledge the full weight of the "crisis of history" in that it positions the subject psychologically, morally, and culturally within specific discursive formations. At its bare minimum, (post)history attempts to fully recognize the complicity of the "I" who is keenly aware that it is not outside looking in, but inside looking around, thus constituting and being constituted by what it sees and what sees it.

While many texts, particularly postmodern ones, engage history in this way, it is the attempt to maintain a certain degree of presence while simultaneously undermining its very possibility that invokes projects taken up by oppressed and marginalized peoples that characterizes (post)history. A (post)historical text attempts to create a space for itself as it negotiates the need to dismantle *and* establish a "history" that could be read as an attempt to establish a provisional system or frame of intelligibility. Jane Caplan points out that discussions of historical events are often caught up in a dualistic metaphysics. What she calls the "derealist" position attempts to mythify the past by making it a "transhistorical event whose real meaning may perhaps only be appropriate in its fullest sense by those who are said to have participated in it," whereas the "hyperrealist" seeks to resist this dehistoricization by fixing explanations of the past in "textual sources and readings that are as precise and incontrovertible as possible..." (1989: 277). Both approaches ultimately share the desire to "*fix* past events" in interpretive or causal terms. (Post)historical representation attempts to do both and neither. On the one hand, a (post)historical text insists on a narrative form that becomes the apparent core of a historical account, often using countless books, photographs, testimonies, and personal visits to fill the gaps and ground the narrative in concrete sources, while on the other hand the text simultaneously foregrounds the inability to fully represent the experience by stressing that all accounts are contaminated, skewed, and infinitely inaccessible.

In its specific engagement with the past, *Barton Fink*, as Hutcheon says of other postmodern texts, self-consciously enacts the "metalinguistic contradiction of being inside and outside, complicitous and distanced, inscribing and contesting its own provisional formulations" (1987: 26). *Barton Fink* begins its engagement with the past by indicting the lack of vision held by leftist artists and intellectuals in 1941. Barton, who leaves New York for Hollywood, feels out of touch with the "common man" whom he pretends to represent, is shocked into reality, and finally writes his greatest work ever which Lipnick rejects as "fruity." Barton invokes the familiar by becoming a typical modernist who seeks integration amid fragmentation, in particular, by focusing on the self located in the psyche. He is afloat in a seemingly chaotic world, and his identity is threatened at every turn. He is in a kind of filmic *Wasteland*, and like a good modernist, Barton turns to art as a final retreat, a last source of reason, stability, and harmony against the peeling walls, burning hallway, dripping ears, and murdered lovers. This glorification of the mind is more than evident when Barton records what almost seems to be his dream — his inner self — and as a result, produces a great work of art that the "monsters" at the USO dance, the "filthy" police officers, and the monomaniac Lipnick cannot comprehend or appreciate. Barton sees himself as an artist who has tried to show us "something beautiful, about

191

all of us," who wants to "forge something real out of everyday experience," presenting the "hopes and dreams of the common man" that are as "noble as any king. The stuff of life...," but he is rejected by the uncomprehending masses. Barton presents himself as the philosopher-poet who has a special relation to the true or the real. Barton wants to play this foundational role, the privileged representative of the real, for this position would then allow Barton to, presumably, reconcile knowledge and power. Throughout all this, however, we recognize Barton as a fraud, as a mere "tourist with a typewriter" who does not listen to or understand the "common man." As Audry tries to teach Barton, empathy comes from understanding, and Barton feigns both.

The figure of Barton Fink invokes many other subtexts, thus reinforcing the postmodern notion that subjectivities, a mere composite of figures, are always already inauthentic and unoriginal. For example, many viewers see the parodic image of Clifford Odets in Fink, for both playwrights involve themselves in the formation of a leftist theater, have their play performed in the same theater, go to Hollywood. Both "fink" in the sense that Odets was a willing witness at the House hearings on Un-American Activities, and Barton betrays the very group of people he claims to represent. But Barton is not just a mirror image of Odets; he also reminds us of Elia Kazan who "finked" on others in Hollywood and most notably played a character based on his own actions in an Arthur Miller play. In fact, Barton invokes Arthur Miller more directly, for Miller wrote, of course, *Death of a Salesman* and "Tragedy and the Common Man," whose terminology and images remind us of Fink's own political declarations. We have Barton's "the hopes and dreams of the common man are as noble as any king" and we have Miller's "the common man is as apt a subject for tragedy in its highest sense as kings were." While Charlie is no Willie Loman in that Willie is crushed by threatening forces and Charlie decapitates those who annoy or insult him, the underlying theme of the unappreciated salesman struggling to attain the American Dream is nevertheless present yet reworked.

Importantly, this notion of rewriting rather than original creation *ex nihilo* is part of the parodic intertextuality that surfaces throughout the film but it too affirms the film itself as an inauthentic compilation. The Coens draw attention to this very process, for the film invokes, as mentioned earlier, a host of other figures. Yes, we have Odets, Miller, Kazan, and Faulkner, but we also get images of such diverse texts as the mythical Maenads, the films *The Shining* and Fellini's *8 ½*, the books of Genesis and Daniel in the Old Testament, Faustus, the Holocaust, and "historical" figures such as Cornell Woolrich, Harry Cohn, Louis B. Mayer, Nathanael West, Orson Welles, and Roland Barthes. The point of this often not-so-subtle intertextuality is multifold. By being so intertextual, the film reinforces the notion that all texts are dependent on and infiltrated by prior concepts, figures, codes, unconscious practices, conventions, and texts. As a result, a search for origins, a search for a definitive signature, only amounts to an endless search into a textual abyss.

A more important effect of this postmodern collage/montage of texts (what Jameson calls "cannibalization") is that each cited element

> breaks the continuity or the linearity of the discourse and leads necessarily to a double reading: that of the fragment perceived in relation to its text of origin; that of the same fragment as incorporated into a new whole, a different totality (Group *Mu*, cited in Ulmer 1983: 88).

The result is an "undecidable reading effect, oscillating between presence and absence..." (1983: 88). This oscillation runs counter to a history of logocentrism which attempts to pin down and fix a specific signified to a given signifier, for the sign becomes repeatable, iterable, or imitable in that "it can break with every given context, engendering an infinity of new contexts in a manner which is absolutely illimitable" (Derrida 1990: 12). Importantly, the working assumption of collage's procedure of direct, massive citation, is that repetition is "originary." The Coens' method mirrors Derrida's in the desire to superimpose one text on another in an attempt to "devise a system of reference or representation which works in terms of *différance*, with its reversible temporality, rather than in terms of the irreversible time of the sign" (Ulmer 1983: 93). This playing with temporality accounts for the postmodern collapsing of space and time in *Barton Fink*. Thus, the film is able to assemble on a single plane a host of figures, events, and time periods.

The Coens, then, loosen up history, presenting it as a collection of fragments in order to make larger psychological and political connections. We could see *Barton Fink* as a kind of machine that couples, regulates, or codifies fragments and partial objects in unexpected but politically charged ways. Spivak helps to clarify this move by explaining that the entire socius (the combination of social text and consciousness) is a "continuous sign-chain" (1988: 198). Here she aptly points out that "the possibility of action lies in the dynamics of the disruption of this object, the breaking and relinking of the chain." Signs may not have fixed referents, but rearranging or relinking signs may confer on the Coens a new kind of political power. With the freedom that cinema affords, they are able to intersect and conflate images and events more readily, thus illustrating possible relationships between leftist intellectuals, fascists, the Holocaust, Biblical history, and the Hollywood film industry. *Barton Fink* may show that connections and narratives are mere constructions motivated by paranoid desires, for consciousness is not set "over against the socius, but sees it as itself also constituted as and on a semiotic chain" (1988: 198), but it simultaneously suggests that the fabrications may be no less real or significant. The paranoid may feel that everything is connected, but it does not mean that the paranoid is mistaken.

While *Barton Fink* is relentless in its attempt to parody and subvert authorship, identity, and the filmic production of reality, the film simultaneously attempts to offer a new form of realism and identity. That is, *Barton Fink* enacts what Deleuze calls a new kind of image: "Making-false becomes the sign of a new realism, in opposition to the making-true of the old" (1986: 213). Deleuze cites Eustache who "makes a character in *La Maman et la putain* say, 'The more you appear false like that, the farther you go, the false is the beyond.' Under this power of the false all images become clichés, sometimes because their clumsiness is shown, sometimes because their apparent perfection is attacked" (1986: 214). Deleuze wonders whether or not this type of image will only remain a cinema of parody or contempt, but inauthenticity may be yet another strategy to establish a contingent identity and create a floating foundation for artistic production. Rather than conceptualizing the relationship in terms of a parasitic economy in which the parasite exploits the host (i.e., the critic's relationship to the artist, the collage to the "originals," Barton to Audry and Charlie), we should perhaps frame the relationship more symbiotically. For example, Greg Ulmer (1983: 105) points out through his discussion of John Cage and mushrooms that

> these fungi are not parasites, but *saprophytes* (any organism that lives on dead organic matter), and exist in a symbiotic, mutually beneficial relationship with their hosts (the green plants and trees which supply the organic 'food').

Ulmer goes on to point out that this symbiotic ecology is a version of what Benjamin was talking about when he compared allegory to ruins, for "it could be said that the saprophyte, living off the decay of dead organisms is a way that makes life possible for living plants, is to nature what the ruin is to culture, or the allegory to thought" (1983: 105-106).

This notion of saprophytes helps us to understand postmodern culture in general, for postmodernism is often characterized by the constant pillaging, reactivating, and reworking of old myths, figures, types, etc. But it also applies to Barton Fink the playwright and *Barton Fink* the film, for both are saprophytes in this sense, since both feed off dead matter. This is not to valorize or even trivialize exploitation, but simply to recognize and map the inevitable exploitation that takes place. There is no innocent ground, just as there is no original text. Artistic production takes place, in Theweleit's terms, as a product of masculine, Orphic creation: as with Orpheus, Barton feels ashamed at outliving "his beloved," whom he was not able to keep among the living. As Theweleit points out, "It is the shame of still being in possession of this beautiful voice, while the most beautiful creature, to whom he was singing, is now dead" (1985: 140). Importantly, the dead woman's absence is the basis for aesthetic production, for the work attempts to make the absence present, to transform the dead body "into the beauty of the poem; to reshape it there; to make loving words of great intensity out of the flesh of the vanished..." (1985: 156). What a postmodern/ (post)historical film like *Barton Fink* provides, then, is a disturbing illustration of the creative process. At this point the question to ask is not so much "how can I quit exploiting?" (i.e., how can I quit writing?) but "whom am I exploiting? Who is exploiting me? Under what terms? For whose gain? At what price?" As we see in *Barton Fink*, Barton's creative explosion occurs at the price of Audry's dead body; she is the repressed "well-spring of success." But Barton is exploited as well, for the "contents of his head are the property of Capital Pictures."

The process of repression, then, is part and parcel with aesthetic production, a point Žižek makes clear when he points out that "reality itself is nothing but an embodiment of a certain blockage in the process of symbolization" (1991: 45). This observation is particularly insightful in light of Barton's central problem — he has writer's block. That is, Barton is unable to assimilate, integrate, or symbolize the real, and as a result, he fails to write his screenplay. From the moment the worker/actor lowers the boom in the first scene, Barton embarks on a journey that finds him anything but integrated and whole. The film, like many other postmodern texts, becomes a reverse *künstlerroman*, for instead of tracing the development of an artist, the film traces Barton's fragmentation and disintegration. Barton is unable to give the chaotic, meaningless world around him a form. In other words, Barton is unable to give consistency to his being, and this act, as Žižek tells us, is "the way we — the subjects

— 'avoid madness,' the way we 'choose something ... instead of nothing' ... through the binding of our enjoyment to a certain signifying, symbolic formation which assures a minimum of consistency to our being-in-the-world" (1989: 75). That is, our very identity, the coherence of the "I," is created by the symptom as a signifying formation or network. It is the element that gives consistency to our being. We literally have nothing without a symptom. We see this clearly in Barton; he feels as though he is "losing his mind" because he is losing his ability to symbolize the real around him. Barton's identity as a writer and as a sane human is in jeopardy.

This blockage, which is really an *inability to block* the onslaught of the real, is embodied in the Hotel Earle, for Barton is surrounded by images of dismemberment: we have, of course, the literal dismemberment of bodies, but we also sense the decay in the hotel atmosphere, the "deco-gone-to-seed," and we see vacuous hallways filled only with empty shoes. His room, with two windows that function as eyes (albeit closed and shaded), suggests a disturbed psyche. Thumbtacks are used to keep wallpaper in place whose melted yellow paste reminds us of the dripping pus in Charlie's ear which he tries to block with cotton. There are corroded pipes, trapdoors, thin walls, faded stationary, and blood-sucking mosquitoes. Everywhere we look we see evidence of decay and fragmentation. Barton is losing his mind to the degree that he cannot give shape to or contain the real, or better yet, Barton is losing his mind to the degree that he cannot make sense of the "common man's" psyche which he now inhabits.

Just as Barton cannot stop the pus-like paste, Barton's inability to contain the real attests to its resisting nature. This failure to symbolize the Other makes sense, for Žižek points out that the attempt to suture the gap in an effort to include it in the regular circuit of life is a vain and impossible attempt, for the real "makes a sudden appearance in the symbolic order, in the form of traumatic 'returns' and 'answers'" (1991: 39). The real is uncontainable, and the images of dismemberment and the various forms of excess — the dripping wallpaper, oozing ears, incessant waves, extraordinary heat, seemingly endless blood, cadavers, well-wrapped packages — all attest to the failure to totalize the real, to fully colonize the Other.

The most disturbing example of Barton's inability to suture all gaps occurs when he confronts the "common man's" image of women. Audry drops by Barton's hotel room to help him with his screenplay, and Audry eventually seduces him. What follows is somewhat surreal, invoked by a slow pan and tracking shot which takes us down Barton and Audry's legs, across an old chair, to the bathroom, and down into a vaginal-like pipe where heavy breathing turns to moaning, suggesting at once an anxiety-filled return to the womb but also a degrading and polluting sexual experience, for the vaginal pipe is corroded and eventually filled with screams. What Barton confronts here is the feminine as his common-man fascist sees her — as a loathsome bloody object bent on destroying men. Even though Charlie enjoys his porno-tie and cannot complain about the "dames," women are for him domesticating forces who demand more than they give. Strangely enough, we get the impression that Charlie kills Audry (we assume he kills her, given the pattern, but we never know for sure — yet another ambiguity in the film) as an act of "kindness," for we learn later that Charlie feels sorry for men who are trapped by women: "Yeah. It tears me up inside, to think about what they're going through. How trapped they are. I understand. I feel for 'em. So I try to help them out...."

Saturated with the real, Barton is paralyzed for a while until Charlie and Lipnick encourage him to repress his anxieties by "putting out of his mind" events that disturb him. Insulating himself in his room, Barton is finally able to begin the process of symbolization, filling up pages non-stop. When Barton does finally complete his "large work," he can only do so by shutting out the real, exemplified by Barton's wearing of ear plugs as he writes his master work. Repressing the real allows Barton to write, but it is unclear whether or not Barton's screenplay "The Burlyman" is a mere repetition of his play, *Bare Ruined Choirs: Triumph of the Common Man* (for we hear the echoes of the play as the screenplay's words become audible and the last couple lines are the same) or whether the play is a product of "dream-work," suggested by the passage Barton reads in Daniel:

> And the King, Nebuchadnezzar, answered, and said to the Chaldeans, I recall not my dream; if ye will not make known unto me my dream, and its interpretation, ye shall be cut in pieces, and of your tents shall be made a dunghill.

Is Barton's screenplay a transformation of his latent dream into an acceptable form or is it an interpretation of Nebuchadnezzar's/Charlie's "dream," an act that ultimately saves Barton's head? In either case, what is interesting is that Lipnick rejects the screenplay as a "fruity movie about suffering." The film should have been about "big men, in tights — both physically and mentally. But especially physically," thus coding suffering and "wrestling with one's soul" as feminine.

197

As a way of briefly summarizing and framing my own narrativizing of the Coens' work, we could say that *Barton Fink* exemplifies a postmodern aesthetic in its relentless parodic gestures that attempt to interrogate humanist assumptions concerning originality, authorship, history, and the real. The film crosses a multitude of boundaries, not only in terms of time and space, but also in the merging of the historical and the fictive, the comic and the tragic, and ultimately of the image and the real, most evident in the final scene when Barton invades the image hanging on his wall, simultaneously implying that the real has interrupted the glossy image as well as suggesting that the frame of the image has enlarged, assimilating Barton into the simulation itself. Given these gestures, the film's function appears to be demystification, for we can find residues of Brecht throughout, for *Barton Fink* uncovers or exposes the present in a Brechtian-like presentation, exposing conditions by interrupting and foregrounding the dramatic process. Much like epic theater, *Barton Fink*, as a filmic social-critiquing machine, estranges the visual by its explicit "striptease" of the social body, stripping the costumes and props that decorate and disguise it. However, it is not so much a striptease as a fashion show, for it highlights the costumes and props decorating and disguising the body we never have access to.

This reading, however, is not without its limitations. Despite the film's unrelenting gestures toward demystification, Žižek points out that deconstructing or unmasking the very unity of experience or meaning by revealing it to be the effect of signifying mechanisms may be ultimately a modernist procedure par excellence. In another register, Shaviro observes that Brechtian techniques have a different impact when they are transferred from the stage to the screen, for "the modernist critical paradigm regards involvement or fascination as a state of ideological mystification, and employs the alienation effect as a tool to undo this state" (1993: 163). He maintains that we would be naive to think we can

> somehow free ourselves from illusion (or from ideology) by recognizing and theorizing our own entrapment within it. Such dialectical maneuvers tend, ironically, to reinforce the very objects of their critique. They achieve their explanatory power at the price of transforming local, contingent phenomena into transcendental conditions or developmental necessities (1993: 11-12).

The problem with postmodern theories of parody, self-reflexivity, and alienation-effects is that we tend to equate "passion, fascination, and enjoyment with mystification..." (1993: 14). It reveals a panic at the prospect of being affected and moved by images. Moreover, this line of reasoning assumes that visual pleasure depends on a stable and centered subject and that editing sutures the spectator and perspectivizes the gaze. What this position denies is that "a wide variety of cinematic pleasures are predicated explicitly upon the decentered freeplay, the freedom from the constraints of subjectivity, that editing and special effects make possible." In fact, spectators are often delighted when there is narrative discontinuity, impossible points of view, and implausible temporal and spatial arrangements. As Shaviro reminds us, foregrounding constructedness has been part and parcel of the film industry's history. There is nothing radical per se in self-reflexive gestures. To the contrary, distancing and alienation-effects serve to "intensify the captivating power of cinematic spectacle" (1993: 42-43).

Shaviro argues that "in film's virtual space, visual pleasure and fascination are emphatically *not* dependent upon any illusion of naturalness or presence." To the contrary,

> in the cinematic apparatus, vision is uprooted from the idealized paradigms of representation and perspective, and dislodged from interiority. It is grounded instead in the rhythms and delays of an ungraspable temporality, and in the materiality of the agitated flesh (1993: 44-45).

Shaviro describes how filmic images essentially attack the spectator in such a way that one is affected before one can reflect or respond. We are touched and altered by images before we have had a chance to become conscious of them. Consequently, cinema "involves the violation of presence and the irreversible alienation of the viewer." In its disruptive play of immediacy and distance, film "enacts, again and again, what Bataille calls the sacrifice of the sacred (auratic) object, or what Benjamin calls the disintegration of the aura in the experience of shock" (Shaviro 1993: 46). One effect of this disintegration is that as viewing subjects, we cannot objectify things and people because we do not ever gain distance from them, for the distance "between subject and object is at once abolished and rendered infinite" (47). As long as we stare at the screen, our responses are not "internally motivated and are not spontaneous; they are forced upon me from beyond" (49). Cinema is strictly material, then, for the images are less phantasmic reflections *to* the viewer as much as real effects *in* the viewer. What Shaviro proposes, then, is that we ask different questions of cinema. Rather than positing a Barthesian (Hutcheonian and even Lacanian) viewing subject who desires possession, plenitude, closure, stability, and reassurance, Shaviro suggests that we ask: "What effects and passions are constructed or expressed by the mechanisms of cinema?" It is only at this point that we will understand the subversive workings of this postmodern film.

Seen in this way, *Barton Fink*'s reproduction of 1941 New York/Hollywood is less a subversive parodic representation than a "tactile convergence" that stimulates the nervous system and invests social power relations. The film exemplifies what Shaviro says of all films in that it affirms raw sensation, provokes visceral excitation, and "hyperbolically aggravates vision, pushing it to an extreme point of implosion and self-annihilation" (1993: 55). *Barton Fink* is less concerned with believability than with our immediate response. The film accomplishes this end by affirming the spectator's desire for *inauthenticity* and by affirming the spectator's *masochistic* pleasure which is derived from submission rather than control.

The parody of Barton as committed leftist and writer now takes on added significance. Rather than simultaneously exploiting and contesting that which went before, *à la* Hutcheon model, the loss of control, fragmentation, abjection, and subversion of self-identity work to excite and seduce us. Rather than being disgusted by Barton's inauthenticity, we revel in it. Rather than maintaining fixed boundaries, we seek to dissolve them. In disabling our ability to process and control its "meanings," *Barton Fink* affirms our masochistic pleasure. That is, rather than avoiding films which produce anxiety, we seek them out, for "fearfulness is itself a thrill and a powerful turn-on..." (1993: 56). The masochist

seeks not to reach a final consumption, but to hold it off, to prolong the frenzy, for as long as possible. Cinema seduces its viewers by mimetically exacerbating erotic tension, in an orgy of unproductive expenditure. Visual fascination is a direct consequence of this masochistic heightening, rather than any secondary movements of suturing and satiation (1993: 57).

It is, then, loss of control, fragmentation, abjection, and subversion of self-identity that excites and seduces us. The body is active and affirmative to the extent that "it does not merely seek to preserve and capitalize itself, but expends and actualizes its capacity to the maximum" (60). As a result, the body is masochistic in that it has a passion for "disequilibrium and disappropriation" (60). The cinematic body does not derive pleasure from mastering or containing the real, but from embracing the real, from pushing itself to its limits, from desiring its own extremity.

Barton Fink, then, has a great deal in common with a film like *Un chien andalou*. Much like the razor which slits the eyeball in an attempt to "extinguish the power of sight" (55) and dispossess the spectator, *Barton Fink* attempts to decapitate its spectators, thus preventing the mind from reflecting on, making sense of, or logically processing the images. The film's principle strategy is, perhaps, overdetermination. The Coens invest an image with so much "meaning" that the image ceases to function as a referential object. Filmed objects become nothing but images that solicit our attention. As Shaviro says of a couple of Godard films, "our gaze is suspended; we are compelled merely to regard these images, in their strangeness, apart from our knowledge of what they represent" (1993: 30). For example, the drain pipe scene invokes, as mentioned earlier, the vagina, birth canal, polluted sex, and anal entry, but Charlie also mentions that he can hear people having sex "through the pipes or something." The corroded pipe reminds us of Charlie's infected ear, and the vacant hallway, the jazz musician's trumpet which we also penetrate, and the mixing of the euphoric moaning and screaming Barton hears in Charlie's room when he first arrives and later when he listens to the couple having sex next door. The connections are excessive, but rather than fleeing from the excess, we are drawn toward it, thrilled by it, and fascinated by it even as we are baffled by it. The waves, the cry of seagulls, the mosquitoes, the mysterious box, the altered Gidean Bible, and the mezzotint are all examples of this excessive signification, for it is ultimately impossible to assimilate all these disparate elements. Meaning is not reduced as much as expanded, disseminated, and defamiliarized. The images ultimately exemplify Baudrillardian seduction, for they do not show anything, but merely demand to be seen. Or, as Shaviro says of *Querelle*, the images are "so hyperbolically visible, so flat and vacuous, so aggressively superficial and stereotypical, that they develop a violently intensive force" (1993: 167). Their explicitness and heavy-handedness arrest the action because they do not refer to other objects; they become intense images in and of themselves. This "frozen quality" or suspension of gestures is, as Deleuze (1991) asserts in his analysis of Sacher-Masoch, certainly part of the waiting and the suffering which are preconditions for masochistic pleasure.

The seductiveness of images and the pleasure that we derive is part of the thematic content of the film, exemplified by Charlie's punning of the phrase "peace of mind." The cliché is multivalent: it suggests solace and comfort, but also functions metonymically, as in a piece is a mere part of something else. Most importantly, there is the sexual association, as in "I got a piece last night." "Piece of mind" refers to a sense of well-being, of course, but also to the decapitated heads and to a kind of violation/rape of the mind, a structuring metaphor that governs the entire film. Charlie does not want a "piece of ass" as much as "piece of mind," both of which are ultimately equated with each other. But the pun also refers to the larger sense of the film, for the film is about "piece/peace of minds" — a pleasurable violation of the mind. Gaylyn Studlar (1992) points out that

> the repetition of loss, of suffering, does not deter or confuse masochistic desire but inflames it.... The eternal masochistic attitude of waiting and suspended suffering is maintained in all its tragedy and comic absurdity to the very end..." (781).

As spectators, we are immobile, passive subjects, submitting ourselves to the images which cannot be controlled, with the unknown contents of the mysterious box perpetuating our pleasure. Knowing the contents of the box may fulfill our desire, for it is analogous to achieving orgasm, but to achieve orgasm means death, as Audry's cadaver so testifies. Studlar clarifies this relationship by pointing out that "masochistic desire depends on separation to guarantee the structure of its ambivalent desire" (1992: 785) whereas sadism depends upon mastery and gratification. We never see into the box, just as we never really find out who killed Audry and the other victims. *Barton Fink* always defers fulfillment.

In sum, *Barton Fink* does not require a spectator to have a knowledge of its parodic subtext or an awareness of its fragmented composition. The film as an assemblage of images offers what Shaviro says of all cinema: "a Bataillean ecstasy of expenditure, of automutilation and self-abandonment...." Shaviro explains that

> In affirming raw sensation, in communicating the violent contents of visual excitation apart from its pacifying forms, and in provoking visceral excitation, film hyperbolically aggravates vision, pushing it to an extreme point of implosion and self-annihilation. As Buñuel says of *Un chien andalou*, a film's "object is to provoke instinctive reactions of revulsion and attraction in the spectator" (54-55).

Within the film narrative, we do not feel attracted to Barton as much as to Charlie. Charlie is the likable character. Charlie is the one who is ignored, patronized, abused. Even when we see Charlie shoot the police officers, it is hard to sympathize with them, for the officers are racist stick figures who, in a machine-like fashion, finish each others' sentences. At the same time, however, we are repulsed by Charlie's penchant for decapitation, by the mutilated body of Audry, the pathetic figure of Barton, and the fanaticism of Lipnick. We are annoyed by the excessiveness of the images and the lack of closure, even as we are drawn toward them, reveling in the film's ambiguity.

It is at this point of convergence, perhaps, that the film anchors desire and perception in the agitated historical body. *Barton Fink* displays a classic postmodern strategy in its attempt to simultaneously install and undermine the object of its critique, but the film is not content merely to critique the ideological apparatus of the filmic production of reality; rather, as a postmodern cinematic assemblage, it explores the material and corporeal basis of fascism — the historical framework of the film — locating it not in sadistic totalization, but in masochistic submission to the totalizing body. Studlar reminds us that "the masochistic fantasy may be viewed as a situation in which the subject (male or female) assumes the position of the child who desires to be controlled *within* the dynamics of the fantasy" (1992: 778). Barton exemplifies this fantasy, for he not only assumes the position of the child in relation to Audry as he seeks her protection in a crisis, a reunion with the mother figure that ends in death, but he ultimately becomes part of the fantasy image once he steps into the frame of the mezzotint in the final moments of the film. Barton is complicit with fascism, and therefore unable to recognize a fascist when one steps through his hotel door. More importantly, the film encourages us to recognize our own complicity. "Decapitating" us with seductive images and violence forces us to locate fascism within ourselves. *Barton Fink* is not a representation of fascism; instead, the film invokes our fascistic impulses as it displays its incorporeal and excessive images which are profoundly material.

Another way to say this is to point out that the film provides us with a fantasy image in which we can only uncomfortably reside. Studlar points out that the masochistic fantasy is dominated by the desire to return to the nondifferentiated body state of the mother/child, *and* the fear of abandonment and loss. Masochism obsessively "recreates the movement between concealment and revelation, disappearance and appearance, seduction and rejection" (1992: 777). It is at this point that the events invoked in the film gain their greatest significance, for the Holocaust, the failure of the political left, the power of Hollywood, and America's weak response to fascism are brought together in a dense nexus that connects paralysis of will to moral decay, that permits intersections of repressed homosexual desire with desperate attempts to maintain heterosexuality, of invasions and penetrations of the body with violation and colonization of the mind.

The masochistic dynamic *Barton Fink* displays, therefore, is multifold and decidedly masculine. First, invoking a list of some of our most ineffectual moments from the recent past, reminding ourselves of our inability to act when a situation demands a response, is coded as a form of pleasurable impotence. The gesture is regressive and potentially subversive in that this powerless position infantilizes the male subject: immobile, surrounded in darkness, he becomes "the passive receiving object who is also subject. The spectator must comprehend the images, but the images cannot be controlled" (Studlar 1992: 785). As agents in history, as spectators in a dark theatre, we receive, but no demands are made of us. Put another way, the Coens' embedded masochistic structure leads to a feminizing of the past and a masculinizing of the spectators. That is, history, much like the female in a masochistic fantasy, is not a discarded object, but a powerful force which is both dangerous and comforting. Watching *Barton Fink* becomes, then, an act of self-abasement and self-punishment in which we willingly submit to the powerful oral mother who must inflict cruelty in love.

On the other hand, *Barton Fink*, with its masochist aesthetic, posits a time before disintegration, a period when "lacking nothing," the mother is "allied with the child in the disavowal of the destruction of the superego" (Studlar 1992: 777). That is, the painful and castrating historic events invoked by *Barton Fink* — the Holocaust, the failure of the left, the inability to displace Hollywood studios — may function as a father's punishing superego which places guilt on the son, where fear of punishment and pain gives way to the wish for it, where cruelty and discipline come to stand for love. As Silverman points out, "the 'ordinary' male subject oscillates endlessly between the mutually exclusive commands of the (male) ego-ideal and super-ego, wanting both the love of the father and to be the father, but prevented from doing either" (1988: 41). The result of this abuse, of this subjection to an infantilizing and feminizing past, is a specific kind of cultural identity that in a modern subjectivity is disavowed but in a (post)historical subjectivity is exaggerated and displayed. The (post)historical spectator is nearly synonymous with the male masochist, for he proclaims that

> his meaning comes to him from the Other, prostrates himself before the Gaze even as he solicits it, exhibits his castration for all to see, and revels in the sacrificial basis of the social contract. The male masochist magnifies the losses

and divisions upon which cultural identity is based, refusing to be sutured or recompensed. In short, he radiates a negativity inimical to the social order (Silverman 1988: 51).

For Barton, his hysteria, impotence, effeminacy, and ultimate ignorance resist suture or compensation and work in opposition to totalizing forces. Moreover, his very identity — a (post)historical identity — is based on societal rejection and unoriginality. This process works in a similar way for the Coens, who, in their rejection of the studio system, in their identity as "independent filmmakers," mimic Barton's own desire to remain outside a totalizing system.

Contrasting this view, Paul Smith points out that the masochistic moment may be temporary, "a kind of trial, a rite of passage that we men know we have to go through but that will not take all our energy." The masochistic moment is ultimately part of a conservative agenda, for masochism "represents a way of structuring into the full subjectivity of the egotistic hero a resistance, a way of beating the father to within an inch of his life before replacing him or allowing him to be resurrected...." (1993: 171). Smith, however, deals primarily with action adventure films with males already coded as masculine and a genre structure that necessitates the return of the hero. The only sense of a resurrection we receive in *Barton Fink* is a parody of Shadrach, Meshach, and Abednego, who withstand the fire which surrounds them, but we can hardly call this a full return, for Barton is promptly humiliated and dismissed by Lipnick in the next scene. Barton remains ineffectual, for he is unable to answer the woman's question on the beach, and he is simply unable to respond as the image absorbs him.

This lack of control reminds us why a new concept of history appears under postmodernism. "History," conceived in Enlightenment terms, posits a centered, autonomous subject who can adequately express the contents of a contained space. Consequently, pleasure derives from mastery and control, or as Barthes's amateur wrestler, from insisting on the absolute clarity of the sign. As Jane Flax points out, "a central promise of Enlightenment and Western modernity is that conflicts between knowledge and power can be overcome by grounding claims to and the exercise of authority in reason." The assumption is that reason "operates identically in each subject and it can grasp laws that are objectively true; that is, are equally knowable and binding on every person" (1992: 447). The "I" is a free-agent in that the "I" is not contaminated or affected by desire or historical experience. The "I" has "privileged access" to the operation of its own reason. Given these assumptions, historical representation takes the form of the "I" discovering or uncovering the social text to secure the basis of cultural power through the claim to knowledge. Under postmodernism, these assumptions are questioned and rejected. Subjects are unable to maintain any boundaries, let alone access a universal and neutral reason. Meanings are not folded back upon the body, but proliferate endlessly and uncontrollably. Historical representation must then take the form of the "I" proclaiming its unoriginality and its inability to control and master. The "post" here suggests capitulation or at least a sober acknowledgment that mastery and control are beyond our ability. Cultural power is never secured. Marginalization becomes a source of pleasure but also a constant point of tension and negotiation. None of this is lost on the Coens who expose the masochistic fantasy as they simultaneously re-enact and repeat it. Like other (post)historical texts, *Barton Fink* satisfies the (post)historical subject's penchant for self-mutilation by forcing us to face our own ineffectual moments even as it tells us why we love it so, reminding us yet again that while we cannot control the painful past, we can surely enjoy it.

References

Barthes, Roland. 1972. *Mythologies*, translated by Annette Lavers. New York: Jonathan Cape Ltd.

Barton Fink. 1991. Directed by Joel Coen. Rank. Circle Films.

Caplan, Jane. 1989. "Postmodernism, Poststructuralism, and Deconstruction: Notes for Historians." *Central European History* 22: 260-78.

Deleuze, Gilles. 1986. *Cinema One — The Movement Image*, translated by Hugh Tomlinson and Barbara Habberjam. Minneapolis: University of Minnesota Press.

———— 1991. *Masochism*. New York: Zone Books.

Derrida, Jacques. 1990. *Limited Inc*. Evanston, IL: Northwestern University Press.

Ermath, Elizabeth Deeds. 1992. *Sequel to History: Postmodernism and the Crisis of Representational Time*. Princeton: Princeton University Press.

Flax, Jane. 1992. "The End of Innocence." *Feminists Theorize the Political*, edited by Judith Butler. New York: Routledge.

Hutcheon, Linda. 1987. "Beginning to Theorize Postmodernism." *Textual Practice* 1, no. 1: 10-31.

———— 1990. "An Epilogue: Postmodern Parody: History, Subjectivity, and Ideology." *Quarterly Review of Film and Video* 12: 125-133.

Huyssen, Andreas. 1986. *After the Great Divide: Modernism, Mass Culture, Postmodernism*. Bloomington: Indiana University Press.

Jameson, Fredric. 1991. *Postmodernism, Or, the Cultural Logic of Late Capitalism*. Durham: Duke University Press.

Shaviro, Steven. 1993. *The Cinematic Body*. Minneapolis: University of Minnesota Press.

Silverman, Kaja. 1988. "Masochism and Male Subjectivity." *Camera Obscura* 17 (May): 31-68.

Smith, Paul. 1993. *Clint Eastwood—A Cultural Production*. Minneapolis: University of Minnesota Press.

Spivak, Gayatri Chakrovorty. 1988. *In Other Worlds: Essays in Cultural Politics*. New York: Routledge.

Studlar, Gaylyn. 1992. "Masochism and the Perverse Pleasures of the Cinema." *Film Theory and Criticism*, edited by Gerald Mast, Marshall Cohen, and Leo Braudy. New York: Oxford University Press.

Theweleit, Klaus. 1985. "The Politics of Orpheus between Women, Hades, Political Power and the Media: Some Thoughts on the Configuration of the European Artist, Starting with the Figure of Gottfried Benn, or: What Happened to Eurydice?" *New German Critique* 36: 133-56.

Ulmer, Gregory L. 1983. "The Object of Post-Criticism." *The Anti-Aesthetic: Essays on Postmodern Culture*, edited by Hal Foster. Seattle: Bay Press.

Žižek, Slavoj. 1989. *The Sublime Object of Ideology*. New York: Verso.

———— 1991. *Looking Awry: An Introduction to Jacques Lacan through Popular Culture*. Cambridge: MIT University Press.

Part IV

Auteurial Presences

Akira Kurosawa's Dreams *(Warner Bros., 1990) Akira Kurosawa*
Harmony of nature in the first episode of Akira Kurosawa's Dreams.
Still courtesy of Jerry Ohlinger's Movie Materials.

CHAPTER 11

SOMETHING LIKE AUTOBIOGRAPHY IN *AKIRA KUROSAWA'S DREAMS*

Marshall Deutelbaum

Throughout his career, Akira Kurosawa has steadfastly refused to discuss the possible autobiographical elements of his films or offer any interpretation of their stories. As Donald Richie explained more than thirty years ago in his seminal study, *The Films of Akira Kurosawa* (1965):

> Kurosawa has said that he could not possibly define his own style, that he does not know what it consists of, that it never occurs to him to think of it. While quite ready to talk about lenses, or acting, or the best kind of camera-dolly, he is unwilling to discuss meaning or aesthetics. Once I asked what a certain scene was really about. He smiled and said: "Well, if I could answer that, it wouldn't have been necessary for me to have filmed the scene, would it?" (184)

Kurosawa reasserted his belief that his most successful creative work is the result of an unconscious process in the "Foreword" he wrote to a catalogue that accompanied a recent exhibit of many of the preliminary drawings and paintings he has executed for his films since *Kagemusha*:

> It is interesting to note that when I consciously tried to draw well, the drawing would not come out well. But when I simply translated onto paper an

image I had in mind for the movie, the drawing somehow seemed to captivate viewers.

Because of his belief in creation as an unconscious process essentially inaccessible through words, Kurosawa has always let his films speak for him. Thus when he was invited to be the guest editor of a portion of the Christmas 1989 issue of *Vogue (Paris)*, he included a photograph of himself as a young man captioned: *"Rien ne révèle plus son créateur que l'oeuvre elle-même"* ["Nothing reveals its creator more than the body of his work itself"] (257). A few pages later, as if to insist upon this claim, he presented a suite of his paintings for a story variously entitled "Tobu," "Ciel," and "Flying," which might have been planned for inclusion in *Dreams*, but which he never filmed. Preceded by a haiku by Buson about someone who has fallen to his death, the brief heading at the beginning of these images states that *Dreams* will consist of nine dreams from Kurosawa's childhood. This suite, identified as story-boards for a tenth dream, are mysteriously described as "Unique et secret," but otherwise unexplained.[1]

The filming of *Dreams* began shortly after the issue of *Vogue (Paris)* appeared. Not surprisingly, Kurosawa told those gathered at the press conference announcing its production only that each of its stories was inspired by a dream he had had (Tessier 1989: 74). In light of his repeated insistence upon the unconscious nature of artistic production, the dream state, that unconscious place of storytelling, seems the perfect source for Kurosawa's tales. All that ties these stories together is the continuing presence of Kurosawa as a character, either as a small child or as a young man, as well as an abiding concern with death. Originally planned as ten or eleven stories — the exact number is not clear — *Dreams* was finally shot and released as eight stories in a different order than initially announced. This shifting number and order underlines the finished film's lack of linearity. In this regard, *Dreams* is quite unlike any other feature film and seems to bear the mark of the postmodern that Jean-François Lyotard describes when he writes of works that

> ...cannot be judged according to a determining judgment, by applying familiar categories to the text or to the work. Those rules and categories are what the work of art itself is looking for (1984: 81).

In opening this discussion with Kurosawa's unwillingness or inability to reveal anything about himself or the creative process behind his films, I want to suggest that much of *Dreams* is designed to reinforce these claims, *even* when Kurosawa draws upon personal material accessible to us in his autobiography, *Something Like an Autobiography*. Indeed, "Crows," the film's highly metaphorical and self-reflexive fifth story, is at one and the same time an enactment of Kurosawa's belief in the essentially unconscious process of creation, as well as a suggestion of what it may be like for viewers to discover meaning in a visual artist's body of work.

In the story, Kurosawa as a young, aspiring artist pursues Vincent van Gogh to ask him about his art. Kurosawa has often acknowledged his admiration for the Dutch artist. A passage in *Something Like an Autobiography* where Kurosawa describes the disorienting effect that studying reproductions of works by painters, including van Gogh, had upon him in his youth, strikes me as the germ of this cinematic encounter:

> After looking at a monograph on Cézanne, I would step outside and the houses, streets, and trees — everything — looked like a Cézanne painting. The same thing would happen when I looked at a book of van Gogh's paintings or Utrillo's paintings — they changed the way the real world looked to me. It seemed completely different from the world I usually saw with my own eyes (1982: 88).[2]

"Crows" develops this experience into a broader, metaphoric explanation of how one can better understand an artist through the contemplation of his works, than through conversing with him.

"Crows" is highly symmetrical in structure. It begins in an art gallery where the young Kurosawa, carrying his painting implements, looks at several of van Gogh's paintings. Focusing on one particular painting, "Pont de Langois," Kurosawa enters its space and begins to search for van Gogh in Arles, eventually finding him sketching in a field. When van Gogh abruptly breaks off their brief conversation and walks away, Kurosawa begins a second pursuit of him, this time passing through several of his landscapes. He emerges from them in the heightened reality of Auvers, and catches sight of van Gogh as the painter crests a distant hill. A flock of blackbirds disturbed by van Gogh's passing take flight from the surrounding wheat fields. A straight cut from this sight suddenly returns us to the gallery where Kurosawa stands before van Gogh's painting of this scene, the famous "Wheat Field under Threatening Skies with Crows." His position and gesture further underline the symmetry of "Crows:" where he stood at the right side of "Pont de Langois" and put on his hat before entering that landscape, he stands to the left of this canvas and takes off his hat.

The passage from gallery space, to the space of Arles, through various spaces constructed from several of van Gogh's paintings, to the space of Auvers, and back, transforms the experience Kurosawa describes in *Something Like an Autobiography* into a spatial itinerary that progressively represents the process of understanding a visual artist. It is a double pursuit because the words of van Gogh prove — much as Kurosawa has insisted in his own interviews — only that he does not have conscious access into his methods and purpose. The second pursuit, wordlessly entering even more deeply into the artist's works, seems to offer the inquiring Kurosawa the insight that van Gogh is incapable of providing. Deep, sympathetic contemplation seems to provide the understanding the artist either cannot or will not offer on his own. Thus even though we cannot know what the young Kurosawa learned from this journey, by removing his hat he seems to signal not only respect, but an epiphanic insight as well.

The first image in "Crows," a van Gogh self-portrait, announces the story's subject in terms of the question of autobiography: what can one tell from how an artist chooses to present himself through his paintings to the world? After looking at this and some other paintings, the young Kurosawa stops to contemplate van Gogh's "Pont de Langois." Whether or not the title is meant to carry the extra weight of an homage to Henri Langois, the cofounder of the Cinémathèque Française, as Max Tessier suggests, this painting of a bridge admits the young Kurosawa, imaginatively at least, into van Gogh's Arles. Putting on his hat, Kurosawa enters the landscape and sets off in search of van Gogh, played by Martin Scorsese — a strong suggestion that this story is as much about cinematic creation as it is about painting. In words that echo Kurosawa's words I quoted earlier, van Gogh tells the would-be painter that the process of creation is not a conscious one:

> van Gogh: A scene that looks like a painting does not make a painting. If you take the time and look closely, all of nature has its own beauty. When that natural beauty is there, I just lose myself in it. And then, as if it's in a dream, the scene just paints itself for me. Yes, I consume this natural setting! I devour it completely and wholly and when I am through, the picture appears before me, complete. But, it is difficult to hold it inside.
> Kurosawa: Then what do you do?
> van Gogh: I work. I slave. I drive myself like a locomotive.[3]

After declaring how he drives himself like a locomotive, van Gogh returns to his sketching as the young Kurosawa watches. A new, driving piano score on the soundtrack, along with shots of a steam locomotive's turning wheels and belching smokestack, intercut with his sketching, underline the force with which he claims to throw himself into his work. After furiously sketching for a while, van Gogh gathers up his implements and walks away, declaring — in what amounts to *his* refusal to speculate any further on his art: "The sun! It compels me to paint. I can't waste my time standing here talking to you." The younger Kurosawa pursues him again. This second pursuit initiates the second spatial transition in the story. Where the first moved from the reality of the art gallery, through the painting of the "Pont de Langois," into van Gogh's Arles, this one moves from the heightened reality of Arles into the even more distorted landscapes of van Gogh's drawings and paintings themselves. The differences between these landscapes is signaled by Kurosawa's passage along a monochrome road between them. Having failed to learn anything from van Gogh himself, Kurosawa literally pursues him now through his paintings.[4]

During Kurosawa's travel through these works, the continuing presence of the steam whistle and driving piano score heard earlier on the soundtrack suggests that we are watching the young man's attempt to understand van Gogh's creative process through contemplation. Indeed the words spoken by van Gogh to describe what happens when he paints seem applicable in describing the experience Kurosawa undergoes here if one rephrases them, substituting "painting" for "natural beauty" in order to shift the focus from the process of painting to the process of contemplative understanding. Thus one might say that the young Kurosawa:

> loses himself in these paintings. And then, as if it's in a dream, the scene's meanings reveal themselves to him. He consumes the paintings. He devours them completely and wholly and when he is through, the pictures' significance appears to him, complete.

The young Kurosawa emerges from his journey through van Gogh's works onto a real path winding through real wheat fields. Van Gogh is visible on the path, some distance ahead. As van Gogh approaches the horizon, the younger painter pauses, and hundreds of crows rise from the fields. Then, as van Gogh disappears from view, the nondiegetic steam whistle sounds again on the soundtrack, and with a freeze-frame the film cuts to van Gogh's famous painting of the scene, "Wheat Field under Threatening Skies with Crows," on display in the gallery. The camera zooms back to reveal the younger Kurosawa standing in the gallery before this painting. After the steam whistle sounds again more softly, he removes his hat and the image fades out to end the story.

What can one make of "Crows"? In an article titled "Memory and Nostalgia in Kurosawa's Dream World," Stephen Prince concludes merely that "Crows" presents Kurosawa's coming to grips with the fact that he had little talent for painting. Prince (1991) writes:

> Clutching his painting tools and wearing Kurosawa's trademark hat, the surrogate is trapped inside the images of this master painter. Beyond the way it makes explicit Kurosawa's reverence and respect for van Gogh, this episode clearly implies that, had he not elected the cinema as his chosen forum, Kurosawa might have been lost as a minor talent in mediums not his own and that were already claimed by true giants (35-36).

This flat interpretation of "Crows" ignores all the marks that indicate the story ends with a more substantial epiphany for the young Kurosawa. The nondiegetic repetition of the steam whistle, the sudden stillness created by the shock cut from fluttering crows to the motionless painted scene in the quiet gallery, as well as Kurosawa's removal of his hat, serve to indicate some insight gained by the young man from his contemplative journey far more significant than the recognition of his inferior talent as a painter. Precisely *what* this understanding is, however, remains unexpressed.

Strikingly, this unspecified meaning seems quite different from the meaning most viewers have found in the painting. The general public has long regarded "Wheat Field under Threatening Skies with Crows" as a straightforward biographical work: the painting's distortion symbolizing the painter's disturbed mental state, with the subject frozen at that precise moment when van Gogh committed suicide. As Pascal Bonafoux (1990) describes so melodramatically in a biography of van Gogh:

> Sunday 27 July 1890: suddenly, over the wheat, the crows flew away, terrified by the report of a gun resounding over the silent countryside. Vincent had just fired: on the little known painter, on the man 'who feels a failure' (144).

Kurosawa presents the crows taking flight, but without any gunshot. In replacing the gunshot most viewers imagine as the cause of the crows' flight with the nondiegetic sound of the locomotive's whistle, Kurosawa seems to want to remind us of how limited popular conceptions can be of how to read autobiography within an artist's work. Perhaps like the young Kurosawa in the gallery, we too should experience an epiphany, forced as we are by "Crows" to see this familiar painting with freshened perception. The self-conscious, contemplative experience of "Crows," then, may well suggest that we redirect our interpretation of the painting away from our knowledge of van Gogh's despair to focus instead on the mystery of artistic creation itself.

From this perspective, Kurosawa could not have chosen a better surrogate to teach this lesson than Vincent van Gogh.

References

Bonafoux, Pascal. 1990. *Van Gogh*, translated by Alexandra Campbell. New York: Henry Holt and Co.

Gogh, Vincent van. 1978. *The Complete Letters of Vincent van Gogh*, second ed., 3 vols. Boston: New York Graphic Society.

Kurosawa, Akira. 1982. *Something Like an Autobiography*, translated by Audie E. Bock. New York: Alfred A. Knopf, Inc.

———— 1988/1989. "*Vogue* Par Kurosawa." *Vogue (Paris)* no. 692 (Décembre/Janvier): 235-272.

———— 1990a. *Rêves. L'Avant-Scène Cinéma* no. 393.

———— 1990b. *Yume.* Tokyo: Iwanami Shoten.

———— 1994. *Akira Kurosawa Drawings.* Tokyo: Ise Cultural Foundation.

Lyotard, Jean-François. 1984. *The Postmodern Condition: A Report on Knowledge.* Minneapolis: University of Minnesota Press.

Prince, Stephen. 1991. "Memory and Nostalgia in Kurosawa's Dream World." *Post Script* 11, no. 1: 28-39.

Richie, Donald. 1965. *The Films of Akira Kurosawa.* Berkeley: University of California Press.

Stone, Irving, ed. 1937. *Dear Theo: The Autobiography of Vincent van Gogh.* Boston: Houghton Mifflin.

———— 1939. *Lust for Life: The Novel of Vincent van Gogh.* New York: Random House.

Tessier, Max. 1989. "Un Film Rêvé: Les Rêves Filmés de Kurosawa." *La Revue du Cinéma* no. 447: 73-74.

Notes

1. Despite this cryptic description, the full suite published in *Vogue (Paris)* strongly suggests his close relationship with his older brother, Heigo, who took him to movies and encouraged his interest in Western culture. In *Something Like an Autobiography*, Kurosawa follows his description of Heigo's suicide with a chapter entitled "Negative

and Positive," in which he reflects briefly on their relationship. The light and dark twin figures with which the suite concludes visualize how the actor, Tokugawa Musei, describes Kurosawa's relation to Heigo: "'You're just like your brother. But he was negative and you're positive.'" Kurosawa rephrases this remark cinematically: "I prefer to think of my brother as a negative strip of film that led to my own development as a positive image" (1982: 87). Five sketches for "Tobu" also appear in *Akira Kurosawa Drawings.*

2. This passage immediately follows Kurosawa's comparison of himself and his brother as negative and positive strips of film.

3. Van Gogh's dialogue is rendered in English on page 84 of *Yume*, the Japanese edition of the script for *Dreams. Yume* also reproduces many of the original paintings made by Kurosawa in planning the film. Considering Kurosawa's well-known aversion to biographical information, it is intriguing how close van Gogh's final words in "Crows" are to Vincent van Gogh's words in a letter he wrote to his brother, Theo, in early September 1888: "Ideas for my work are coming to me in swarms, so that though I'm alone, I have no time to think or feel, I go on painting like a steam engine. I think there will hardly ever be a standstill again" (letter 535, III, 33). The source from which Kurosawa may have taken van Gogh's words is uncertain. Irving Stone, who edited van Gogh's letters and used them as the basis for a biography of the painter, also wrote the script for the MGM film biography of van Gogh, *Lust for Life* (directed by Vincente Minnelli, 1956). In the film, van Gogh describes himself in a voice-over as painting like a steam engine *while* he is shown painting the "Pont de Langois." Whichever the source, the use of van Gogh's actual words indicates that "Crows" involves more than pure dream. And, considering how much van Gogh's remarks about not having the time to think or feel while he works are strikingly similar to Kurosawa's description of his own unconscious creative process quoted earlier from *Something Like an Autobiography,* the Dutch painter seems all the more the perfect model and spokesman for the mature Kurosawa's refusal to explain himself or his films.

4. Most of these works by van Gogh are identified in notes to a French translation of the film's script published in *L'Avant-Scène Cinéma* no. 393.

CHAPTER 12

NOT WAVING BUT DROWNING BY NUMBERS

Peter Greenaway's Cautionary Tale

Philip Holden-Moses

YAN

Nobody heard him, the dead man,
But still he lay moaning:
I was much further out than you thought,
And not waving but drowning.

Poor chap, he always loved larking
And now he's dead.
It must have been too cold for him,
His heart gave way, they said.

Oh, no no no, it was too cold always
(Still the dead one lay moaning)
I was much too far out all my life
And not waving but drowning.

Stevie Smith, *Not Waving But Drowning*

TAN

While the notion of postmodernity is no longer a novel one, it is, nevertheless, still contentious and has become no less so after a great deal of debate and discussion — only some of which has been friendly. What remains, regardless of the tenor of these exchanges, is a lasting dissatisfaction and deepening disillusionment with our current social condition. Modernity brought with it an implied social order and a structure of knowledge ranging from blind positivism to the extraordinarily systematized "automatism" of the surreal movement. It was an order that seemed equally applicable to the sciences and industry as it did to the genteel social life of the rapidly increasing middle classes. Such conditions suggested the possibility of a leisure class who were as much concerned with enlightenment and knowledge as they were with economic power and the maintenance of the social status quo. Postmodernity, however, which currently boasts a new "world order," only seems to frustrate reactionary forces by suggesting a new series of disorders — both intellectually and socially. Having, at last, understood ourselves to be only the product of modernism and modernity,

Drowning by Numbers (*Miramax, 1988*) *Peter Greenaway*
Cissie Colpitts 1 (Joan Plowright), Cissie Colpitts 2 (Juliet Stevenson), Cissie Colpitts 3
(Joely Richardson). Still courtesy of Jerry Ohlinger's Movie Materials.

not its practitioners, we now also understand why such notions of postmodernity seem to fit. They accord with the strong sense of doubt and the creeping anxiety that arises once we realize that we are actually modernity's heirs. We discover with apprehensiveness and consternation that we have, unwittingly, become the custodians of History (where all too often the emphasis falls on the first syllable, only now it is spoken through clenched jaws so that the sound is spat in one seething hiss).

It was modernism, however, that weakened the links in the chain of history. It posited the idea of history as a series of events locatable within the object itself, rather than external to it, and not necessarily as a unified system of cause and effect — traceable, definable, and knowable. Foucault's *The Order of Things* served only to cast renewed doubt on the singular nature of history and the role of historian/history-man as the sole keeper of these events. History then became subject to the grudging awareness that what we experience is merely, to use Foucault's own words, "a succession of discursive practices." More importantly, these are practices that illustrate, even illuminate, the relationship between knowledge and power. They are a testament to the marginalization of "the other," seen in terms of race, gender, class, and ethnicity. Finally, of course, they represent histories of discontinuity, of difference and disorder.

The tendency of institutions, of vested authority, has been to attempt to efface those differences. In an effort to solidify the past, to manufacture a distinct and knowable history, a mythic dimension has been introduced while the cracking seams have been overlooked in favor of a "golden-age" past that informs the present. Such conservatives — and I mean this in its literal sense here — are, not surprisingly, incensed by the bricolage of styles and periods and the insistence upon seemingly unrelated quotations of postmodern thought and production that both simultaneously evoke and alienate it from its own past. Nevertheless, in postmodern art forms, the past is being reworked and reorganized along different lines — sometimes along the highly artificial lines of game and role playing — to readdress the present and the issues of power therein. *Drowning By Numbers* (1988) attends to such a reorganization, where counting and game playing provide the only structure with which the characters and audience may comprehend events; where the film's diegesis speaks to a post-war England that never really existed. It is a late-empire England, still reeling from rationing and only vaguely aware of the effects of its own crumbling influence — an irony not lost on its contemporary, mid-Thatcher, audience.

Drowning By Numbers constitutes an example of postmodern role-playing activities that confuse the issue and the levels of reality. These

221

artificial activities create the kind of pastiche that Jameson might well have been describing when he suggested that it "is not incompatible with...a world transformed into sheer images of itself and for pseudo-events and *spectacles*. It is for such obstacles that we may reserve Plato's conception of the *simulacrum*, the identical copy for which no original has ever existed" (Jameson 1991:18).

TETHERA

Shepherds in Yorkshire used to count their sheep in a language that was, it is said, derived from Icelandic. The numbers from one to twenty run as follows:

Yan	Yandeek
Tyan	Tyandeek
Tethera	Tetheradeek
Methera	Metheradeek
Pimp	Bumfit
Sethera	Yanabumfit
Lethera	Tyanabumfit
Othera	Tetherabumfit
Dothera	Metherabumfit
Deek	Jiggit

To the west, in the Lake District, it ran a little differently:

Yan	Sethera
Tan	Wineberry
Tethera	Wagtail
Methera	Tarrydiddle
Pip	Den

This counting system is both rhythmic and repetitious, and bears little or no resemblance to English or any northern dialect with which I am familiar. It is an arbitrary organizational system, colorful but nevertheless functional, intended to facilitate keeping track of sheep. It is similarly employed here in an effort to organize my ideas, and hopefully might even evoke the extraordinary sensitivity of the sheep who form an essential component of the game of "Sheep and Tides," rather than provoke the customary, sleep-inducing, reaction. It is an organizing system, nevertheless, of which Peter Greenaway, perhaps the quintessential formal filmmaker, might well approve. Quite remarkable is, in fact, his predilection for systematization and cataloguing. In an interview with *Film Comment* (issue of May-June 1990) he noted that:

> Systems are always deeply, deeply faulted — and absurd. Like the alphabet. Our whole lives are governed by this wretched, artificial construct: our medical records, our police records, the way we approach our academic life — all based on this stupid system of A-Z. The whole world is now clued into this — even the people who don't use the sort of alphabet that we do. It's absurd. The time band system and the lines around the Equator — which are so artificial — have been systemized and empiricized to make chaos somehow more readable. More usable (57).

In *Drowning by Numbers* Greenaway employs a system which rivals in magnitude the earthly organization of time, and that is space. As the film opens, the star system by which mankind structures space is being enumerated by the teenage girl as she counts out her skipping game. It is the first game of the film and its rules are the simplest, only its terms are difficult to understand.

One — Antares	Eleven — Vega
Two — Capella	Twelve — Golubin
Three — Canopus	Thirteen — Spica
Four — Arcturus	Fourteen — Capra
Five — Agreetor	Fifteen — Acrab
Six — Anektor	Sixteen — Deneb
Seven — Duendin	Seventeen — Sapho
Eight — Algerib	Eighteen — Castor
Nine — Agena	Nineteen — Pollux
Ten — Lalandry	Twenty — Stocha

And so on to one hundred, when we are reassured that the other hundreds are all alike, no matter how many stars there may be in the sky. The skipping girl is the film's guide and hostess. She leads the audience into the central organization of the film — counting in the game being played. In this role she also governs Greenaway's "wretched, artificial construction," an attempt to make the "chaos" of the film's diegesis "somehow more readable. More usable."

Few things are more artificial than a film, while still appearing to be natural. More often than not, the structure of a film is its narrative. In this film the structure is twofold — the narrative and the representation of numbers from one to one hundred, either on screen or in the dialogue of the characters. Usually the narrative propels the film forward; here the narrative is as predictable as the progression of the numbers. There are three Cissie Colpitts, each has a husband and each husband will drown at the hands of his wife. The male protagonists will drown — until the ultimate demise of the duplicitous coroner, Madgett — at which point the narrative has been, almost literally, exhausted.

METHERA

Most surprising, even shocking, is the death of the skipping girl followed by that of the boy, Smut, who hangs by the luminous rope of his female, teenage counterpart: deaths that bring together the film's underlying themes of frustrated romance and mortality (Smut's death by strangulation is suggestive of an auto-erotic mishap). In the playful world(s) of *Drowning by Numbers,* children no longer serve the classic Shakespearian dual function as the innocent wit/idiot savant or wise jester. Smut and the skipping girl are thirteen, an age at which childhood recedes and adulthood looms with its attendant anxieties. Smut is the child of a coroner for whom corpses are yet another occasion for cataloguing and counting in "The Great Death Game."

The Great Death Game

One of Smut's major preoccupations involves the skewering of butterflies and insects, counting, labeling and burying corpses with a burst of fireworks in order to mark the event with sufficient dignity and ritual. He explains:

> A great many things are dying very violently all the time. The best days for violent deaths are Tuesdays. They are the yellow-paint days. Saturdays are the second best — or worst. Saturdays are red-paint days. The Great Death Game is therefore a contest between red-paint days and yellow-paint days. So far yellow-paint days are winning by thirty-one corpses to twenty-nine. Whatever the color, a violent death is always celebrated by a firework.

Certainly, the games featured by *Drowning by Numbers* (Bees in the Trees, Dawn Card-Castles, Strip-Jump, Sheep and Tides, Dead Man's Catch, etc.) suggest a strategy for gaining the attention of the childlike. It is a narrative devised around the model of a children's tale, but it is for adults, whose strong memories of childhood games, counting rituals, fantasies from illustrated children's books and childhood imagination reign. There seems to be a preoccupation with childhood food. Madgett, at times of great stress, reverts to eating chocolate pudding from an oversized bowl, rather as a child would clean the batter from a bowl after the cake has gone into the oven. Cissie Colpitts II and Hardy eat popsicles — although their use of them as sex-aids clearly indicates their status as adults. The same Cissie also concocts a mixture of Corona, the iconic British equivalent of Kool-Aid (a sweet carbonated children's drink that comes in a limited range of flavors and is strangely packaged), together with added sugar in order to sabotage Hardy's typewriter.

This childish impulse is here played out with added irony as Cissie then attempts to type a childlike imperative to her husband, "Kiss me, Hardy" (Nelson's apocryphal last words at Trafalgar). Finally, the skipping girl details the party food that she expects to eat that night. The locations and objects within the film hint at a universal memory of childhood — the large glossy art books, the tree house, and a fascination with fire and fireworks. The games and events of childhood which are meant to be the learning processes of our youth, artificial constructions perhaps intended to show us how to win and lose and to learn about the harsh realities of life without ever having to face the consequences of such reality, here leave the male figures of this film sorely unprepared for reality, and it is through them that Greenaway plays out past and present anxieties.

PIP

Such anxieties are worked out through game playing and the losers literally die. Smut is the principal game player, and he explains the rules of each game in a dry monotonous voice, as if he were reading instructions from the box top. Each game has clear and distinct rules that work toward an eventual goal. For instance, the cock must crow three times before Smut will answer the telephone in the morning or, in the game of Reverse Strip-Jump, he must first complete an entire circuit, concluded by a safe landing, before he can put on another article of clothing.

Dawn Card-Castles

He explains that "in the game of Dawn Card-Castles, fifty-two playing cards are stacked up into a castle in a draught free space: the player can determine the dreams of the next night if he awakes before the castle collapses. Those players who wish to dream of Romance build their castle with the seven of hearts." The pack of cards has always held the promise of magic and prophesy. Linked both to the stage magician, gypsies, and the tarot cards, Smut imbues the cards with the ability to predict the future. It is a fantasy that takes place at the juncture of night and day — the place where the indeterminacy of the dark gives way to the clarity of the light of the following morning. If the ritual is carried out correctly, with the appropriate card (the seven of hearts), the game even has the ability to determine the romantic content of dreams, once again signalling the preoccupations of the thirteen-year-old Smut, caught between an implicit belief in games and a newly acquired interest in love. The game is, of course, a mystical attempt on Smut's behalf to foretell the outcome of his romantic interest in the skipping girl. The object of Smut's affections is, however, unimpressed by his interests and suggests circumcision as a suitable gesture of love. She goes on to describe the "bad-men" that her mother says are out on the streets. We have indeed seen direct evidence of the truth of this statement when Jake passed by with the object of his amorous pursuits, Nancy, at the beginning of the film. What the girl fails to mention, however, is that it is Jake who dies and not Nancy. He may have been a reprobate, but the result of his games was death — by misadventure, according to Madgett!

Smut's games though are, solitary diversions. The consequences to Smut of his failing or losing one of these games is only ever witnessed by the documenting Polaroid camera with which he records everything. The anxiety over the result of these games is, therefore, artificially induced. However, Smut is merely the game-playing pupil. It is Madgett who is the master and in Madgett's life the games that are played carry with them a different set of rituals, role-playing, and competitiveness, representing restrictions on civilization and its Freudian discontents. Madgett plays the larger, collective games like "Sheep and Tides," where human estrangement from the natural in favor of the cultural is replaced by sheep who are sensitive to the motion of the tides.

SETHERA

Hangman's Cricket

The more important identities are the Emperor, the Widow, the Judge, the Hangman, the Ghost, the Red Queen, the Fat Lady, the Dunce, the

Business Man, the Adulterer, the Harlot, the Gravedigger, the Maiden, the Twins, the Chinaman, the Cook (one might also add the thief, his wife, and her lover), the General, the Prisoner, the Beggarman, the Thief, and the Priest. The Adulterer can only pair with the Harlot when each has an even number of lives above twelve, though the Dunce can cancel this, provided that the Sailor is not batting. The Mother-in-law is only allotted five runs at a time after which she must defer to the Gravedigger who is allowed to add the number of lives or runs of each competitor he bowls out to his own.

Madgett has been a game player for a long time. He has reference books for game statistics (an interest in statistics is somewhat less common in England than here, where it is a practiced art), his room is presided over by the great cricketing W.D. Grace, a man in English sporting lore similar in stature, both physically and in legend, to Babe Ruth, with the exception that W.D. Grace was a gentleman. Madgett reads aloud from a book of cricketing accidents. It is a book something akin to *Wisden's Cricketing Almanac*, but entirely more gruesome. A great deal more abstract than Smut's games, Mudgett's games have to do with recreating, analyzing, photographing, and documenting the past. He seeks to determine the even more subtle nuances of a game long-since played, with the kind of zeal which only the most ardent of positivists could muster. What this approach masks is Madgett's inability to grasp any real notion of how to deal with the subtle nuance of society. The only game that engages anything like a community is the beach game of Hangman's Cricket, a corruption and embellishment of the very English children's game of French Cricket, in and of itself is a piece of adult chauvinism intended to belittle eastern neighbors: cricket is an adult game of skill and elegance; its simplistic, inelegant version is named after the French. In the game of Hangman's Cricket, however, the players take on strictly defined roles. Society is present, but, mirroring Madgett's world, the rules only produce the appearance of order; in reality they make no sense.

Unlike cricket, its civilized counterpart, which is played in teams with breaks for lunch and tea, Hangman's Cricket is played by individuals. There is no winner to the game, only "an outright loser is found and is obliged to present himself to the Hangman...who is always merciless." We are left to wonder whether there is any relationship between the number of runs and lives earned and the determination of the loser, or whether the word loser is being used here in the American, colloquial sense of the word. Regardless of which is the case, the description of the rules makes it clear that the gender of the loser is always male.

WINEBERRY

The men continually fall short. In personality they are far from attractive. Jake is a philandering drunkard who seduces the prim Sunday school teacher, Nancy. Hardy is a cold fish (without the ability to swim like one) who is unable to heed the advice of every good mother who tells her children to wait an a hour before going swimming. If as children we often wondered what the result of not waiting would be, Hardy provides us with adequate evidence. Finally, Bellamy is moody, rough, and only learns to swim because it is one of only two conditions for matrimony laid down by the third Cissie Colpitts. So unwilling is she to recognize him as a an acceptable partner that she insists, after the wedding, as the only other condition, that he only ever "take her" from behind — a condition to which he readily agrees, unlike his reaction to swimming lessons. Madgett and Smut are free from such pejorative notions only if we care to leave aside Madgett's continual playing with the three Cissie Colpitts for sexual favors. Even then they can best be described as somewhat dull or a little lack luster. Smut's relationship with the skipping girl mirrors that of Madgett with all three of the Cissie Colpitts. He consistently attempts to engage her with stories and ideas and is invariably corrected by some wiser source, most often the girl's mother. Each time Smut approaches her with ideas about romance he is rebuffed. Similarly, Madgett attempts to be the agent of law and order, but is continually undermined by the each of the Cissie Colpitts, who not only correct him in his legal pronouncements, but also decline his sexual advances in order to secure favorable drowning verdicts from him in his capacity as the coroner. The wisdom and guile of the three women turn Madgett's appeals to law and science into yet another form of game playing. However, the rules to the game are now as fluid as the water in which men drown, and the women who were once subject to Madgett's rules have now become the ones who dictate them. What were thought to be constants — law and natural order as represented by science — have been thoroughly undermined.

WAGTAIL

Peter Greenaway has often commented, in a manner that sounds not too dissimilar to Smut's, on the fact that an author does not necessarily have to sympathize with the moral behavior and the opinions of his characters. Nor is it necessary or obligatory for him to blindly believe in the tenets of his own construction — all of which is a disclaimer to the notion that the author of *Drowning by Numbers* believes that all men are weak, loutish, coarse, and generally inadequate and incompetent as partners for women.

Drowning by Numbers is, then, a dismal exploration of male potency and sensitivity, peopled by opportunists and cowards. Its bravest representative is the unknowing boy, Smut, who, in the name of love, willingly circumcises himself with a pair of scissors, at the risk of bleeding to death. In search of knowledge, Smut questions his father about Samson, but in the face of apathy or ignorance from his father, opts to remove his foreskin rather than his hair. The ritual is empty, however, and far from joining the ranks of men in controlling and possessing women, the skipping girl rejects Smut and he is left to recoup his strength, propped-up in bed as an invalid — or rather, one whose attempt at seduction has become invalid. It is Hardy, the obese and abusive husband of Cissie Colpitts II, who has the fetish for haircuts. He willingly submits to the hand of his wife as she removes his hair, unable to understand that he has aided in his own emasculation. Even after death he is given a trim — injurious insult is added to fatal injury.

TARRYDIDDLE

Smut is the scapegoat: he is needlessly and painfully circumcised; he is sent out into the bushes while Madgett sexually propositions all three of the Cissie Colpitts, and he takes on the burden of guilt for two of the narratives strongest issues. Firstly, he considers his advice to the skipping girl to move out into the road as the cause of her death — at the hands of a hit-and-run driver. The car is actually carrying a load of runners who represent the closest thing to a thread of the film's narrative, running from beginning to end, tossing about a trail of brightly colored pieces of paper. The audience, like the perusing runners, are grateful for all such devices in the film — the most noteworthy of which has been the counting game of number spotting — and are horrified by the senseless killing of the semi-innocent girl at the willful hands of a capricious narrative. This, combined with Smut's second transgression — the dropping of the rope during the tug of war in response to an inquiry by the police — leads him to believe that he has selfishly betrayed the two people that he loved most, the girl and his father. In his final game he dashes any potential hope for men which his character had insofar embodied.

The End Game

The object of the game is to dare to fall with a noose around your neck from a place sufficiently high off the ground such that a fall will hang you. The object of the game is to punish those who have caused great unhappiness by their selfish actions. This is the best game of all because the winner is also the loser and the judge's decision is always final.

DEN

Finally the film moves toward its resolution. The three Cissie Colpitts have done away with their useless husbands and bludgeoned Madgett into favorable verdicts. The men have all been tarred with the same damning brush, and the women have examined their own status as representatives of their gender. Cissie Colpitts III asks Madgett if he believes that they are all the same woman. Indeed, they could be representative of one woman at three stages of life. They are, however, obstinate in their insistence that they are distinct, separate people. It does not matter whether they are or are not. What the film has demonstrated is that these women are in touch with their own sexuality and their place in the world, and they understand how to get things done. They are survivors, sometimes duplicitous, but always heavily motivated. They take on their husbands, the Water-Tower conspirators (in a plot development which apes the testosterone-laden machinations of Watergate) and hoodwink the coroner. Once the tug of war is lost by Madgett, their victory is secured and the last vestiges of male authority are sent to a watery grave as Madgett is abandoned in a sinking boat bearing the number "100." Full fathom five, my father lies...and for good reason. The failure to move beyond the seeming limitations of their gender, freezes-out the men in this film. They have, however, been too cold and too far out their whole lives...and not waving, but drowning.

REFERENCES

Foucault, Michel. 1973. *The Order of Things*. New York: Vintage Books.

Jameson, Fredric. 1991. *Postmodernism, or, The Cultural Logic of Late Capitalism*. Durham: Duke University Press.

Smith, Gavin. 1990. "Food for Thought." Interview with Peter Greenaway. *Film Comment* 26.3 (May-June): 54-60.

Smith, Stevie. 1958. *Not Waving But Drowning*. London: A. Deutsch.

CHAPTER 13

A DOUBLE VOICE

The Dual Paternity of *Querelle*

Mary M. Wiles

Yet each man kills the thing he loves
By each let this be heard
Some do it with a bitter look
Some with a flattering word.
The coward does it with a kiss,
The brave man with a sword!

Some love too little, some too long,
Some sell, and others buy;
Some do the deed with many tears;
And some without a sigh;
For each man kills the thing he loves;
Yet each man does not die

Oscar Wilde

Genet's "theatre of the double" forecasts postmodernist pre-occupations. Rainer Werner Fassbinder will use it to structure his film *Querelle* (1982), the adaptation of Jean Genet's 1948 novel, *Querelle de Brest*. I will show how in both the Genet novel and the Fassbinder film, the Genetian theatrical notions of dramatic placement, psychodrama, and mistaken identity are used to open up critical differences between the actor, his fictional role, and the role played by the

Querelle (Columbia Tristar, 1982) Rainer Werner Fassbinder
"Each man kills the thing he loves." Querelle entranced as he slays the sailor Vic.
Still courtesy of Jerry Ohlinger's Movie Materials.

characters. This "destroys" character in the traditional sense and exposes the spectator as participant in the spectacle. Genet's postwar dream of a "théâtre sur le théâtre" echoes the Artaudian "theatre of cruelty" in the demand for the destruction of dramatic character and especially in the insistence on a theatre that would place the spectator on stage. During the 1930s, Antonin Artaud had insisted on a "theatre of cruelty" that would invert the authority of the text, placing the spectator on stage alongside of the actors and giving precedence to mise-en-scène. In *The Theater and Its Double*, Artaud searched for a theatrical language that would privilege movement as opposed to mimesis, spectacle as opposed to meaning, and vision rather than voice (Oswald 1989: xiv). Genet's transposition of Artaud's theatrical language of space in the novel *Querelle de Brest* points ahead to postmodernist preoccupations with process, participation, and performance, rather than the authoritative and finished work of art (Oswald 1989: xiv). In my postmodern reading of Fassbinder's film adaptation *Querelle*, I will draw on discussions of postmodernism that point to "a diversity and simultaneity of forms and strategies" that "replay past avant-gardes and the history of modernism, as well as aspects of what might be termed the classical" (Turim 1991: 188). I will show how the Genetian trope of the double provides the unifying principle for the rehearsal and replay of Hollywood as well as high-art avant-garde discourses, determining our productive engagement with antecedent and contemporary modes of ordering experience.

The initial frame of the Fassbinder film provides an introduction through the linguistic signifiers: "*Querelle,* a film about Jean Genet's *Querelle de Brest,* by Rainer Werner Fassbinder." The Genet novel was read in the postwar years as the violation of an aesthetic norm and the name "Genet" itself would have carried a subversive surcharge of signification for the public of 1948. The name "Fassbinder" was marketable to the international film-art echelon in 1982, the release date of the film, while serving as a trademark and signifier of cinematic quality. Within the context of the European art cinema of the early 1980s, the physical persona and image of the director fulfill an essential role within the sphere of distribution; the director provides exchange value and a context of meaning. As with painting and sculpture, the persona of the artist influences reception of the art object. Each supports the other, for together they must attract the interested gaze of the public (Elsaesser 1989: 75). As film historian Thomas Elsaesser has observed in *New German Cinema,* the Fassbinder persona, his overt homosexuality and flagrant abuse of drugs and alcohol, was familiar to Europeans as well as to Americans (1989: 292). In utilizing the star Jeanne Moreau, the film gains the prestige of all her previous roles, which treat such subjects as identity crisis, homoeroticism, insanity, and death. Does the film *Querelle* seek simply to cater to the international film art market, pandering to its neoconservative nostalgia for "poetic" stylization and for art-deco? I will suggest that, on the contrary, this nostalgia for the past, this seemingly exploitative search for a viable "tradition" does express a genuine dissatisfaction with modernity and "the unquestioned belief in the perpetual modernization of art" (Huyssen 1984: 12). Film historian Maureen Turim aptly describes this late twentieth-century phenomenon:

> If the line of artistic production seems to loop back (rehearse modernism, pastiche earlier forms, replay traditions) more than it leaps ahead, this too may be a part of the refusal to continue the vector of aesthetic developments, a refusal not necessarily voluntary or conscious but itself the most salient evidence that indeed the late twentieth century is finding its own creativity in the astute articulation of the pause and rewind modes (1991: 189).

Insofar as the postmodern, as Andreas Huyssen defines it, operates in a field of negotiation "between tradition and innovation, conservation and renewal, mass culture and high art" (1984: 48), and does not automatically privilege the second terms over the first, my reading places the film adaptation *Querelle* within postmodern parameters where it may be viewed as an "anti-art art film" (Elsaesser 1979: 38).

Querelle suspends and deforms rules that govern the ritual of cinematographic identification. In "The Imaginary Signifier," Metz has described this structure of vision in the cinema as that of voyeurism and exhibitionism, and has definitively named it as a specific form of the sexual drives (1977a: 59). All the sexual drives depend on a lack, the perpetual absence of that which could satisfy the desire (Doane 1979: 28). The desire of the look is a condition of the possibility of the cinema, and thus, Metz concludes that the film is automatically projected onto the side of the imaginary. The voyeur can never attain the object of his desire without violating the fundamental condition of its voyeurism. The aesthetic boundary between spectator and actor provides the necessary condition of a ritual that permits identification. The spectator can typically relax his/her defensive posture and project him/herself into the moving images that invite his affective participation. In one sense, the spectator can risk everything indirectly, because according to the rules of ritual he/she actually risks nothing.

For Metz, the cinema retains its imaginary character, for the object of the look is not present. The image is a trace of the presence of the actor — it is only a copy (Doane 1979: 31). Thus, the voyeur and the exhibitionist in the cinema never meet. In "Story/Discourse: A Note on Two Kinds of Voyeurism," Metz concludes that the film, the classic traditional film, remains ignorant of its spectator.

> The film is not exhibitionist. I watch it, but it doesn't watch me watching it. Nevertheless, it knows that I am watching it. But it doesn't want to know. This fundamental disavowal is what has guided the whole of classical cinema into the paths of 'story,' relentlessly erasing its discursive basis, and making it (at best) a beautiful closed object which must remain unaware of the pleasure it gives us (literally, over its dead body), an object whose contours remain intact and which cannot therefore be torn open into an inside and an outside, into a subject capable of saying "Yes!" (1977b: 94-5).

Metz situates the classic cinema as a form of history for it hides the traces of its source of enunciation. The stories it presents are simply there, already complete, and they come from nowhere. For our present needs, this description upholds the notion that the cinema is not exhibitionist. Authentic exhibitionism always demands the interplay of two persons: its form is analogous to that of dialogue (Doane 1979: 33).

In the cinema, the look of the spectator relates to the "eye" of the camera. This initial inscription of the spectator in the film defines primary identification. Primary identification is the requisite condition for secondary identification in which the spectator is implicated across the looks of characters. The movement between primary and secondary identification depends on the identification of the look of the camera and of characters, which is achieved in the cuts between shots, the shots of a character who is looking at the object of his look. The alignment of shots at the level of the eye of a character and the continuity established between a character and the object of his look are the subcodes of the code of secondary identification.

Usually, this movement between primary and secondary identification occurs smoothly, for it resembles the movement between the discourse of an omniscient narrator in the third person novel and the direct discourses of characters who speak in the story. To identify with characters within the story, we must completely ignore the mask worn by the narrator. In the domain of the cinema, the identification of the spectator demands that he be willing to project himself into the place of the character (into the domain of the imaginary). In *Querelle*, our perceptual position is put into danger for the classic rules that govern the ritual of cinematic identification are transgressed, and, consequently, the "self" of the spectator is exposed to the menace of absolute identification, of a collapse of the borders between subject and object (Sandro 1974: 7). It is this menace of absolute identification — the sense that the loss of self is imminent — that we can trace in *Querelle* as a spectre of psychosis.

This reflection upon the rules of cinematic ritual will inform our discussion of Genet's principle of the "double" as a discursive formation in both the Genet novel *Querelle de Brest* (1948) and its filmic adaptation directed by Fassbinder. Laura Oswald's notion of "the double" as articulated in *Jean Genet and the Semiotics of Performance* serves as a privileged theoretical source, for she addresses the question of postmodernism in Genet in terms of a performance aesthetic that collapses the boundaries between novel, film, and theatre.[1] Oswald's conceptualization of a postmodern performance aesthetic was inspired by the poststructuralist approach of Jacques Derrida who stages Genet with Hegel in *Glas*. While this provocative work constructs a postmodern textual space, combining widely diverse writing styles, levels, and modes of discourse, and even typefaces, Derrida does not discuss the theory of a performance aesthetic. As Oswald notes, performance constitutes the main event with postmodern writers, moving the subject of narrative, cinematic, and theatrical representation in "a kind of philosophical or psychological mise-en-scène"(1989: xiv). By examining those aspects of discourse that trace the subject's movement in textual performance, rather than focusing on the form and function of structural models, Oswald has been able to account for the evolution of Genet's famous "theatre of the double"(1989: xiii). In the course of my analysis, I return to Oswald's conception of the double to bring to light a discursive formation that supports both the structuration of the Genet novel *Querelle de Brest* (1948) and its filmic adaptation directed by Fassbinder, *Querelle*. With Fassbinder, the figure of the mask permits the opening of critical differences between the actor, his fictional role, and the role that the characters play, thus reinforcing the dispersion of narrative voice.

The Double: *Querelle de Brest* by Genet

First, let us look at Genet's *Querelle de Brest*. Laura Oswald has remarked that in the novels of Genet, the narrative discourse not only creates an image of the narrator, but is included in the discourse of characters (1989: 38). On the other hand, the personal idiolects of characters not only produce images of fictional personages, but are incorporated into the flow of narrative discourse. In this passage, the metanarrational voice intervenes to comment on this phenomenon:

> Finally, in order to be palpable to you, to become the character in a novel, Querelle must be shown as existing outside ourselves. Only in this way will you be able to appreciate the apparent — and real — beauty of his body, his attitudes, his exploits, and their slow disintegration (1966: 25).

Genet exploits the differences between argot, literary preciosity, and personal idiolects to show the participation of reported discourse and narrative discourse. The accentuated differences in the styles of discourse within the narration represent the movement between the discourse of the narrating subject, the first person of the discourse, and the discourse of the other. Here, the voice of narration directly addresses the reader, pointing to the character Querelle's unconventional idiolect:[2]

> We must try to bear this fact in mind in order to understand Querelle better, for his mental make-up and his thought processes, indeed his sentiments, are

dependent upon and assume the pattern of a certain stylized syntax and unconventional pronunciation. We find in his vocabulary such slang expressions as: "Let the ribands rip!" "I'm squatting on me bollucks," "You can't come copper," "Chop-chop!" "He's caught the boat up," "Take his picture as he climbs aloft!" "He's shot his roe," "See here, baby, I'm on the dot" (17).

Here, the metanarration calls attention to the discourse of characters as verbal constructs, revealing the stamp of an authorial signature in the production of character as well as within the production of narrative discourse. Contrary to the French novelists of the nineteenth century, such as Balzac, Hugo, and Sue, who utilized slang in reported discourse to add local color and verisimilitude to the representation of character, Genet exploits the contrasts between the characters' forms of discourses to represent a struggle between the speaking subject and the discourse of authority (Oswald 1989: 39). In this manner, Genet defines the narrative representation as a problematic of identification and imbrication of discourses. He thereby throws into question the Aristotelian ideal of mimetic closure between discourses and the speaking subject.

If the narrator wears a mask in order to represent a character in *Querelle de Brest*, this mask insinuates itself into the relation between the reader and the narrator. In the following passage, the metanarrational voice intervenes to recast images, created by the narrative discourse, into the mold of cinematic style:

> The presentation of the story of this last adventure was given purposely in slow motion; not with the intention of instilling terror into the reader, but of giving the murder the effect that is sometimes to be derived from an animated cartoon (1966: 78).

In the film *Querelle*, Genet's self-conscious narration finds its formal equivalent in the intermittent eruption of white intertitles, which demarcate divisions between scenes. Reminiscent of introductions to book chapters, these select quotations are taken from outside authors, Plutarch and Paganel, as well as from the canonical literary source. Although these framed quotations do not comment on the film's form per se, they do force us to reflect on the presentational style of the voice-over narration by insistently pointing to the notion of literary authorship as well as to the linguistic source text. In Fassbinder's earlier film adaptation *Fontane Effi Briest* (1974) based on the well-loved nineteenth-century novel by Theodor Fontane, every scene transition fades into the pure white of the printed page. As Elsaesser points out, it seems as though the images rose from the words of Fontane, which are spoken in voice-over by Fassbinder himself (1996: 282). In the later adaptation *Querelle*, Fassbinder places literary citations within white intertitles to destroy aesthetic distance, while introducing the problem of the double into the filmic narration, for the double voice of the narrator is reflected in the troubled identification of the spectator with the narration.

Although the self-conscious narration of Genet has precedents in a literary tradition that can be traced to Joseph Sterne's *Tristam Shandy*, the doubled narrational voice of *Querelle de Brest* is redoubled not only within the register of the characters' reported discourses, but in the Janus-faced roles that the characters play. Oswald has remarked that the relation between the discourse of the narrator and the discourses of the characters have evolved from one novel to the next (1989: 39). In Genet's early works like *Notre Dame des Fleurs*, the verbal styles of disparate characters infiltrate the narrator's voice. In later works, like *Pompes Funebres* and *Querelle de Brest*, the characters abandon their spoken style to adopt the literary style of the narrator. In *Querelle de Brest*, the periodic shifts in spoken style correspond to changes in position of the narrating subject, the first person of the discourse. Thus, one can read the voice of the narrator incorporated within the discourse of Querelle in this scene between Querelle and the Lieutenant:

> Querelle smiled at being so very near the brink of shame from which no escape was now possible, and in which he might well discover lasting peace... "I shall know no peace other than being kissed by him, and such a way that he shall watch over me, as I lie struck down across his knees, as Jesus is watched over in a *Pietà*" (1966: 318).

In this manner, Genet reveals the play of masks underlying the mimesis of the novel. These periodic shifts from personal idiolects to literary preciosity, from popular slang to standard French give rise to what Henri Godard has termed a "halo of uncertainty" in the reading (Watts 1995: 212). Genet's plurivocal style is transposed to cinematic style in *Querelle*, where the integration of narrative voice with that of Querelle is even more pronounced:

> I am very close to that point of disgrace from which there is no return; but I think that it is also a place where I shall find eternal peace... I shall not find this peace until you have taken me. But you must do it in such a way that afterwards I may rest across your thighs, as in a *pietà*, and you will watch over me as Mary watches over the dead Jesus (1982: 167).

The Double: The Voice of Seblon

The voice of Lieutenant Seblon occupies a unique place vis-à-vis the narrative discourse, both in *Querelle de Brest* and in the film *Querelle*. The narrator in *Querelle de Brest* makes explicit the position of Seblon with respect to other characters, in this aside to the reader, marked by parentheses:

> (Inasmuch as the other characters may be by their nature incapable of the lyricism with which we invest them, the more efficiently to reconstruct them within you, the reader, Lieutenant Seblon must be regarded as being solely responsible for the part he plays) (1966: 31).

While the voice of Seblon is often distinguishable from the voice of narration due to its more literary style, it is always cast within the framework of a "reverie." The narrator describes with precision the special status of Seblon: "but Seblon is *not* in the book" (1966: 92). Fassbinder translates the parenthetical discourse of Seblon into filmic terms in *Querelle*. The film opens with these words spoken by a voice off, "The thought of murder often awakens in us, thoughts of the sea and sailors" (1982: 57). Further on, the voice off narration continues with a description of the sailors, accompanied by a medium shot of the lieutenant, a point-of-view shot of the sailors, and another medium shot of Seblon. The quotation which follows seems to be attributable to the lieutenant, due to the shot/reverse shot code (the supposition that a shot which follows the shot of a character who is looking out of the filmic frame becomes the point of view of the character):

> When you brush past them, past these shoulders, profiles, curly hair, those strong and supple boys, you can't help imagining that they are also capable of murder (1982: 60).

What follows this introductory voice off narration is the voice of Seblon taking up the narrative relay with an elaborate description of sailors, a description that is both logically consequent and formally equivalent to the previous passage:

> I shall press these boys close to my naked body. These boys as bold and hard as rocks; they are elevated so high above me that I am shattered... My tears soften me. I dissolve. With their wetness on my cheeks I luxuriate. I disintegrate in tenderness at the thought of the hard flat cheekbones of these lads (1982: 62-3).

The sensuality and the quality of the image conveyed by this description provide the logical continuation to the voice off narration that preceded it. The voice that will become attributable to Seblon also shares a formal similarity with the preceding narration. The unsourced voice opens accompanied by a shot/reverse shot (medium shot of Seblon, a close-up of photos, a medium shot of Seblon). The voice is extinguished with the final medium shot of the lieutenant, in which the true source of its emission is definitely localized with the magnetophone that plays back the text both for the lieutenant as well as for us.

This series of shot/reverse shots that can only retroactively be attributed to the voice of Seblon, formally recalls the shot/reverse shot that accompanied the original voice off narration. While we are retrospectively tempted to attribute the entire opening narration to the voice of Seblon due to the formal equivalencies existing between the two segments of film, the idiolect of Seblon (played by the actor Franco Nero) that accompanies the second segment definitively forecloses this possibility. In this manner, Fassbinder underlines the movement, the oscillation between the narrating "I" and the discourse of the other, revealing the masquerade at stake in the inscription of the spectator into the narration.

It is clear that the interaction between the narrative voice and the discourses of characters in Genet's novel *Querelle de Brest* has shaped Fassbinder's notion of filmic representation. The figure of the mask permits the opening out of critical differences between the actor, his fictional role, and the role that characters play, thereby reinforcing the doubling of narrative voice. This process "destroys" the character in the traditional sense and reveals the spectator as a participant in the spectacle.

This staging of the subject of cinematic representation within what Oswald has termed, "a kind of psychological or philosophical mise-en-scène" (1989: xiv) draws not only on Genet's prose style, but recalls Artaud's theatre of cruelty. As Oswald points out, Antonin Artaud had considerable influence on Genet (1989: xv); so it seems unsurprising that his concept of a "metaphysical" performance theatre should surface to shape Fassbinder's adaptation of *Querelle de Brest*. Indeed, Artaud's theatre had a direct impact on Fassbinder's style, which first became evident within the performance pieces produced by his avant-garde Action Theater troupe, a collective that existed on the margins of Munich's cultural scene (Shattuc 1995: 95). Working within the countercultural climate of the late 1960s, as film historian Jane Shattuc points out, "The Munich troupe adapted and systematically perverted canonical German and classical plays and their performance traditions"

(1995: 95). One critic reviewing the group in the June 1968 issue of
Theater heute comments:

> It of course strikes one as grotesque that the Action Theater refers to Brecht
> and that [idea] has threatened the continuation of his ideas... The Action
> Theater... comes out of the world of the pop and hippie culture (an example
> being the staging of *Leonce* and *Lena*) and visually out of the world of comic
> strips and film (Shattuc 1995: 95).

Although film critics have scrutinized the structural Brecht theater
influence on Fassbinder's films,[3] I will argue that *Querelle* draws on the
theatrical performance style of Antonin Artaud, who Shattuc describes as,
"the *other* theorist of modernist theater" (1995: 96). Indeed, Fassbinder
definitively rejected the notion that Brecht's theatre had influenced his
filmmaking style, remarking, "No. Kluge's alienation is intellectual like
Brecht's, while mine is stylistic" (Shattuc 1995: 87). His lifelong
admiration for Artaud, however, is amply documented in the homage
paid to him within numerous films:[4]

> The film *Satansbruten* (1975-76) begins with a quotation from Artaud's *The
> Theater and Its Double: Despair* (1977) is dedicated to "Artaud, Vincent Van
> Gogh, Unica Zurn." And in 1981, the year before his death, he wrote and
> directed a film, *Theater in a Trance,* that combined dance pieces with Artaud's
> writings (Shattuc 1995: 96).

The metaphysical dimension of Artaud's theatre, which Oswald describes
as "the scene of the transcendental subject's performance in the space of
spectacle" (1989: xiv), is transposed to cinematic style in *Querelle*. Unlike
the spectator's identification with the personal identities of characters,
Artaud's metaphysical theatre emphasized the spectator's response to
mise-en-scène, which he defined as "a language in space and in
movement" (Oswald 1989: xiv). Artaud's aesthetic theory outlined in *The
Theater and Its Double* affected Fassbinder's ideas about the cinema, and
these ideas later take shape in his adaptation of Genet's *Querelle de Brest*
in terms of dramatic spacing, role-play, and mistaken identity.

The Uncanny Double: Querelle

The film introduces the spectator to Querelle through Lysiane, who while
dealing tarot reveals that Robert has a brother who shares a physical
resemblance and is his "double." In the film Lysiane says: "You're quite

alike, aren't you?" (1982: 59). In the novel *Querelle de Brest*, Genet insists on the strange resemblance between the two brothers:

> As soon as she (Lysiane) caught sight of the face of Querelle coming through the door into the salon, she experienced the same disturbing feeling that had so worried her when she first noticed that the two brothers' features were both united, as it seemed in one face, so exactly alike was the cast of each. So powerful was the resemblance between Querelle and her lover that she even went so far as to suppose, without really believing it, that Robert must have disguised himself as a sailor...the monstrosity of this so perfect resemblance took possession of her thoughts (1966: 131).

According to Freud, the instances where we meet the phenomenon of "the double" are among the most marked instances of the uncanny. The Freudian uncanny overlaps with Gilles Deleuze's description of a double, which is defined in terms of a virtual image and an actual image (1989: 68). In Deleuze's terms, the actual image itself has a virtual image that corresponds to it like a double or a reflection. The real object is reflected in a mirror image as in the virtual object which, from its side and simultaneously, envelops or reflects the real: there is a coalescence between the two (Deleuze 1989: 68). There is a formation of an image with two sides, actual and virtual. Freud has described this phenomenon as follows:

> Thus we have characters who are to be considered identical because they look alike. This relation is accentuated by mental processes leaping from one of these characters to another — by what we should call telepathy — or it is marked by the fact that the subject identifies himself with someone else, so that he is in doubt as to which his self is, or substitutes the extraneous self for his own. In other words, there is a doubling, dividing and interchanging of the self (1955: 234).

Thus, "the double" is in alliance with spirits and phantoms, the immortal soul being perhaps the first "double" of the body. If we review the impressions, events, and situations in which the sentiment of the uncanny has erupted in a particularly precise and powerful way, the most striking instance is the one where:

> doubts as to whether an apparently animate being is really alive; or conversely, whether a lifeless object might not be in fact animate, referring in this connection to the impression made by waxwork figures, ingeniously constructed dolls and automata (1955: 226).

An ambiguity remains in the text of Genet as well as in the film *Querelle*: is the character Querelle human or supernatural?

In the film, Lysiane and Robert conjure up his image while playing tarot. His visual introduction is made on board the ship "Vengeur," the image violently stained in a reddish-orange vermillion and is accompanied by a music that is at once haunting and ethereal. Genet in *Querelle de Brest* precisely describes the scene:

> ...the rating (Querelle) has become an angel for Lieutenant Seblon...that is to say, as turning into a character less and less human, as something from another world, ethereal, remote, about whose person is wafted a mysterious music unrelated to any known harmony, a haunting music that remains after all earthly harmony has been assimilated and distilled. In this rarefied atmosphere the vast angel of his creation is free to roam, slowly, unwitnessed, his feet resting upon the waters of the sea, but his head — or where his head should be — the multiple confusion of the rays of supernatural sun (1966: 15).

The ethereal and distant quality of Querelle brings us to an aspect of the uncanny described by Freud as "an animistic conception of the universe" (1955: 240), which includes the belief in the omnipotence of thoughts and in the magic that ensues. In the film, Lysiane not only makes Querelle appear by magic but attributes certain magic and superhuman powers to him in return. She remarks to him, "You're destroying me! You've got some kind of power that goes on multiplying forever. Querelle, you're not human; You don't come from this world" (1982: 173). Querelle's supernatural power is evoked in the film by Brad Davis's bluish waxen persona and enhanced by his flat, laconic deliverance of dialogue lines, setting him apart from the characters who inhabit the orange decor of "Vengeur" and the Feria. Toward the end of the film, Lysiane chases Querelle away like a bad dream while, once again, playing tarot. She remarks to Robert:

> I was wrong all along. You don't have a brother. Can you understand? I made a mistake. Did you hear me Robert? I made a mistake; you haven't got any brother! He hasn't got any brother. Did you hear me everybody? (1982: 174)

This commentary by Lysiane is accompanied by a bluish image of Querelle, who is spatially segregated from the narrative space of the Feria. The haunting laughter of Lysiane saturates this image as well as the closing shot of sailors aboard the "Vengeur." These final images of the film and the sound track that accompanies them instill doubt in the spectator's mind: was the character Querelle human, or was it a phantom magically evoked by Lysiane at tarot?

The uncanny, as Freud points out, only seems strange or unknown, but is something already familiar, firmly entrenched with our consciousness and buried there by the process of repression (1955: 241). Gilles Deleuze has described this phenomenon as follows:

> It is as if an image in a mirror, a photo or a postcard came to life, assumed independence and passed into the actual, even if this meant that the actual image returned into the mirror and resumed its place in the postcard or photo, following a double movement of liberation and capture (1989: 68).

We can suppose that the spectral image of Querelle evoked in the film is the reincarnation of the homosexual Robert, the frightening element that must be repressed. Thus, we can surmise that the return of Querelle to the seaport of Brest acts as the return of the repressed, homosexual "double" of Robert. This double, the character Querelle, will serve as relay with other characters who play a double role in the film (Seblon, Mario, Nono, and Gil).

Double Vision: The Voyeurism of Seblon

Lieutenant Seblon plays a double role in the film for he incarnates and expresses the discourse of authority, a role that brings in its wake the more transgressive pose of pederast and of voyeur. Querelle functions both as the object and as the relay of the transgressive voyeurism of Seblon. According to Freud, voyeurism not only displaces the sexual drive onto the look, but is accompanied by sadism, since the object of desire is subjugated by the mastering look of the subject (1957: 77). The voyeur engages the physical presence of the other simply by remaining at a distance behind a wall, a door, or a window. The voyeurist practice of Seblon is visually demarcated in the film for he is typically seen behind a window, framed with a much larger frame, the screen itself. The position of Seblon in the diegesis reflects our position at the cinema — inasmuch as the screen functions as the invisible wall and the aesthetic limit procuring the requisite condition of cinematic identification. In *Querelle*, the break with the normal functioning of the code of looks that defines the relation between voyeur and the object of the look invites us to recognize our situation before the film (that which constitutes a return to the real) and to become conscious of our identification with the voyeuristic gaze of Seblon.

In order to retrace the intervention of the I/eye of the narrator, we must examine the scene in which Seblon clandestinely watches as Querelle meets the sailor, Vic, to discuss an opium deal. It is in this scene that Seblon is included in the secret of the relation between Vic and Querelle, which will subsequently furnish Seblon with the identity of Vic's murderer. The scene opens on a series of shot/reverse shots (Seblon in medium shot, followed by a long shot of Querelle and Vic on board the "Vengeur," return to Seblon in medium shot, long shot of Querelle and Vic). This long shot of Querelle and Vic, which is framed from the point of view of Seblon, is followed by an extreme close-up of Querelle's hand in his pocket. The close-up of Querelle's hand is shot from a frontal perspective and thus, due to the camera angle could be attributable to the point of view of Seblon, to his focal point of attention in this scene. Yet, the shot is too obviously close to be attributable to Seblon's point of view without rupturing the code of spatial verisimilitude within the scene. Such modifications in the code of cuts between shots do not disturb the continuity and coherence of the diegesis: rather, they point our attention to the look of the camera as an autonomous narrative presence (independent of the glances of characters within the diegesis).

After Querelle and Vic have agreed upon the shipment of opium, the camera returns to a medium shot of Seblon. This shot is followed by a long shot of Querelle seen from behind, then a return to a medium shot of Seblon. It is patently obvious for the spectator that this series of shot/reverse shots between Seblon and Querelle are impossible in terms of the logic of narrative space as it has been elaborated within the preceding segment, in terms of the distance and angle of the camera. We are forced to recognize the autonomous narrative presence of the camera (independent of the glances of the characters). This recognition of the camera as an autonomous narrating presence causes a doubling of reference for the look, the first-person discourse. We are forced to admit that the I/eye refers as much to the autonomous narrator as to the voyeur Seblon. This movement of discourse transforms the film into a "bad object," inscribing a sentiment of bad faith into the shot composition that structures the scopic drive. Disturbing the state of half-dream characterizing spectatorial consciousness by introducing a bothersome reflection on the predisposition of the camera to voyeurism, Fassbinder places the spectatorial subject on stage, a participant in the play of images.

Despite the frequent allusions to a provocative eroticism that invades almost every scene in this film, the eroticism in *Querelle* is subversive insofar as it exceeds the rules permitting our transgression and proscribing our pleasure. For example, in the scene where Mario seduces Querelle, the spectator is forced to recognize his voyeuristic complicity with the events occurring on the screen. Each time that the spectator, forgetful of his situation, of his position, begins to respond with pleasure to the events in this theatre of desire, his own desire is transformed by the character of Seblon, the voyeur who intervenes to surveil the process of seduction in the film.

The seduction scene between Mario and Querelle begins with a full shot, and we notice Seblon in the background of the frame watching the conversation without being seen. Later, when Querelle descends into a dark tunnel, the series of shot/reverse shots between Querelle and Mario is interrupted by an extreme low angle shot of Seblon who is climbing the stairs and watching from above. The spectator could be tempted to attribute the following medium shot of Querelle, who continues to look upward into space, to the point of view of Seblon. However, the spectator must remember that the initial full shot of Querelle and Mario on the docks terminates with the presence of Seblon climbing the stairs in the extreme background of the frame. Thus, in terms of narrative logic and spatial continuity with the preceding scene, it is impossible to attribute the medium shot of Querelle to the point of view of the lieutenant. In this seduction scene, we are again forced to admit that the I/eye simultaneously refers to the autonomous narrator and to the voyeur Seblon. This movement of the discourse disturbs the fascination that can entrance the spectator before a provocative erotic scene. Here instead, a troubling reflection on the voyeuristic predisposition of the cinema and of the spectator is introduced. The apogee of this scene of seduction is replaced by a dazzling white page where a citation from Genet's *Querelle de Brest* is recorded. The whiteness of the screen shocks the spectator, breaking down aesthetic distance, while the intervention of a linguistic intertext destroys the spectator's identification with the characters who perform in the erotic scenario unfolding on the screen. The dephasing, unsettling of the spectator achieved through the formal device of authorial citation could easily be seen as a debt to Brecht, interpreted as the filmic equivalent of the famous alienation effect of the Epic Theater (Elsaesser 1996: 47-8). Yet, the scene does not develop the class-based or sociopolitical awareness that was Brecht's reason for such a method. As Shattuc pointedly notes, Fassbinder was a product of the German counterculture of the 1960s and consequently, condemned the high seriousness of Brecht's political theory (1995: 102). It was instead the antirationalist Artaud's demand for a visceral theatre of cruelty designed to "call into question, organically, man, his ideas about reality, and his poetic place in reality" (Oswald 1989: xiv) that had inspired Fassbinder, shaping his filmmaking style.

The Double Role of Seblon: Authority and Transgression

The spectator is implicated in the transgressive voyeurism of Seblon who fixes his look on Querelle, the relay of his role as pederast. Yet, the dramatic role of Seblon is doubled at the diegetic level, bestowing on his point of view the complicity that exists between his official role as lieutenant and his private role as pederast. This complicity between official and private roles is displayed in the scene where Seblon is interrogated by Mario about the murder of Vic. Seblon categorically denies the voyeuristic relation that he entertains with the sailors and Querelle, "I do not go around spying on my people! I believe their rendez-vous are shrouded in great secrecy. These repulsive types are wonderfully organized" (1982: 131). And Seblon goes even further in his denial as to knowledge of the murder of Vic:

> It is not my business to be interested in the physical relationships among the young men aboard. Even if Seaman Vic was murdered in connection with such episode I would hardly be the one to come to for information (1982: 131).

In denying the voyeuristic relation that he has exhibited vis-à-vis Querelle and his knowledge of the meeting between Vic and Querelle, Seblon becomes an accomplice to murder. In this scene, the discourse of Seblon as authority on the sea is complicit with his discourse as pederast, underscoring the permanent movement of perversion which taints the construction of "official" discourse.

The Double Role of Mario: Authority and Transgression

The double role of Seblon is found reflected in the dramatic role of Mario. Similar to Seblon who heads a maritime territory representing the institution of the navy, Mario governs the seaport of Brest, representing police authority (Knapp 1968: 65). In his role as "chief of police," Mario holds the discourse of authority, but this institutional role is undercut by his transgressive role of pederast. If we remember the seduction of Querelle, Mario is wearing his police officer's cap and using interrogation tactics in order to seduce Querelle. In the course of this seduction scene, Mario is filmed in extreme low angle, suggesting his position of power over Querelle, and his look tilted downwards over Querelle suggests the rapport between a hero vis-à-vis a captive criminal or victim.

247

Later in the film, Mario again adopts his role of "police chief" to interrogate Roger Bataille on the subject of the murder of Vic. The sexual connotations dispersed throughout the questions asked by Mario during the course of this police interrogation parallel the form of the preceding seduction scene between Mario and Querelle. The discourse of Mario as an institutional authority on land intersects with the discourse of Mario the pederast. Yet again, this doubling of discourse exposes the continuous movement of perversion in the construction of "official" discourse. During the interrogation of Roger Bataille, a narrative voice off intervenes, perverting respectable and conventional signification of words through its use of double entendre. The narrator comments, "They couldn't *pull anything out of him*... Crime enabled him to *penetrate a world* where feelings are violent" (1982: 113, my italics). Here, the police interrogation, an institutional discourse, intersects with the sexual transgression of language.

Querelle: The Doubled Roles of Nono and Mario

At the opening of the film, we observe that Querelle functions as a relay between the transgressive characters of Mario and Nono at La Feria. As Querelle meets Nono and Mario together there, he must also recognize their double game. Although Nono is both the patron of La Feria and the heterosexual husband of Lysiane, he has his "own preoccupations." Although Mario is the chief of police, he is recognized within the limits of La Feria as their true "safety guarantee." The uncanny quality of Querelle provokes the homosexual triangle among the three men. Querelle enters into the filmic field framed by the two men as a mirror image of them, a reflection that confirms the uncanny quality of his character. Freud reminds us that a "double" always has to do with mirrors, spirits, and shadows (1955: 235). At the same time as the "official" pretext of the conversation between Nono and Querelle unravels revealing a plan on an opium shipment, Querelle is distanced from the orange background of La Feria by the blue and ethereal luminosity enveloping him. A voice off narrator intervenes to describe the homosexual phantasms that Querelle projects onto Nono and Mario:

> Querelle appraised the great strength of the boss and the beauty of the policeman. Never before had he been confronted with such power of male rivalry as he now saw manifest in the figures of these two men (1982: 71).

The "official" pretext of the conversation between Nono and Querelle, the passage of opium, is undermined by a pun made by Querelle *the sailor*: "There's nothing *fishy* about this deal, is there?" (1982: 71, my italics). In the final scene of the film, the strangeness attached to the figure of Querelle, the relay of homosexual relations among these three men, is magically made to vanish by Lysiane and reintegrated into, "the lofty region where mirror images converge and are united" (1982: 174).

The Double: Gil

The character of Gil plays a double role in the film, for it is the same actor Hanno Pöschl who interprets both the role of Gil and that of Robert. "Gil" is in fact "Robert." It is Querelle who establishes a fraternal relation with both Robert and Gil, functioning as relay between the two characters. The fraternal relation that unites Giles Turko with Querelle is established at a figurative level, "Querelle was excited. For the first time, he would now meet an other criminal, a murderer of his own class, someone with whom he could discuss business" (1982: 135). But the fraternal relation is formally established at the moment in which Querelle disguises Gil as Robert in order to attack and rob Lieutenant Seblon. In this ceremonious manner, Querelle clothes Gil in the starched suit of Robert and finishes by attaching a mustache to perfect the disguise. It is only when Gil becomes "Robert" that Querelle falls in love with him, "Querelle's friendship for Gil intensified to the point where love begins. Gil was a little Querelle for whom Querelle cherished a strange feeling of admiration mixed with curiosity" (1982: 150). The Judas kiss between Querelle and Gil is simultaneously an act of love and treason, for Querelle will hand Gil over to the police. The ambiguous relation of love/hate between Robert and Querelle is thus reflected in this kiss between Gil and Querelle.

"Gil" is "Robert" both literally and figuratively. This confusion of identity is revealed within the film in the final scene where Lieutenant Seblon enters La Feria and by mistake identifies Robert as the mustached thief who attacked and robbed him. Even here, critical differences are instituted between the actor Hanno Pöschl and his fictional double role. This process "destroys" the character in the traditional sense and projects the spectator into a participant position of that which unfolds on the screen.

Even minor characters like Roger Bataille play a double role in the film. Roger is often confused with his sister Paulette who resembles him so much. Gil remarks to Roger:

> She (Paulette) really turns me on. Man would I screw her. You've got the same chops.
> You've got the same eyeballs (1982: 75).

The figure of the mask opens out onto a critical difference between the fictional role of "Roger" and the phantasm of "Paulette" that Roger plays for Gil Turko:

Gil: Boy your sister. She's so cute!

Roger: She looks like me.

Gil: I know but she's even prettier. If I were holding her now, the way I'm holding you, I'd make out with her like crazy. Too bad you're not a girl. You're definitely as pretty as one (1982: 134).

This double sexual identity of Roger Bataille recalls the division of sexual identity of Seblon. Seblon describes his feminine double in the instant in which the spectator is tuned into the close-up of the photo of a nude woman seated on a bed. This representation of a double sexuality is thus a verbal as well as a visual discourse in the film. He ruminates, "The more I love Querelle, the more defined the woman in me becomes and the more sensitive, delicate and sad, because she cannot be fulfilled" (1982: 111). *Querelle* is the story of a man divided, of a man who struggles against himself. This Genetian principle of the double that structures the story and character of *Querelle* overlaps with the German expressionist notion of the "double" or "*Doppelgänger*," thus constituting a foliated discourse.

The Double: Expressionism and Melodrama

This notion of the "double" is part of the world of E.T.A. Hoffmann, the celebrated theme of the *Doppelgänger*, the shadow or reflection that takes on an independent existence and turns against its model. In *Elixire des Teufels*, Hoffmann, terrified by his own being, exclaims:

My whole being, turned into the capricious toy of a cruel fate, surrounded by strange phantoms, floated without rest upon a sea of events whose enormous waves broke over me roaring. I can no longer find myself... I am what I seem, yet I seem not to be what I am. I cannot solve the problem myself: my "self" is split in two (Eisner 1977: 109-110).

The theme of double identity is traceable throughout the history of the German expressionist film movement. The central character in Robert Wiene's *The Cabinet of Dr. Caligari* (1919) is both an eminent doctor and the hypnotist of a gypsy fair. Later, in F. W. Murnau's *Nosferatu* (1921), the vampire, who is also master of a feudal chateau, wishes to purchase a house from a seemingly ordinary businessman who himself is permeated with the diabolic. And the duplicitous character of Death in Fritz Lang's *Destiny* (1921) is also an everyday voyager in quest of land to purchase. In the ambiguous world of German cinema, characters are unsure of their identity and could undergo radical transformation at any instant (Eisner 1977: 110). The character of Querelle who is "in danger of finding himself" (1982: 59), if we are to believe the declarations of Lysiane, plays the role of *Doppelgänger* to his spectral double, Robert. As Lotte Eisner writes, "...for the Germans, the demoniac side to an individual always has a middle-class counterpart" (1977: 110). It does seem curious that Robert should first differentiate Querelle in terms of class difference:

Lysiane:	You have a brother?
Robert:	So what if I do?
Lysiane:	You've never even mentioned him. You're quite alike aren't you?
Robert:	Well, that's what people say. But it's not true. *Querelle is a sailor.*

(1982: 59, my italics)

This tendency is obviously demonstrated in Otto Ripert's *Homonculus* (1916) where the protagonist, a sort of Fuhrer, has the possibility of dividing his personality at will; disguised as a worker, he incites the poor to rebel against his own dictatorship (Eisner 1977: 110). In *Querelle*, class differences intersect with sexual differences, for Robert is not simply a bourgeois but the only heterosexual male of the film. Querelle, the demonic mirror image of Robert, truly takes up an independent existence and turns against his heterosexual model, Robert. When Robert learns of the homosexuality of Querelle, a ceremonial joust takes place in the streets of Brest.

The expressionist intertext presupposes certain themes and codes that traverse the film text. Eisner has characterized the orientation of German expressionist cinema in its classic form, "Mind, Spirit, Vision and Ghosts seem to gush forth, exterior facts are continually being transformed into interior elements and psychic events are exteriorized" (1977: 15). In the haunted universe of E.T.A. Hoffmann, bewitched objects seem to possess an insidious life. This expressionist tendency can be perceived in the opening shots of *Querelle*. Accompanying the conversation of sailors, at the moment they arrive at Brest, a long panoramic shot uncovers the port of La Feria. An attentive spectator will have noticed that the towers are nothing other than gigantic phalluses that reflect the competitive character of the conversation between men:

— Land Finally!
— And Broads.
— Juicy cunts. Greedy soft.
— Ever been to Brest before?
— Why?
— Because I hear they have the raunchiest whorehouse in the world there.
(1982: 60)

Here, the psychic reality of men is exteriorized in architectural representation. Other visual jokes appear in the film, such as the sexually transgressive images that appear in the latticework in the brothel La Feria: a penis, balls, as well as miniature people who are in the midst of coitus. In *Querelle*, Fassbinder makes use of conventional architectural structures to interlace visual jokes of a sexually transgressive nature. Thus, the meaning transmitted by the image is doubled, referring on one hand to a rhetoric of respectability and convention and, on the other hand, to a rhetoric of sexual transgression. Semantic orientations are displaced and in constant conflict.

Evidence of expressionist influence reoccurs persistently throughout the film. Within the expressionist repertoire of film techniques, deformed decor and the creation of ambiance due to high-contrast lighting eloquently convey the terrors of agitated dreams and morbid psychological states. The scene in which Seblon is attacked by Gil belies this expressionist influence, due in part to the presence of angular and oblique lines that fill the screen. The moment the theft scene opens, a slanting bar masking the foreground of the screen, as well as the staircase under which Gil is hidden, form an opposing diagonal. Insofar as expressionism attached a metaphysical sense to oblique lines and to curves, the presence of oblique lines in this scene would necessarily generate an entirely different psychic reaction than if straight lines were used. The branches of trees and the menacing shadows that haunt the mise-en-scène of the theft seem to possess a life of their own, recalling the bewitched objects of the Hoffmannian universe. The scene closes on the transmogrified, wounded Lieutenant, his reflection captured in a concave mirror. The use of convex and concave mirrors to transmit emotionally subjective states was a typical expressionist technique found in films such as *Uberfall* (1928) of Metzner, *Variété* (1925) of Dupont, or even *Phantom* (1922) by Murnau (Eisner 1977: 31). German expressionism sought to create states of terror and anxiety as part of a modernist project of social transformation (Eisner 1977: 21).

The monologic consistency of style found in such expressionist works as *Caligari* involved what cultural theorist Jim Collins has termed "a discursive self-enclosure" of an avant-garde vision that erased even the slightest evidence of other visual languages (1989: 76). As Collins points out, when the satanic Caligari visits the city hall, all of the elements of the mise-en-scène, from the painting of the walls to the costuming and make-up of the actors, are determined by the same graphic design (1989: 76). This self-enclosured stylistic purism that was characteristic of the expressionist work defined its quintessentially modernist vision. Indeed, the assertion of its "difference" as a revolutionary vision depended on its total rejection of discursive heterogeneity. In the film *Querelle*, however, the themes and codes of German expressionism overlap with Fassbinder's signature melodramatic style, offering an affront to the "seriousness" and "self-enclosure" of the modernist project. While the influence of German expressionism is everywhere apparent in the film *Querelle*, as Jane Shattuc notes, "Fassbinder's greatest influence was felt at the level of style, or through what I term his 'melodramatic mode'" (1995: 110).

Insofar as dramatic symmetry characterizes the classical melodrama, it seems important to point to the number "2" that appears throughout the film in one manner or another: in the characters (2 brothers), in the events (2 murders), in the contrast between masculinity and femininity, in the contrast between land and sea and in the film's symmetrical commencement and closure at the tarot table. This doubling of events provides the skeletal foundation for Fassbinder's broad melodramatic strokes. In melodramas such as *Effi Briest* (1974), *Fear Eats the Soul* (1974), or *The Merchant of Four Seasons* (1972), Fassbinder had recourse to such melodramatic devices as dramatic symmetries, character types (villain, victim, and hero), amplified music, and excessive mise-en-scène. The film *Querelle* is full of such melodramatic mannerisms. Each costume in the film casts characters in terms of sexual and social class stereotypes. The police chief and the lieutenant are types, lords of land and sea respectively, cast in duplicitous roles by their densely codified costumes, jewels, capes, and caps. During the robbery of Seblon, Gil's mustache creates the generic villain, while Robert's suit paradoxically types Gil as both heterosexual and bourgeois. Music, the hallmark of film melodrama, functions as a strong subjective device, intoning the haunted heroics of Querelle, while a melancholy Oscar Wilde ballad becomes habitually associated with the character of Lysiane. Organ chords struck in minor keys accent the erotic suspense of scenes, punctuating their outcome.

Derived from the musical term "modus," what Shattuc terms the Hollywood "melodramatic mode" designates a set of recurrent features historically associated with textual "realism" (1995: 110). As film scholar

Christine Gledhill has pointed out, the melodrama is not incompatible with realism but, on the contrary, "it has power on the premise of a recognisable, socially constructed world" (1987: 37). Melodrama, Gledhill asserts, "takes its stand in the material world of everyday reality and lived experience" (1987: 33) and its ethical conflicts, "though symbolically rendered, are not produced as allegorical abstractions" (1987: 30). *Querelle*, however, does not simply amplify realist narrative conventions to achieve a melodramatic effect. The film reworks those conventions associated with textual "realism" that include duplicitous character typing, dramatic symmetries, and repeated events, to reinvent the theme of the double associated with the German expressionist *Doppelgänger*. Thus in *Querelle*, the melodramatic mode is replayed in two distinctly separate keys, invoking both the classical realist tradition as well as the high-art avant-garde tradition of abstract film.

This use of melodramatic mannerisms fits well with Fassbinder's appropriation of American pop art iconography. Shattuc notes that in the Hollywood melodrama, all expressive resources of mise-en-scène work to convey subjective psychological states (1995: 112). In *Querelle*, Fassbinder's melodramatic mode appropriates the bright neon colors and sensual forms of pop art, to celebrate the intense "trivial" emotion (Shattuc 1995: 101). In the scene in which Seblon slips beneath an underpass to chalk the obscene inscription "The navy needs men with big cocks," a dissonant electronic whining accompanies his lewd grin as he stands transfixed before an etching of a cock and balls drawn across the transparent glass of the "screen." These eerie sonic waves seem to mimic the undulations of his lewd homoerotic fantasies surfacing in this scene. In the following scene, these sounds are sourced in the pop iconography of a video game at La Feria and "climax" there with the crash of a car being zapped by its competitor. Here, the "intense" competitive character of homosexual male rivalry at La Feria is exteriorized in the garish colors and sounds of a video road game. Fassbinder's melodramatic mode and its appropriation of American pop art iconography converge with the themes and codes of German expressionism at nodal points in the text. The Hollywoodian melodramatic mode pinions the German expressionist intertext not only in its rearticulation of the trope of the double through duplicitous character typing, dramatic symmetries, and repeated events but in its reinscription of excessive mise-en-scènes to convey inner states. Fassbinder's appropriation of the brilliant, visceral immediacy of American pop art overwrites the German expressionist intertext, contesting the "seriousness" and "self-enclosure" of its modernist project, while simultaneously galvanizing the canonical literary source. The polylogic relationships established between multiple intertexts in the film *Querelle* seem coincident with Bakhtin's description of intertextuality, "Bakhtin has in view writing as the reading of an anterior literary corpus, the text as absorption of and reply to an other text... every text [is seen as] a mosaic of citations" (Doane 1979: 91).

If *Querelle* offers us a polyphonic discourse, it proposes a dual paternity. The final shot demonstrates gratitude toward the author Jean Genet, as the initial shot carries the mark of Fassbinder:

> His birth certificate reads as follows:
> Born on the 19th of December, 1910, at ten o'clock in the morning.
> Mother: Gabrielle Genet
> Father: Unknown
> Apart from his books, no one knows anything about him; not even the hour of his death, which he feels fast approaching (*Querelle*).

In the European art cinema, the director is identified as an "author," while his films are viewed as an extension of a personal vision. Fassbinder extends this personalism to commemorate the film's dual authorship in a closing dedication that can be interpreted, in retrospect, as darkly confessional. In *Querelle*, Fassbinder moves beyond the confessional tradition of modernist European art cinema, however, to interrogate the viability of any ideological stance, including his own. As Shattuc points out, Fassbinder's confessional work can be distinguished from that of other confessional filmmakers such as Fellini or Truffaut due to its appropriation of the crass conventional eroticism of American pop art iconography (1995: 98). Indeed, the unique juxtaposition of discourses within the film text *Querelle* plays out the unresolvable tension present in the director Fassbinder between his transgressive public persona as a homosexual drug addict and his institutional persona as an artist who was sanctioned by the same public for whom his personal life represented a provocation (Shattuc 1995: 98). As the authorial double of Jean Genet, the *enfant terrible* of the French theatre, Fassbinder looked to violence and physicality as a means to transcend social or even sexual control.

Fassbinder's fascination with the violent, ritualistic nature of film as a source of its power can be traced to the theatre aesthetics of Artaud. Artaud's aesthetic theory had called for catharsis as the crucial experience of the theatre of cruelty, which would surpass the social constraints of language to communicate on all sensorial levels (Shattuc 1995: 97). As

Martin Esslin points out, Artaud, "exemplifies the profound identity of all political attitudes based on the primacy of emotion over reason…" (Shattuc 1995: 98). Artaud's performance theatre incarnated the essence of modernism insofar as, "modernism had a fundamental respect for creative cognition and the role of the arts as stimulation" (Turim 1991: 188). In *Querelle*, the tactile and immediate quality of American pop art iconography combines with the anarchistic subjectivity of the avant-garde form that is derived from the Artaudian tradition. The visceral violence acted out in Artaud's political Action Theater is acted out in Fassbinder's film *Querelle* as an assault on the spectator's perceptual position. In the film, the "self" of the spectator is exposed to the menace of absolute identification, of a collapse of the borders between subject and object (Sandro 1974: 7). It is this menace of absolute identification — the sense that the loss of self is imminent — that we have attempted to trace in our analysis of *Querelle*.

In conclusion, I have tried to locate in Genet's novel, *Querelle de Brest,* several types of doubling as retranscribed to the screen by Fassbinder — the voice of the narrator, the identities of characters, and the effect of the incessant mirroring of narrative and reported discourse. While a retranscription of types of doubling necessarily determines specific codes associated with high-art cinema, the film *Querelle* actually engages a broader, mass cultural audience through its use of the crass conventionality associated with Hollywood melodrama and American commercial iconography. Fassbinder grafts the intertextual frame of Hollywood melodrama and its appropriation of American pop art onto a European high-art avant-garde work. In this manner, Fassbinder foregrounds unresolvable tensions between the disparate discourses of Hollywood and high-art, but also unifies these diverse styles around the well-defined trope of the double. Such intertextual tension prevents the film *Querelle* from being appropriated and politically anesthetized within the high-art avant-garde tradition of abstract film. The postmodern aim as articulated in the film *Querelle* is not unmotivated, random pastiche, but specific intertextual combinations for particular purposes. Jim Collins's description of Charles Moore's Piazza d'Italia provides the perfect architectural parallel to the postmodernist project of this film:

> His (Charles Moore's) design for an Italian cultural center incorporates Roman arches, neon bars, and skyscrapers, utilizing stone as well as highly polished aluminum in its various columns. But the juxtapositions here are not without a precise guiding principle. Moore has included most of the important styles that have been used within the Italian city-space since ancient Rome. This

juxtaposition of seemingly contradictory styles makes perfect sense, given the Piazza d'Italia's function as a center intended to celebrate cultural traditions in the 1980s (1989: 138).

The film *Querelle*, like the Piazza d'Italia, is a contemporary postmodern work built from seemingly contradictory styles. The Genetian trope of the double provides the unifying principle for the precise combination of styles in the film, determining our active engagement with antecedent and contemporary modes of ordering experience. Fassbinder's wholly new postmodern film necessarily resides in a schizoid, yet not at all antagonistic, coexistence with its literary source. In both the Genet novel and the Fassbinder film, the Genetian theatrical notions of dramatic placement, psychodrama, and mistaken identity are used to explode critical differences between the actor, his fictional role, and the role played by the characters, thereby reinforcing the doubling of narrative voice. This "destroys" character in the traditional sense and exposes the spectator as participant in the spectacle. Fassbinder's transposition of Genet's theatrical language of space in his filmic adaptation of the novel *Querelle de Brest* reflects postmodernist preoccupations with process, participation, and performance, rather than the authoritative work of art (Oswald 1989: xiv). In the film *Querelle,* writing must be viewed as double and also perceived as perpetually delayed in an impasse that is reflected in the character Querelle. The film upholds the momentary and violent pleasure of manic sexual expenditure, while simultaneously exposing and betraying this perverse mania and its pretensions (Stoekl 1985: 19). In effect, it becomes clear that excessive sexual expenditure cannot be severed from what unequivocally opposes it — loss and silence. It is possible to see the film *Querelle* as a metadiscourse on the writing of excess as well as a provocative, postmodern inquiry into the dilemma of the Writer as Metteur-en-Scène.

REFERENCES

Collins, Jim. 1989. *Uncommon Cultures: Popular Culture and Post-Modernism.*
    New York: Routledge.
Deleuze, Gilles. 1989. *Cinema 2.* Minneapolis: University of Minnesota Press.
Doane, Mary Ann. 1979. "The Dialogical Text: Filmic Irony and the Spectator."
    Ph.D. Thesis, University of Iowa.
Eisner, Lotte. 1977. *The Haunted Screen.* Berkeley: University of California Press.

Elsaesser, Thomas. 1979. "Afterword: Murder, Merger, Suicide: The Politics of Despair." *Fassbinder*, edited by Tony Rayns. London: BFI, 37-53.

——— 1986. "Primary Identification and the Historical Subject: Fassbinder and Germany." *Narrative, Apparatus, Ideology*, edited by Philip Rosen. New York: Columbia University Press.

——— 1989. *New German Cinema: A History.* New Brunswick: Rutgers University Press.

——— 1996. *Fassbinder's Germany*. Amsterdam: Amsterdam University Press.

Fassbinder, Rainer Werner. 1982. *Querelle: The Film Book*, edited by Dieter Schidor. New York, NY: Grove Press.

Freud, Sigmund. 1955. "The Uncanny." *The Standard Edition of the Complete Psychological Works of Sigmund Freud*, vol.17. London: Hogarth Press.

——— 1957. "Instincts and Their Vicissitudes." *A General Selection from the Works of Sigmund Freud*, edited by John Rickman. Garden City: Doubleday Anchor Books.

Genet, Jean. 1966. *Querelle of Brest*. London: Anthony Blond Limited.

Gledhill, Christine. 1987. "The Melodramatic Field: An Investigation." *Home Is Where the Heart Is*, edited by Christine Gledhill. London: BFI.

Huyssen, Andreas. 1984. "Mapping the Postmodern." *New German Critique* 33 (fall): 5-52.

Knapp, Bettina. 1968. *Jean Genet*. Boston: Twayne.

Metz, Christian. 1977a. "The Imaginary Signifier." *The Imaginary Signifier: Psychoanalysis and the Cinema*. Bloomington: Indiana University Press.

——— 1977b. "Story/Discourse: A Note on Two Kinds of Voyeurisms." *The Imaginary Signifier: Psychoanalysis and the Cinema*. Bloomington: Indiana University Press.

Oswald, Laura. 1989. *Jean Genet and the Semiotics of Performance*. Bloomington: Indiana University Press.

Querelle. 1982. Directed by Rainer Werner Fassbinder (with Brad Davis, Jeanne Moreau, Franco Nero, Michael McLernon and Hanno Pöschl). Munich: Planet-Film/Paris: Gaumont.

Sandro, Paul. 1974. "Assault and Disruption in the Cinema: Four Films by Luis Bunuel." Ph.D. Thesis, Cornell University.

Shattuc, Jane. 1995. *Television, Tabloids and Tears: Fassbinder and Popular Culture*. Minneapolis: University of Minnesota Press.

Stoekl, Allan. 1985. *Politics, Writing, Mutilation*. Minneapolis: University of Minnesota Press.

Turim, Maureen. 1991. "Cinemas of Postmodernity and Modernity." *Zeitgeist in Babel*, edited by Ingeborg Hoesterey. Bloomington: Indiana University Press.

Watts, Philip. 1995. "Postmodern Céline." *Céline and the Politics of Difference*, edited by Rosemarie Scullion, Philip Soloman, and Thomas Spears. Hanover: University Press of New England.

NOTES

1. Also see Thomas Elsaesser's "Primary Identification and the Historical Subject: Fassbinder and Germany" in *Narrative, Apparatus, Ideology: A Film Theory Reader* (1986), in which he traces the obsession with mirroring, doubling, and illusory self-images from its origins as a generalized cinematic theme to its current status as a specifically German theme. Elsaesser characterizes his discussion of Fassbinder as "the occasion for historicizing the obsession" (541).

2. This passage is a British translation from the original French text, Jean Genet's *Querelle de Brest* (1948).

3. See Rob Burns, "*Fassbinder's Anst Essen Seele Auf*: A Mellow Brechtian Drama," *German Life and Letters* 48 (1), 1995: 56-74, who discusses the film in terms of the contrasting traditions of Hollywood melodrama and Brechtian stylization. See also Judith Mayne, "Fassbinder and Spectatorship," *New German Critique* 12, Fall 1977: 61-70, who analyses the Fassbinder frame in terms of Brecht. Finally, see Hans-Bernd Moeller, "Fassbinder's Use of Brechtian Aesthetics," *Jump Cut* 35, April 1990: 102-107, who examines the film trilogy *The Marriage of Maria Braun, Veronika Voss,* and *Lola* in terms of Brechtian aesthetics.

4. See Jane Shattuc who, in "Shock Pop: Fassbinder and the Aesthetics of the German Counterculture" in *Television, Tabloids, and Tears: Fassbinder and Popular Culture,* provides an excellent discussion of Artaud's influence on Fassbinder. Shattuc reminds us that while Brechtian analyses of Fassbinder's films are based on ample textual evidence, these analyses fail to take into account the historical context of the reception of Brecht. During the late 1960s, Brecht's plays and his name no longer carried a destabilizing threat in Germany, for he was viewed as a sanctioned playwright. Shattuc remarks: "Although Brecht's works stood as a major model of leftist cultural resistance, the young German counterculture directed its wrath primarily against any established culture... In fact, so established was Brecht as a sanctioned playwright that Fassbinder's avant-garde/political Action Theater in Munich never produced even one of Brecht's plays in its countercultural repertory" (1995: 89).

NOTES ON THE CONTRIBUTORS

Cynthia Baron is a visiting assistant professor at Washington University in St. Louis. She is currently writing a book on drama schools, theories of acting, and the production of film performances in the Hollywood studio era.

Christine Bolus-Reichert, a doctoral candidate in English and Comparative Literature at Indiana University, is currently completing her dissertation on nineteenth-century British and French eclecticism. She has taught numerous courses on film, literature, and the other arts and has served for two years as the book review editor of *Victorian Studies*.

John Bruns is a Ph.D. candidate in the Program of Film, Literature, and Culture within the University of Southern California's Department of English. He is currently writing a dissertation on Mikhail Bakhtin and the cultural politics of festive laughter. He also teaches in the University's Writing Program and works in the University's Writing Center as an instructional coordinator.

Cristina Degli-Esposti is an assistant professor at Kent State University where she teaches courses in Italian Studies and Film Studies. Co-editor of *Perspectives on Federico Fellini*, she has written articles on Umberto Eco, Italo Calvino, Michelangelo Antonioni, Federico Fellini, recent Italian Cinema, Martin Scorsese, Peter Greenaway, and Sally Potter for *Forum Italicum, Voices in Italian Americana, Italica, Cinefocus*, and *Cinema Journal*. Her reviews on a book on Antonioni, and on contemporary Italian cinema appeared in *Italica* and *Screen*. She has contributed to a volume on the International Film Industry, and has written entries on directors, film composers, and film journals for the *Routledge Encyclopedia of Italian Studies*. Both volumes are forthcoming. Her research interests focus on the neo-baroque aspects of postmodernism.

Marshall Deutelbaum is an associate professor of English at Purdue University where he teaches courses in film history and film theory.

Janina Falkowska is a professor of Film Studies at the University of Western Ontario. She is the author of books on Andrzej Wajda and the new Polish Cinema.

Philip Holden-Moses holds a Ph.D. in Comparative Literature-Film Studies from Indiana University. He is now teaching courses in English and Film Studies at Tokai University.

Marwan M. Kraidy is assistant professor of Critical/Cultural Studies and International and Intercultural Communication in the School of Communication at the University of North Dakota. He has published and presented papers in international communication, postcolonial and critical theory, and film theory and criticism. His current research interests focus on cultural hybridity and include developing conceptual formulations for native ethnography and a theory of glocalization (not to be confused with globalization).

Barry Laga is assistant professor of English at Mesa State College where he teaches literary theory, contemporary American literature, film, and cultural studies. He is currently at work on *(Post)history: Negating and Negotiating Representations of History*.

Rosanna Maule is an Italian film scholar at present, completing her Ph.D. dissertation in Communication Studies at the University of Iowa on the construction of film authorship as a resistant practice in 1980s' and 1990s' French, Italian, and Spanish cinemas. Her primary interest in film studies is investigating how cultural identity is mediated by the concept and practice of authorship, with particular reference to European contemporary cinema, early cinema, and Hollywood Classical Cinema. Her theoretical frame of reference includes intellectual and social history, Marxist criticism, cultural studies, feminist film theory, post-structuralist and postmodern criticism.

Timothy Shary is a doctoral candidate in the Department of Communication at the University of Massachusetts. His dissertation is entitled "Generation Multiplex: The Image of Youth in American Cinema, 1981-1996." He has published articles and reviews in *Film Criticism, Journal of Popular Film and Television, Film Quarterly, Post Script,* and *Wide Angle.*

Ellen Strain is currently an assistant professor within Georgia Tech's School of Literature, Communication and Culture, where she teaches undergraduate film classes as well as multimedia design and digital video classes within the graduate program in Information Design and Technology. She is working on a book entitled *Pulic Places, Private Journeys: The Tourist Gaze and Technologies of Immersion* and on a CD-ROM about D.W. Griffith's *The Birth of a Nation* with co-author Greg VanHoosier-Carey.

David Weinstein (Ph.D., University of Maryland, College Park, 1997) is a documentary video producer and historical researcher in Washington D.C. He has published several articles on television, radio, and popular music history.

Mary M. Wiles is a doctoral candidate in the English Department at the University of Florida. Ms. Wiles received an M.A. in French and an M.A. in Film Studies from the University of Iowa and has also studied at Paris III, Sorbonne in France. She has published essays on the articulation of feminine desire in both literature and film. Her dissertation concerns French New Wave director Jacques Rivette, and she plans to return to Paris to pursue her research interests.

INDEX OF PROPER NAMES

Printed in the United States
114020LV00001B/191/P